HAGIA SOPHIA

Architecture, Structure and Liturgy of

Justinian's Great Church

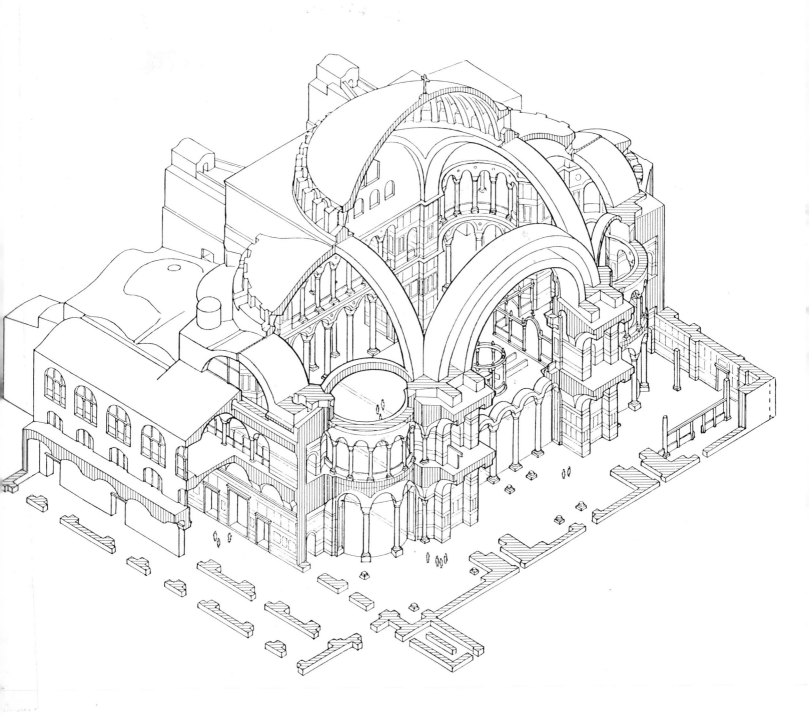

Rowland J. Mainstone

HAGIA SOPHIA

*Architecture, Structure and Liturgy of
Justinian's Great Church*

with 305 illustrations, 56 plans and drawings

Thames and Hudson

Half title: Cut-away isometric drawing of
Justinian's church as it was finally completed in
562 after an early partial collapse

Frontispiece: Justinian presenting the church to the
Virgin and Child as shown in the mosaic over the
inner doors of the south-west porch

© 1988 Rowland J. Mainstone

First paperback edition 1997

British Library Cataloguing-in-Publication Data
A catalogue record for this book is available
from the British Library
ISBN 0-500-27945-4

Designed by Pauline Baines

Printed and bound in Hungary

Contents

Note on terminology and units of measurement

Because of the complexity of the structure, somewhat arbitrary names, whose significance is not always immediately apparent, must be given to some of its parts. These names are shown on illustrations 88 and 89. Also the orientation is not strictly eastwards but closer to the south-east. Nevertheless it is easier and has seemed less confusing to follow the usual practice of denoting directions and further identifying different parts in terms of a nominal (or liturgical) eastward orientation.

Technical terms have been avoided except where they seemed essential. Those structural terms that have been used will be found in the glossary in my *Developments in structural form*, London and Cambridge, Mass., 1975. Terms relating to the Christian furnishings are shown in illustration 252. Other terms likely to be unfamiliar are explained as they are introduced.

The principal units of measurement used are the metre and millimetre for lengths (1 metre = 3.28 English feet; 1 millimetre = 0.0394 inch) and the meganewton for force (1 MN = 100 tons).

In discussing the design and construction of Justinian's church in Chapters 7 and 8, it has, however, been necessary to do so in terms of the unit of the length used at the time – the Byzantine foot. All references to feet in these chapters are to this unit. It will be seen that it was slightly longer than the present English foot (1 Byzantine foot = 0.312 metre = 1.024 English feet).

Photographic Sources

All new drawings and all photographs of the church and of related structures are by the author, as are the photographs of the earlier published views of Grelot and Fossati, and of subjects from other early publications. Photographs of original illuminations and early drawings in private and public collections and of the San Vitale apse mosaics are reproduced by courtesy of the following, whose kindness is hereby acknowledged: Bibliothèque Nationale, Paris, 1; Royal Institute of British Architects, 16; Nationalmuseum, Stockholm, 99, 131, 133, 146; Soprintendenza alle Gallerie, Naples, 182; Julia Elton, 194; Archivio Fotographico, Vatican Museum, Biblioteca Apostolica Vaticana, 241, 255; Photo Alinari, 253, 254.

Preface

THE GREAT CHURCH OF HAGIA SOPHIA is a daunting subject, but to anyone moved by the supreme creations of man's genius it presents a challenge to the understanding that is not easily set aside. For later generations the achievement of Justinian's architects was comprehensible only in terms of repeated divine intervention. How did they, urged on by the greatest of Byzantine emperors, achieve what any normally prudent man would have deemed impossible?

It would be presumptuous to claim to have found a definitive answer. Before even seeking an answer it is necessary to identify what survives intact of the original structure and to visualize it as it was more than fourteen hundred years ago. But it is hoped that a long familiarity with it and almost thirty years of questioning have resulted in some worthwhile new insights.

Even these would not have been possible without the earlier and parallel work of others. Chapter 9, in particular, could not have been written without drawing heavily on other studies of the early liturgy, especially those of Mathews and Taft – though here, as elsewhere, I have looked at the evidence afresh to draw my own conclusions.

My chief debt, in common with all recent scholars, is to the meticulous survey of the existing structure by Robert Van Nice, in association initially with William Emerson of MIT and subsequently under the auspices of Dumbarton Oaks. I had the great privilege of working with him during several seasons in Istanbul between 1964 and 1969, during which time some aspects of the complex structural history were first elucidated by developing the approach described in Chapter 4. It was a corresponding disappointment that the joint publication then envisaged by Dumbarton Oaks became impracticable.

During that time we were greatly indebted to the late Feridun Dirimtekin, then Director of the Ayasofya Museum. During the further researches over the past five years which form the principal basis for the present book, I have been similarly indebted to Bey Ergin Uksal and, especially, to Bey Sinasi Basegmez, also of the Museum. It is a great pleasure to acknowledge their help and many kindnesses.

I owe a parallel debt to Dr John Thacher, late Director of Dumbarton Oaks, to Ernest Hawkins, Professor Ernst Kitzinger and Professor Cyril Mango, who were also associated with the project at the time, and to the librarians and staffs of the British Architectural Library, the British Library, the Society of Antiquaries, the Victoria and Albert Museum, and the Warburg Institute.

Finally I wish to record my more personal thanks to a number of friends and colleagues who have, in one way or another, furthered the enquiry or assisted in the appearance of this book. Among those not already named who have shared their experience, supplied copies of their papers, or offered welcome hospitality, have been Koksal Anadol, Professor Sedad Eldem, Professor Martin Harrison, Professor George Majeska, Professor Thomas Mathews, Professor Lee Striker, and Professor Mufit Yorulmaz. Birgul Biktimir kindly translated one paper for me from Turkish, and my daughter Anita Pepper gave similar assistance with translations of recent German papers. For his skill and care devoted over a long period to the processing and printing of most of the photographs, I am most grateful to Michael Caldwell. And all might have been in vain but for the good-humoured forbearance and further encouragement of my wife, Rhoda.

ROWLAND MAINSTONE
September 1985

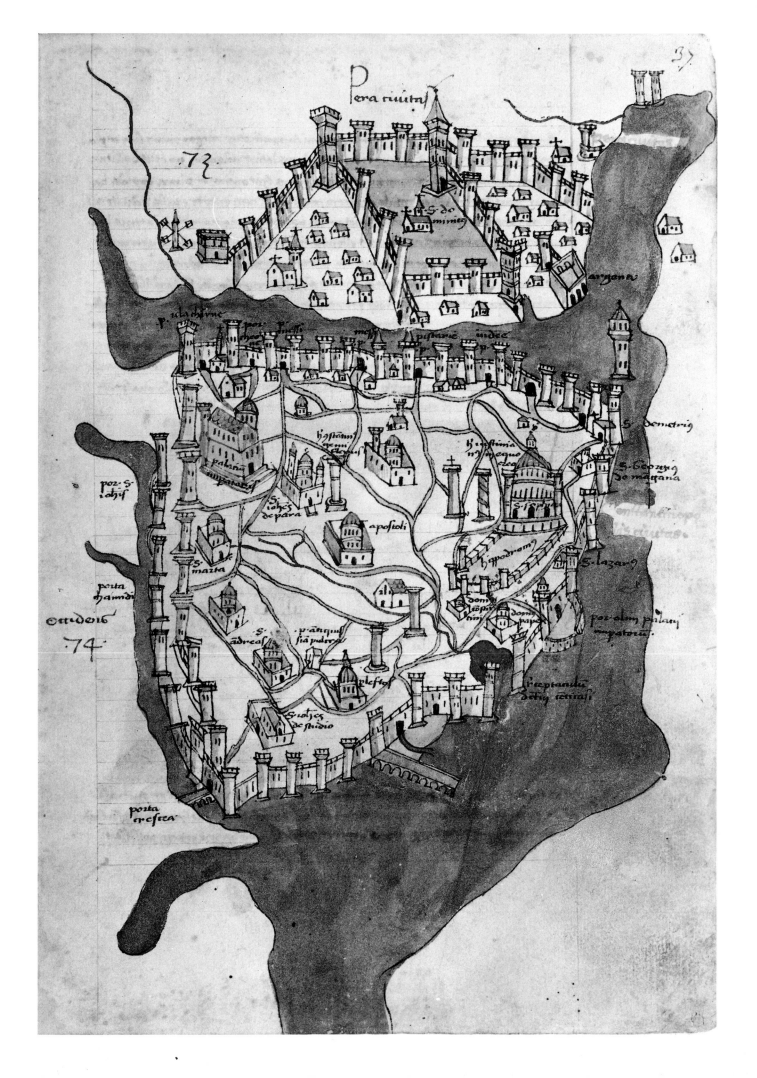

CHAPTER I

Introduction

JUSTINIAN'S CHURCH OF HAGIA SOPHIA or Divine Wisdom was first dedicated in 537 and received its definitive form in 562 after a reconstruction of the central dome. By an unprecedentedly daring combination of structural forms, Justinian's architects created an immense interior of wide-spanning vaults and subtly interpenetrating spaces that has never been surpassed and has never ceased to excite and amaze.

As the patriarchal seat in Constantinople until the Ottoman conquest – apart from the period of the Latin occupation that followed the Fourth Crusade – the church was both the centre of the religious life and the setting of much of the ritual and pageantry of the Byzantine state for the best part of a millennium. Further afield, its splendour and treasures became a legend and a challenge to those responsible for the new wave of church building in the West in the twelfth and thirteenth centuries. After the Ottoman conquest and its conversion from church to mosque its challenge was felt more directly, and can be seen reflected in the designs of a succession of later purpose-built mosques.

Today, though it survives only as a museum considerably impaired by the loss of all its Christian furnishings and much of its original setting and atmosphere, it is still sufficiently intact to be seen as the supreme architectural expression of Eastern Christianity and as one of the greatest architectural and structural achievements of all time.

1 Even the site is a commanding one, on the crest of the promontary that juts out from Europe towards Asia where the Sea of Marmara contracts into the deep narrow channel of the Bosphorus. The Sea of Marmara lies to the south, with Asia on the far shore. To the north is the long natural harbour of the Golden Horn, where ships could put in at ease in the worst weather.

---

1 An early fifteenth-century map of Constantinople, showing Justinian's Hagia Sophia as the large domed building just within the sea-wall at the right. Below it is the Hippodrome. The Sea of Marmara extends to the foot of the map, the Golden Horn runs into it from left to right near the top, dividing the city proper from the later development of Pera, and the Bosphorus enters from the direction of the Black Sea at the top right. (From *Liber insularun archipelagi* by Buondelmonte, Bibliothèque Nationale, Paris, Cod. Lat. 4825)

Already in the seventh century BC, Greek settlers had recognized the advantages of this site, and had established there the colony of Byzantion. Its acropolis had been built along the crest. In the second century AD, Byzantion fell to the Roman emperor Septimus Severus and became the Roman city of Byzantium or Colonia Antoninia. It was not yet of great importance. But, after Constantine had defeated Licinius in 324 and thereby made himself the sole ruler of the empire, he chose this already Romanized city as his new capital in the East – New Rome or Constantinople. Then, as Old Rome declined, this New Rome progressively supplanted it and became in its own peerless right simply The City – as it still is under its present Turkish name of Istanbul. 157

Justinian's church was not the first on the site. It was preceded by two others and by the nearby Constaninian church of Hagia Irene or Divine Peace, which seems to have served as the episcopal church or cathedral until the first Hagia Sophia was dedicated under Constantius in 360. After this dedication, Hagia Sophia became and remained the principal church, though the two churches functioned essentially as one.

The first rebuilding was made necessary by a fire on the occasion of the second banishment of St John Chrysostom, then patriarch, in 404. The restored church was rededicated under Theodosius II in 415 and was, in turn, severely damaged by fire in the Nike riot of January 532, which almost cost Justinian his throne. This disaster gave Justinian the pretext, at least, for erecting in its place his completely new and far more magnificent church. 3–8

Its great scale and novel design must soon have become almost frighteningly apparent to all observers as work started later that year, or early the following year, on the construction of the piers that were to carry the high vaults of the nave. Their clear spacing was half as much again as the span in any known building in the Eastern Empire, and considerably greater even than that in the most nearly comparable structure in Old Rome – the Basilica Nova of Maxentius and Constantine, built two centuries earlier. Here there was to be no progressive development of a new form through a sequence of related experiments, such as that which produced the great Gothic cathedrals of the Ile de France, but a venture to be likened only to the construction of the Roman Pantheon four centuries earlier, and the much later construction of the dome of Florence Cathedral.

9

2 A detail of the Theodosian land-wall (seen on the left side of the Buondelmonte map)

the other buildings we are accustomed to and much more decorous than those which are huge beyond measure and abounds exceedingly in sunlight and gleaming reflections. Indeed one might say that its interior is lit not by the sun from without but by a radiance generated within, such is the abundance of light that bathes this shrine all round.[2]

Justinian's exclamation has the ring of truth, even if the actual words were not his. The reaction recorded by Propocius is also wholly understandable in the context of the time, as is his later reference to the terrifying seeming insecurity of the eastern semidome, which 'seems somehow to rise on no firm basis, but to soar aloft to the peril of those below',[3] and which was, in fact, soon to suffer the partial collapse that also brought down part of the dome.

Still later in his description, Procopius refers to the gold mosaic that covered the vaults, the marble revetments of the walls, the different hued marbles of the many columns, and the silver embellishments of the sanctuary, all of which must have contributed to the 'gleaming reflections', and then to the overall impression made by the interior on the worshipper:

The whole ceiling is overlaid with pure gold which is beautiful as well as ostentatious. Yet the reflections from the marbles prevail, vying with the gold. . . . Who could recount [their] beauty? One might imagine that one had chanced upon a meadow in full bloom. For one would surely marvel at the purple hue of some, the green of others, at those which glow with crimson and those which flash with white, and again at those which Nature, like a painter, has varied with the most contrasting colours.

And whenever one enters the church to pray, one understands immediately that it has been fashioned not by any human power or skill but by the influence of God. And so the mind is lifted up to God and exalted, feeling that He cannot be far away but must love to dwell in this place which He has chosen.[4]

The partial collapse occurred in 558, and the rededication almost five years later, after the necessary reconstruction, led Paulus Silentarius, a court official, to write his much fuller metrical description which is now our other principal literary source for the Justinianic church, and the primary one for its liturgical furnishings.

During the succeeding years of Christian use, there were two further partial collapses of the dome calling for local rebuilding. There was also a major rebuilding of the great window walls or tympana on the north and south sides beneath the dome, and there were numerous additions of buttresses and other changes on the exterior which considerably affected the natural lighting of the interior.

The liturgical furnishings suffered greatly during the Latin occupation, and must have suffered again through

Equally remarkable was the rapidity with which the new building rose from the ground. Less than six years elapsed between the fire and the first dedication.

According to a late and largely legendary account – the so-called *Narratio* – Justinian was then moved to exclaim: 'Glory to God who has thought me worthy to finish this work. Solomon I have outdone you.'[1]

A more reliable source is the contemporary historian Procopius. Writing some twenty years after the dedication, he opened his long account of Justinian's buildings with a full description of the new Hagia Sophia. He prefaced this with the following assessment:

So the church has become a spectacle of great beauty, overwhelming to those who see it and altogether incredible to those who only hear of it. For it soars to a height to match the sky and . . . looks down upon the rest of the city . . . Its breadth and length have been so fittingly proportioned that it may rightly be said to be both very long and unusually broad. And it exults in an indescribable beauty. For it subtly combines mass with harmony of proportions, having neither excess nor deficiency, inasmuch as it is both more pompous than the second of the two further partial collapses. But after the end of iconoclasm in the ninth century, new figural mosaics were added on some of the principal vaults, on the tympanum walls, in the galleries, and on the lunettes over two of the entrances.

Thus, although the internal aspect progressively changed, the splendour of the overall effect is unlikely to have been greatly diminished up to the Ottoman conquest. The impression made on those attending the divine liturgy on great feasts, with both the emperor and patriarch taking part, must have been even more overwhelming. A well-known testimony to this is furnished by the account in the Primary Russian Chronicle – even if apochryphal in its precise detail – of the report by emissaries of Prince Vladimir of Kiev on a service they had attended:

> We knew not whether we were in heaven or on earth. For on earth there is no such splendour or such beauty, and we are at a loss how to describe it. We only know that God dwells there among men, and their service is fairer than the ceremonies of other nations. For we cannot forget that beauty.[5]

When a much impoverished Constantinople finally fell to the Ottomans on 23 May 1453, Hagia Sophia was again looted as it had been earlier by the Latins. But its spell worked sufficiently on the young sultan, Mehmet II, for it to be spared the fate of Justinian's other great church in the city – the already somewhat dilapidated Church of the Holy Apostles. After being handed back for a time to a new patriarch to serve as the patriarchal church, this was later swept away to make room for the first of the new imperial mosques that now share the Istanbul skyline with Hagia Sophia. Hagia Sophia was merely adapted to a new use as the Mosque of Aya Sofya, and continued to serve this use until it was secularized by Ataturk in 1934.

The initial adaptation probably involved little more than the removal of the principal Christian liturgical furnishings, their replacement by a mihrab and mimbar oriented towards Mecca, and the construction of a temporary wooden minaret. The cross over the dome was replaced by the crescent, but surprisingly little was done to deface or cover the Christian figural mosaics. Many of those in the vaults remained visible until the eighteenth century, and the wings of the seraphim in the eastern pendentives were never hidden.

3 A composite view of the church from the south-east minaret, looking towards the junction of the Golden Horn and the Bosphorus and with the church of Hagia Irene at the upper right

4 The church from the south west

Externally the silhouette was progressively changed in later years by the building of tall permanent minarets in the four corners. The immediate surroundings also gradually changed with the demolition of most of the old patriarchal palace and other Byzantine structures, and the construction of several imperial tombs to the south, and other new buildings on the remaining sides. At various times further structural repairs were also undertaken, including fresh additions to the external buttresses.

Nineteenth-century views showing the interior before and after the last major repairs in 1847–49 give some idea of the changes after almost four hundred years as a mosque. By the early nineteenth century most of the high-level mosaic figures in the nave had been painted over, large square panels bearing arabic inscriptions had been hung against the faces of the piers, and the richest colour must have been that of the prayer rugs which covered the whole floor. Countless small oil lamps were suspended in great hoops only a little above the heads of the worshippers. The light from these lamps, the vastness of the space under the dome, and the strange effect of the skew alignment of the prayer rugs and furnishings and the rows of the turbaned congregation were what most impressed the few non-Muslims who then gained admittance.

During the repairs, most of the surviving mosaics were briefly uncovered and then painted over again, rather for their protection against the more fanatical imams than on account of religious zeal. The redecoration took its inspiration from the geometrical and other non-figural motifs of the surviving original mosaics of Justinian's time. In addition a large new Sultan's box was constructed to the left of the place of the original sanctuary, new windows of stained glass were installed in the apse, new discs with arabic inscriptions were set in place on the faces of the piers, and the big suspended hoops of lamps were replaced by a larger number of smaller hoops.

When newly completed, the redecoration probably made it easier again to appreciate the superb and unique spatial quality of the interior, despite the insensitivity of execution of the crudely stencilled simulations of gold-ground mosaic. Unfortunately it soon deteriorated and became more of a distraction. Early photographs already show it badly discoloured by damp or dirt, though Mark Twain's characterization of the structure after a brief visit in 1869 as 'the rustiest old barn in heathendom'[6] was doubtless more the venting of an unhappy tourist's spleen than a dispassionate appraisal. Some further deterioration occurred as a result of the 1894 earthquake.

9, 10

5 The interior today from the west gallery

Secularization, followed early in 1935 by the opening of the building as a museum, brought to an end almost fourteen hundred years of virtually uninterrupted use as a place of worship by three faiths – Orthodox, Catholic and Muslim. With the removal of the prayer rugs that covered the floor went also the warmth that comes from use – a much more continuous use in the mosque than that of most churches today. In its place there is now too often the distracting presence of large groups of tourists, adding to the other impediments to appreciation that arise from the even worse present condition of the nineteenth-century decoration and the discordant notes introduced by the remaining Muslim furnishings and calligraphic inscriptions.

Thus reactions today are mixed. The expectations raised by the descriptions of Procopius and Paulus Silentarius, and by the report of Prince Vladimir's emissaries, are easily dashed. No one sensitive to the character of spatial enclosure can fail to respond to the experience of stepping through the imperial door into the nave and moving forward towards the great dome. This can still take one's breath away, even after repeated visits, and remains one of the supreme architectural experiences of all time. But to relive the experience of those who first used the building in Justinian's time, to see it as they saw it and feel something of their excitement, calls now for a great effort of imagination. In some ways this effort is easier in the empty shell of an isolated and deserted ruin.

6, 7 Interiors looking eastward from the end bays of the side galleries

Yet secularization has also helped. It has helped most directly and obviously by facilitating the cleaning of the surviving figural mosaics and some of the earlier decoration. It may be hoped that in due course it will permit the cleaning of the remainder, and an appropriate redecoration of surfaces from which the mosaic has been lost.

Less directly it has helped by making possible a precise, measured survey of the existing structure, and other detailed studies of its construction and structural history.[7]

Through these investigations a clearer picture has emerged not only of the quality and character of the decoration, but also of the form of Justinian's church and the changes it has undergone. Other evidence can now be set alongside that furnished by the surviving documents to provide a firmer basis for the necessary efforts of imagination. Somewhat more speculatively, it is even possible to suggest how the design may first have been conceived, and how it evolved, and was, in some ways, modified as construction proceeded.

To arrive at this picture, it has been necessary to bring together evidence of many kinds – documentary, graphic, architectural, structural, archaeological – and to look at it from as many different points of view. To complete the picture, it has also been necessary to look well beyond the church itself and to consider its use as well as its form.

In presenting it and the evidence for it, it is necessary to weave all these threads together and to move both backwards and forwards in time. Some overlap in the discussions (in Chapter 4 and 8) of the early changes that occurred before the church acquired its definitive Justinianic form in 562 is unavoidable. Later changes in form and furnishing and decoration will be considered only to the extent that is necessary to identify and allow for them. This means, for instance, that we shall not look in detail at the figural mosaics, the later additions to the structure, or Ottoman furnishings.

The great size of the church, its complexity of form and structure, the unique spatial quality of its interior, and the changes associated with such a long history, together make unusual demands on the choice of suitable drawings and photographs to accompany the text.

The visual impression one actually has of the interior is always a composite one, in which consciousness of what lies well outside the principal focus of attention plays an important part. Photographs taken with ultra wide-angle lenses do not convey it because they give too much emphasis to this field of peripheral consciousness unless they are viewed from almost impossibly close. The early interior views of Grelot, Loos and Fossati come closer to presenting what one really sees, but only by introducing compensatory distortions. Those that are reproduced will be supplemented here by photographs taken mostly with a 35 mm lens, including some composite views taken from single viewpoints with a roving camera standing in for the roving human eye.

8 Cutaway isometric view of the church today, omitting the present furnishings and all peripheral buttresses, access ramps and other adjacent structures. Below the east-west centre-line the ground plan is shown in full line and the reflected plan of the vaults in broken line

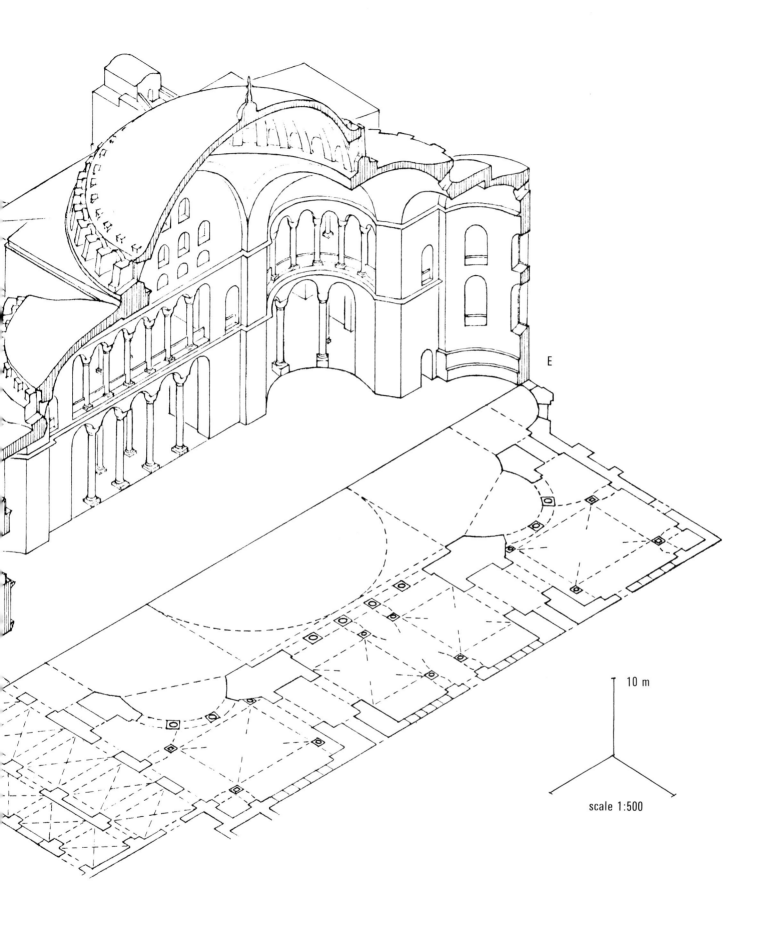

E

10 m

scale 1:500

As a meticulously accurate large-scale record of the present forms with all their deviations from regularity, the survey drawings already referred to are an indispensable tool for all further research. But their value is largely lost in small-scale reproduction, and they give a doubly misleading impression of the Justinianic form in showing not only the results of deliberate later changes but also the marked increases in deformations that have occurred since Justinian's time. In fact, as we shall see later, the present deformations are roughly twice as great as the maximum reached then, even for elements that have survived otherwise unchanged.

To represent Justinian's church with similar accuracy it would be necessary to show it several times over, as construction proceeded, as the early deformations developed, and as the first changes were made. Since this is impracticable, the main series of plans, sections and elevations (placed at the back for ease of reference) shows A2–*f* the final form in 562 as nearly as possible as it may be assumed it was intended to appear – that is, without any of the deformations. The representation of features now lost is, of course, somewhat speculative. But, apart from the liturgical furnishings, these are relatively unimportant, being chiefly peripheral structures, and minor fenes-

10 The same view in 1849 after the Fossati restoration (Fossati, plate 3)

tration. This series of general drawings is supplemented at appropriate points in the text by others of particular elements, drawn to a larger scale and showing the likely actual deformations at particular times as well as successive changes in form.

Finally it may be noted that, for the interpretation of the evidence of the precise present geometry of some of the forms as well as for the elucidation of choices open to the designers and of the behaviour of the structure during construction and afterwards, considerable structural analysis has been necessary. This has been performed with the full resources of modern theory and computational techniques, supplemented where necessary by laboratory tests.[8] But it has not been thought necessary to give details of the calculations, or to quote the results to any greater accuracy than the accuracy of the basic data warrants. If this limited presentation disappoints those who hanker for a single definitive analysis of the way the structure behaves, it must be emphasized that such an analysis is no more possible than is a single precise representation of Justinianic form of the church. The structure is a living organism subject to a continually changing pattern of internal stresses, and, as will become apparent in due course, it always has been so.

CHAPTER 2

The church today: exterior and interior

THE CHURCH AS IT STANDS TODAY is the obvious starting point for any attempt to visualize it as it was in Justinian's day. We shall look first at what can readily be seen by an observant visitor, approaching from a distance, walking round it, entering, and mounting finally to the highest levels, to which access would have been as restricted in the past as it is today.

The distant view

Despite all later changes, Hagia Sophia still dominates the immediate surroundings with almost the same authority as in Justinian's time, challenged only by the nearby Mosque of Sultan Ahmet, the so-called Blue Mosque. From the Bosphorus to the north, it rises above the present Saray Point and the pavilions of the Ottoman palace, and only slowly drops behind these as one approaches. From the Sea of Marmara to the south east, its form is most clearly revealed, with the later additions that crowd around its lower flanks and its east end well hidden by the trees and lower buildings on the slope down to the shore. Between the sharp pencils of the four minarets, the dome sits majestically on its square base with the rounded forms of a cluster of semidomes mounting towards it on the nearest side, and strong buttressing arms embracing it on each flank. Dome and semidomes are sheathed in lead, while nearly all wall surfaces are now covered by a dull yellow rendering.

The dome has a flattish external profile, closer to that of the Roman Pantheon than to the raised profiles of most later domes. Here, though, in place of the steps at the foot of the Pantheon dome, is a ring of low buttresses between windows that are cut into the lower part of the dome itself. These buttresses, linked to one another above the windows, almost create the impression of a low drum. Windows similarly cut into the main and lesser semidomes, and separated by stepped buttress-like additions to the semidome masonry, give to these semidomes a broadly similar look.

The cluster of semidomes at the east is repeated at the west with two differences. At the west, most obviously, there is a large, almost semicircular window in place of the central small semidome at the east. This is the largest single window surviving in the building. It stands a little forward of the drum-like base of the main semidome and is framed to left and right by walls which continue the plane of its arched head and are capped by small domed turrets that rise a little above this head.

The second difference is best seen from the direction of the Mosque of Ahmet to the south, or from the opposite direction of Topkapi Palace. Both main semidomes are then visible together in profile, and that to the west is seen to be markedly stilted in its lower part and correspondingly flattened at the top, although not sufficiently to keep its crown below the top of the dome base. It also has a generally heavier look. We shall see later that this second difference has come about through the partial rebuilding of these semidomes at widely separated dates.

If we ignore the added minarets, the strong buttressing arms that project from the north and south sides of the dome base are the chief contrasting elements. They rise above the roofs of the side galleries almost, but not quite, to the springing level of the dome. Narrow slit windows in their end walls hint at internal stairs.

Between each pair of buttresses spans a deep arch that carries one side of the square dome base, and smaller squinch-like arches bridge the internal angles between the tops of the buttresses and the dome base. The deep projection of these arches in front of the walls that fill the spaces beneath them creates, on the south side, the only strong shadow of this kind on the whole exterior, and accentuates the contrast with the east and west ends, where the forms all swell outwards and there are no significant recessions. Each infill wall – or tympanum – beneath the arches has two ranges of windows whose opening have been narrowed and made slightly pointed at the heads in a manner that is typically Turkish.

Below, the roofs of the side galleries gently swell as they rise over each domical vault, closely following its curvature near the crown. Around their edges they undulate further as they rise and fall over arched vaults above the windows. Like the dome and semidomes which they flank on both sides, these lower roofs are sheathed everywhere in lead, as is the gently sloping roof of the western gallery.

In most distant views, however, the lower levels of the church are only glimpsed, and their possible extent is suggested chiefly by the placing of the minarets. In fact, all the minarets stand slightly outside the eastern and western boundaries of the church proper. Its width, including side aisles and galleries, is that indicated by the full lateral extent of the great north and south buttresses, and it extends longitudinally (if we exclude the narthex and outer narthex) from the west window to the small eastern semidome over the apse.

12 The church from the north west, with the main dome of
Hagia Irene to the left and that of the Mosque of Ahmet to the right

13 The church from the Sea of Marmara

14 The church from the west

15 The church from the south

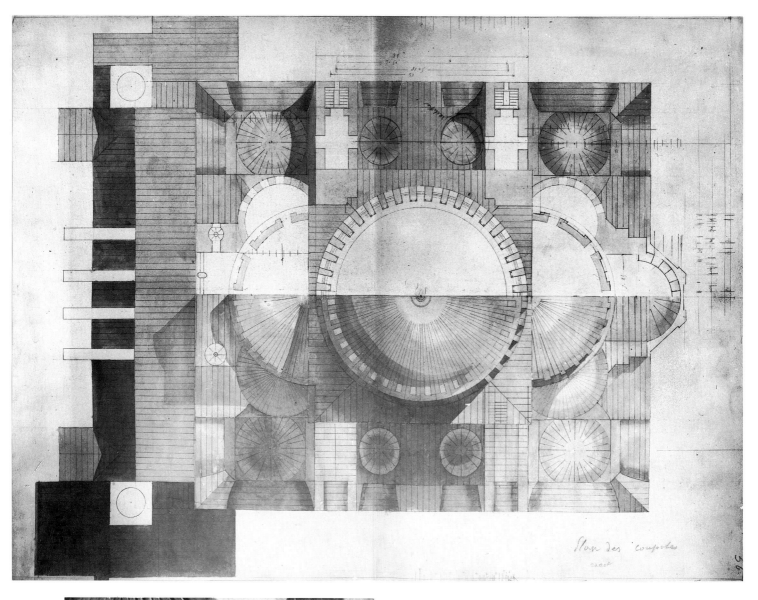

Plan des coupoles

To see properly the gallery roofs and appreciate the lively interplay of surfaces acting as a perfect foil to the bolder swellings above, it is necessary to climb up to thcm, 19 or to climb further to the dome base or one of the 16, 17 minarets, and look down.

The nearer view

Most nearer views are less immediately intelligible than they must once have been because later outer buttresses, rising to the gallery roofs, stand against the church on all sides, and the view is often further obstructed by trees and other nearby structures.

In an enclosed garden to the south are several Turkish tombs as well as the baptistery. In a similar enclosed area to 20 the north behind a higher wall are several workshops and other buildings and, more notably, the skeuophylakion. 161 This last is, in its lower part, probably the earliest structure now standing on the site, and it will be discussed further in Chapter 5. The east and west sides are more accessible. But on both these sides the ground soon falls away rapidly from the crest on which the church stands.

16 Plan of the roofs (drawing by
Charles Texier, 1834. RIBA
Drawings Collection, reproduced
here to approximately the same
scale as plans A2 to A4

17 View of the roofs of the south-
west exedra and the western bay
of the south gallery from the
dome base

18 View on the roof of the south
gallery below the arch that carries
the dome base

19 View from the south, showing,
in the centre, the same area of
roof as that visible in plate 17

One now usually approaches through the garden at the west, which occupies the site of the sixth-century atrium. The eastern side of this atrium survives, somewhat modified, between the projecting masses of masonry that carry the two western minarets. In front of it towards the left may be seen the only excavated remains of the pre-sixth-century church that are still exposed and *in situ*, while the principal architectural fragments discovered in the excavation are displayed nearby in the garden. These remains also will be described and discussed further in Chapter 5.

Looking towards the west end of the church from this garden, one sees the first range of outer buttresses. Here they strongly resemble the flying buttresses characteristic, in the West, of Gothic cathedrals from the late twelfth century onwards. The buttress piers project forward from the outer wall of an outer narthex, and the flyers above reach over to the outer wall of the west gallery below the great west window.

The complex groups of forms around the north and south ends of the narthex and western gallery are more difficult to understand without reference to detailed plans. At both ends they include enclosed ramps which project outside the main rectangle of the church proper to provide access to the galleries. But at the south they include also what remains of the adjoining patriarchate building, as well as the surviving baptistery and some smaller Turkish additions. There is evidence of repeated remodelling, including the blocking of the entrance to the baptistery narthex along its western side.

The outer buttresses along the sides of the church are more varied in form and have greatly altered the original appearance of the exterior just as – by blocking windows and obstructing light – they have altered the character of the interior. Most of them are now seemingly solid masses of stone masonry, built directly against the aisle and gallery walls, with slightly battered outer faces and wide, sloping leaded roofs. Not all, however, are as solid as they appear.

At the east there are more similar buttresses and two more flying buttresses alongside the apse. But these two are of much heavier proportions than those at the west and have, again, slightly battered outer faces in contrast to the vertical outer faces of the piers of the western buttresses.

Embedded in the present enclosing wall to the south of the apse is a porch with a pointed arch. The wall itself and a number of low buildings behind it are of Turkish date, as are the bases of the two eastern minarets. But the southern base probably incorporates part of an original access-ramp to the gallery, and between that at the north and the adjacent corner of the church the north-east ramp still survives.

Most of the surviving original aisle and gallery windows are, like the great west window, large screens of marble and glass which fill virtually the whole of the bays they occupy up to the rounded soffits of the vaults behind. Like the great west window again, they are divided into three sections by intermediate columns. But the division is now in two tiers separated by an architrave on the chord of the window arch, on account of their taller proportion. Marble grills fill the intervening spaces to carry the small panes of glass. Elsewhere – notably in the corner bays of the north and south aisles – the glazed area is reduced. Groups of three narrower round-headed windows separated by brick piers take the place of single windows filling the whole available space.

20 Ottoman tombs (left) and the baptistery (upper right) in the south garden. At the lower right are the roofs of some of the outer buttresses on the south side

21 Looking across the site of the atrium towards the west end of the church

22 The south-west corner of the church, with the baptistery to the right, the south-west entrance a little to the left of centre, and the south-west ramp and remains of the patriarchate above and to the left of this

23 The north-west corner of the church, with part of the outer wall of the atrium to the right of the base of the minaret, and the north-west porch and ramp to the left of it

25 (*Below right*) Looking westwards towards the buttresses on the north side of the church, with the outer buttresses at the foot and the ends of the main buttress piers above them

24 (*Below left*) The south-east corner of the church seen from the foot of the south-east minaret

26 (*Facing page*) The east end of the church

Narthexes

There is clear evidence of original entrances on all sides of the church, including several that gave direct access to the aisles. Only two of the less direct western entrances are in normal use today. The principal one is approached through the western garden and leads first into the outer narthex. The other (now used chiefly as an exit) is on the opposite side of the south-west minaret and leads into the south end of the inner narthex through a porch between the base of this minaret and the projecting south-west ramp.

27   The outer narthex is a long transverse space, largely devoid of decoration, and approximately as high as it is wide up to the springing level of a series of nine domical cross vaults. There is a door from the garden in each of the three bays that are framed by the piers of the projecting central group of flying buttresses, the central door being the one normally in use. In the two bays on each side of this group of doors there are windows to light the interior. One of these windows fills the whole bay in the manner of the first of the two types described above; the others are grouped smaller windows resembling the second type, but they do not appear to be original. In each end bay is a further door on the garden side that must originally have communicated with the atrium. In alternate bays of the long east wall facing the entrances there are five doors to the inner narthex.

These doors, like most others at this end of the church, each have two leaves sheathed in dark bronze with simple relief decorations.[1] Large crosses predominate, sometimes rising from chalices or rocks, sometimes set within architectural frames. The stiles and rails are also decorated, the hanging stiles being rounded at the outer edges, and continued above and below the top and bottom rails to serve as pivots about which the leaves turn.

The alternative entry through the porch at the south   22 end passes initially two door leaves with bronze decoration of a different and unique kind. These doors are   28 now held permanently open against the side-walls by a raising of the floor level. Each face has two recessed panels bordered with bands of rinceaux, studded meanders and other motifs within a boldly studded outer frame. The panels are incised with ninth-century monograms set around crosses, each within a circle. Outside the studded outer frames are attached broader bands of rinceaux and other ornament.[2]

The porch is roofed by a vault that is clearly of later date than the side-walls, and the lack of correspondence between these side-walls suggests that the space was originally unroofed. At its end, above the south door of   29 the narthex, is one of the principal figural mosaics.[3] Justinian (on the left) and Constantine (on the right) are shown presenting models of the church and the city to an enthroned Virgin and Child. Though the model of the   30 church is, as usual in such representations, greatly simplified, it bears a recognizable resemblance to Hagia Sophia and emphasizes the crowning central feature of the dome.

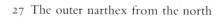
27 The outer narthex from the north

28 Detail of the eastern leaf of the doors at the entrance to the south-west porch

29 The south-west porch

30 The mosaic above the inner door of the
south-west porch

31 Looking into the narthex from the south-west porch

The inner narthex is a much more impressive space, whether entered from the west or from the south. It is considerably taller and wider than the outer narthex, and its walls and vaults are richly decorated. But its length, being the same as that of the outer narthex, is still much greater than its width. This makes it appear smaller than it really is, an effect which the size of the doors does nothing to diminish.

The walls are sheathed in coloured marbles almost up to cornice level, and the vaults are covered in gold-ground mosaic decorated with crosses, stars and other geometrical motifs. Light comes chiefly through windows set high up in each bay above the roof of the outer narthex, so that it is directed towards the opposite long wall containing the doorways leading into the church, and brings out the dull sheen of the marble alongside them.

There are three groups of these doorways, and three in each group. Each door is again sheathed in bronze and decorated in simple relief panels, the largest panels having originally contained crosses whose outlines only can now be distinguished. In contrast to the lack of differentiation between the doors from the outer narthex, the central group of these doors is taller than the others, and the one in the middle of this group – known as the Imperial door – is tallest and widest of all, and is further emphasized by a bronze casing to the head of the doorway, by panels of dark marble decorated in shallow relief at each side, and by another figural mosaic in the lunette above. This shows a prostrate emperor at the feet of an enthroned Christ, to either side of whom are busts of the Virgin and the archangel Gabriel set in circular frames.

It also becomes apparent, if one looks back from these doors to those that open from the outer narthex, that only the central doors directly line up with one another. The remaining doors line up only very approximately, or have no counterpart on the outer side. Looking up, one also sees that the vaulting bays – which do correspond to those in the outer narthex – are consequently unrelated to the placing of the doorways into the church.

This is but the first of several such lacks of correspondence. Visually it is made less obtrusive than it might otherwise be by the lack of any pilaster responds to break the flatness of the wall containing the doors to the church, and by the interposition of a deep continuous frieze between the marble facings of this wall and the springings of the transverse arches of the vaults.

32 The narthex seen from the north west

33 The central group of doors into the nave, with the
Imperial door in the middle of the group

◁ 34 Looking through the Imperial door into the nave   35 The mosaic above the Imperial door

Nave

From the narthex, only the apse at the far end of the nave is
34 seen at first through the open central door, with a mosaic
of the Virgin and Child looking down from its semidome,
marble facings on the wall below and Turkish stained glass
in the windows, and a sultan's box to one side and a
Turkish mimbar to the other. With nothing between to
give scale but a receding perspective of low-slung lamp-
hoops, and bands of green across the white marble floor,
its distance from the viewer is not immediately apparent.

As one moves forward, one sees next that the piers
bounding the apse are flanked by similar but shallower
36 curved recesses or exedrae, angled inwards to the centre of
the nave. But these recesses are only partly visible. They
disappear behind projecting broader and nearer piers
whose visible faces are parallel to the main west-east axis.
These are two of the main piers that carry the dome.
Against their faces, as against the faces of the secondary
piers flanking the apse, hang large circular Turkish plaques
with arabic inscriptions in gold on a dark green ground.

Unlike the apse, the exedrae are not wholly bounded by
solid walls. Between the piers there are open arcaded
colonnades in two storeys; and there is a surprising
37 difference between these storeys. The lower colonnades
are not only taller than the upper ones with a wider
column-spacing. Having only two columns each as
against six above, they are also considerably shorter. There
is no real correspondence. The lower columns are
monolithic shafts of porphyry standing on white marble
pedestals; the upper ones shafts of *verde antico*. The
spandrels above the arches of the lower colonnades are of
fretted marble with inset darker discs. Those above gallery
colonnades are of multi-coloured *opus sectile*. Behind the
colonnades, the outer spaces of aisles and galleries can be
glimpsed, but little is visible of them from this distance.

Extending westwards from the main piers are more
open arcaded colonnades, now in two parallel straight
38 lines. The pier faces have slight setbacks behind the
Turkish plaques, and the colonnades are similarly set back
to increase the overall width of the central part of the nave.
Again the columns are more closely spaced at the gallery
level and this – together with a similar use of fretted
marble and *opus sectile* in the spandrels above the arches at
both levels – reinforces the horizontal continuity
39 established by continuous cornices around the entire nave.
The only significant difference from the exedrae
colonnades is that the columns of the lower colonnades are
here slightly taller monolithic shafts of *verde antico* without
pedestals.

At the east, semidomes over the exedrae and a barrel
vault in front of the semidome of the apse merge into a
much larger semidome as wide as the nave itself. This
semidome is bounded at its forward edge by an arch
spanning from one main pier to the other, though the
soffit of the arch is continuous with that of the semidome.
There is a ring of windows in the lower part of each
semidome. But some of those visible on the outside of the

exedrae semidomes have been blocked and are now
represented in paint – the same badly discoloured
nineteenth-century paint as elsewhere takes the place of
lost mosaic.

To each side, arches of similar apparent span rise high
above the side colonnades and enclose large walls or
tympana, each containing two ranges of windows above a
row of shallow niches. As these arches rise from the piers
and separate from the forward arch of the eastern
semidome, the intervening spaces are filled by the curved
triangles of the two eastern pendentives, each bearing a
mosaic seraph whose face is concealed by a gilt star.

Above the pendentives is the topmost cornice, and
above this, the ring of windows at the base of the dome.

The dome itself is hardly seen at first. But the eye is
irresistibly drawn up to it by the brighter light coming
through its windows, and by the upward movement of
semidomes, arches and pendentives. It appears surpris- 40
ingly shallow for its great span. Ribs between the windows
die out towards the crown, where another, even larger,
circular plaque with arabic inscription hides the central
feature of the gold mosaic that covers the rest of the
surface.

Moving further forward between the two western
secondary piers that carry the barrel vault over the
westernmost part of the nave, one sees to left and right two
western exedrae similar to those at the east, with the aisles
more clearly visible between the tall porphyry shafts of the 41
ground-level colonnades. Overhead is a large semidome
similar to that at the east, rising from similar smaller
semidomes over the exedrae.

Only now does the full extent of the completely open
central space become apparent. Its length from west to east 42
is more than twice its width, even ignoring the narrower
barrel-vaulted extensions between the secondary piers in
front of the apse at the east and inside the Imperial door at
the west. Its width, about 30 m, is about three times that of
the typical Gothic cathedral nave. And the dome, rising to
about 56 m above floor level, would overtop the tallest
Gothic vault.

Equally striking, if not more so, is the character of this
space. The nearest comparable space at the time the church
was built, and for long afterwards, was that of the
Pantheon. But that of Hagia Sophia is far more complex
and subtle. The Pantheon interior is completely
centralized – a hemispherical dome set on a cylindrical
drum – and its enfolding boundaries are simply and clearly
defined and immediately comprehensible. The interior of
Hagia Sophia combines the centrality of a dome with the
axiality typical of a normal basilica, and its true boundaries
are elusive. They alternately advance and recede,
sometimes solid though faced in insubstantial-looking
marble, and sometimes no more than open screens. Never
being fully visible at one time, they appear continuously to
change as one moves around, and there are ever-changing
partial glimpses of the peripheral spaces of aisles and
galleries.

37 The south-east
exedra

Facing page
38 The nave,
looking eastwards

39 Looking across
the nave from
within the central
bay of the south
aisle

40 Looking up towards the dome from the west

41 Looking down the nave and into the south aisle, from the south-west exedra

42 (*Facing page*) Looking back towards the western end of the nave from the north-west exedra

43 Detail of the arcade carried by the ground-level colonnade on the north side of the nave

44 Detail of the upper-level colonnade and arcade on the ▷ north side of the nave

As soon as one looks more closely, expectations are confounded by such features as the lack of correspondence between the colonnades at ground and gallery levels. Unity is achieved, on the one hand, by an underlying geometrical discipline that becomes obvious only at the level of the semidomes and dome, and, on the other, by details like the horizontal cornices that sweep unbroken across the piers and above the arcaded colonnades, and by an overall unity-within-diversity of the colonnades themselves and the decorative treatment of the wall surfaces – even, perhaps, by a consistent absence of the precise uniformity typical of a modern machine age.

We have already noted how the porphyry columns raised on low pedestals in the colonnades of the ground-level exedrae give way to taller columns of *verde antico* without pedestals in the side colonnades beneath the dome. But closer inspection shows that the columns of each group differ significantly in their proportions, and that all columns have a certain irregularity of surface. The differences are greatest in the exedrae columns, presumably because of the difficulty of obtaining perfect porphyry monoliths of this size. All columns of both groups have bronze collars at top and bottom, where earlier classical columns would have had integral neckings. But all columns of the western exedrae and one at the north east also have two or more intermediate collars – one having no less than seven. Minor variations in height within the groups are taken up by variations in the equally unclassical pedestals and bases.

There is more uniformity in the columns of the gallery colonnades, in the capitals of both colonnades, and in the treatment of the spandrels and soffits of the arches they carry at each level – but still no mechanical repetition.

The superb capitals of white marble are even less classical then the almost cylindrical column shafts.[4] At both levels they are of the same basic bowl-form, capped by small Ionic volutes which make the transition to integral flared impost blocks. The surfaces of the bowls are fretted with sharply cut (and undercut) acanthus and palm leaves, stylized but by no means rigid. Bosses in the centres of the faces that contain the volutes carry monograms, mostly of Justinian or emperor (Basileus), or, less frequently, Theodora or empress (Augusta). But no two are quite identical.

42

43–5,

45 Detail of the east end of the ground-level colonnade and arcade on the north side of the nave

46 Looking up to the cornices and upper-level arcade on the south side of the nave

The decoration of the lower spandrels is similar to that of the capitals in its lace-like undercutting and flowing leaf forms. So, also, is that of two narrow bands running around the arches in the slabs fixed under their soffits. That of the upper spandrels and of their soffits is different. The *opus sectile* work on the spandrels was probably intended to read similarly at a considerably greater height. Rinceaux and other vegetal and bird forms in white marble are set against a background of dark marble. In the soffits is gold-ground mosaic with rinceaux and geometric borders in red, green, blue and silver.

The dominant decoration is, however, the marble facing of the wall surfaces. It is of the same general character as that already seen in the inner narthex, with tall slabs of different colours set between narrower bands of lighter colour (plate 16 of Sanpaolesi, *Santa Sofia*). Often two taller slabs that have been sliced from a single block are opened out like a book, so that their natural veining creates a symmetrical pattern. Such pairs, some of the tall single slabs, and all horizontal bands are framed by simple white fillet mouldings, or (in the case of the principal bands of tall slabs that rise almost to the capitals of the colonnades) by wider carved margins of the same white marble. In a few places – notably in the apse and over the Imperial door – small panels with designs cut in relief, and sometimes also inlaid, are again incorporated, as they were in the narthex.

All this facing is executed with great freedom, as Lethaby noted long ago. Slabs and mouldings are usually simply butted against one another, even at angles and other changes of direction. The wider carved margins have simply been cut to length as required, without any concern for the continuity of their decoration. Plane surfaces are not perfectly flat but slightly waved. And there is no suggestion of heavily stressed masonry behind the skin.

Finally, the ambiguity of the relationship between the wall surface and the more expressively structural colonnades and arcades should be noted. At ground level, for instance, the surface decoration of the capitals carries over almost unbroken into the arch spandrels. At each end of each arcade, the spandrel decoration is then carried over into the adjacent wall, and terminated by a simple vertical fillet. But there is no suggestion of column or pilaster on the pier-face below the arch. Round the corner, on the pier respond, there is indeed the suggestion of a pilaster, capital, and base (or pedestal and base), matching those of the colonnade. But each has the same flat character as the facing of the wall in which it is set, in spite of the incongruous suggestion of three-dimensionality given to the capital by showing its volutes as they would appear if viewed face-on from the nave.

47 (*Above*) The north-west main pier seen from across the nave

48 (*Right*) Detail of the east end of the ground-level colonnade and arcade on the south side of the nave

Aisles

Low stylobates of varying depth mark off the aisles from the nave where these communicate through the open colonnades. Today the only other barriers between the two are those created by Turkish tribunes and other balustraded platforms, or, in the two western exedrae, by large marble urns. There is also unobstructed passage from nave to aisles at the west end through barrel-vaulted passages that penetrate the western secondary piers in a north-south direction, and, but for modern barriers, there would be similar passage at the east end through the eastern secondary piers.

To move from nave to aisles is to enter a very different space. In most churches the aisles simply echo the nave on a smaller scale. Here they do not, and they are even more complex in plan.

The difference arises primarily because of the complex side-boundaries of the nave, which look very different when viewed from the direction of the aisle. The added complexity results from the fact that nearly all the bulk of the main piers that carry the dome is within the space marked out by the nave colonnades as belonging to the

48, 5▮

50

50 View northwards from the western bay of the south aisle

49 Looking into the nave and down the south aisle from its western bay

51 View into the central bay of the south aisle from the nave

aisles. In addition, each main pier is faced across the aisle by the answering bulk of a buttress pier. Main piers and buttress piers together bring about a pronounced division of each aisle into separate bays.

Entering either aisle through one of the doors near the ends of the narthex, one thus looks down a succession of bays of varying shape and size, the larger bays being separated by shorter and narrower barrel-vaulted sections between the intrusive main piers and associated outer buttress piers. The largest bay is that in the centre: those at the two ends behind the exedrae are only slightly shorter, and highly irregular in overall plan.

A single, slightly domical groined vault spans over the central width of each end bay, and two similar but smaller vaults span over that of each central bay. To carry (or assist in carrying) these vaults, four free-standing columns are set in each bay. Most of these columns, together with their capitals and bases, are similar to the *verde antico* columns of the central nave colonnades, though considerably shorter. However, the western pair in the west bay and the eastern pair in the east bay are of white marble, square in cross-section, slightly tapered, and with different capitals

52 (*Opposite above*) Looking down the north aisle from its western bay (Fossati, plate 5) – compare with the view on the south side in plate 49

53 (*Opposite below*) Looking from the central bay of the north aisle towards the nave (Fossati, plate 6) – compare with the views on the south side in plates 39 and 54

54 (*Above*) The central bay of the south aisle looking westwards

surmounted by decorated impost blocks. Similar impost blocks on the other pair of columns in each of these bays are slightly elongated to project back into the nearby faces of the main and buttress piers. The columns in the central bay stand behind the two central columns of the main nave colonnade, and the main groined vaults span from them in the east-west direction directly to the faces of the piers.

Barrel vaults of various spans and alignments link these principal vaults to the outer walls and to the rear of the nave and exedrae arcades. Any awkwardnesses that result on the nave side from differences in span and springing levels are made less noticeable by an overall mosaic covering of the vaults. As in the inner narthex, this is now partly obscured by nineteenth-century overpainting, but it still shows a broadly similar pattern of large crosses and other symbols on a gold ground (plate 32, Sanpaolesi, *Santa Sofia*).

Multicoloured marble facings cover the walls, much as in the nave, with some panels decorated in shallow recessed relief, and with the addition of a frieze on the pier-faces at the springing level of the vaults.

The overall impressions are of height, richness of surface, and unexpected juxtapositions of columns of different heights and arches and vaults of different line and form.

The blocking or shading of many of the aisle windows means, however, that at most times the light now comes chiefly from the nave. This, together with the openness of the main bays towards the nave, soon draws the eye in that direction. The closer one approaches the main colonnades, the more fully the nave is revealed, now framed and given more scale by the foreground columns.

Facing page
55 Looking northwards from the eastern bay of the south aisle

56, 57 Capitals in the eastern bay of the south aisle

58 Vaults of the central bay of the south aisle looking westwards

59 Looking into the eastern bay of the south aisle from the exedra – compare the lighting here with the imagined lighting in the Fossati view reproduced in plate 52. Markings on the floor between the two columns against the outside wall suggest that the principal imperial metatorion was located here

Access ramps, galleries and south rooms

Three surviving ramps, projecting from the main rectangle of the church and providing access to the galleries, were referred to in the description of the exterior.

Normal access today is by the ramp which projects from the north-west corner of the church. It is entered from a vestibule that opens off the northern end of the narthex. Seven roughly paved straight ascents on alternate sides of a spine wall are joined by ramped anticlockwise 180 degree turns around it. They end in a short flight of steps up to a doorway in the end bay of the north gallery (seen at the far left of the view in Chapter 4).

Of the other two ramps that remain accessible, that at the south west is entered from the south through a door a little to the right of the entrance to the south-west porch, though there is also clear evidence of a previous entrance from within what is now this porch. It is similar to the north-west ramp, except that its last three ramped ascents up to the end bay of the south gallery no longer exist. They, and the preceding turn, have been replaced by flights of steps which climb much more rapidly, the principal flights being in one straight run to the east of the spine wall.

The north-east ramp, on the other hand, differs considerably. It is differently sited in relation to the corner of the church it abuts, and its longer axis is from west to east rather than from north to south. It can be entered more directly from the church itself through a door at the end of the easternmost bay of the north aisle. Internally there is a central light-well instead of a simple spine wall, and there are short straight ascents after each 90 degree turn around this well. At the top, a door opens into the corner of the corresponding bay of the gallery.

Because of the need for a large measure of vertical continuity of the piers and other supports, the plan at this level corresponds closely to that at ground level. The west gallery corresponds exactly to the inner narthex. It communicates with the side galleries through arched openings directly above the ground-level doorways from the narthex to the aisles. The side galleries correspond almost as closely to the aisles below. But they do also show certain significant differences.

First, there are the differences that have already been noted in the colonnades that flank the nave and curve round the exedrae – the closer spacing of the columns, and the greater length of the exedrae colonnades at the expense of contractions of the secondary piers. Earlier similar extensions of these exedrae colonnades at their opposite ends at the expense of similar contractions of the main piers is suggested by the present partial embedding of the end columns in the piers, and by continuations of the *opus sectile* decoration of the arcade spandrels across the nave faces of the piers as if there had previously been one more opening. Second, the north-west pier is further reduced in cross-section by being tunnelled through from north to south. The other main piers are now solid at this point. But

60 Interior of the north-west ramp

61 Interior of the north-east ramp

62 Looking from the west gallery into the western bay of the north gallery

63 Looking northwards from the western bay of the south gallery. The left side of this view corresponds to the view at ground level in plate 50

64 Looking southwards from the
western bay of the north gallery
through the opening in the north-
west secondary pier, the west gallery
being off to the right

65 The east window of the south
gallery. An external wooden stair
once rose to the door seen at its foot
on the left

there are unmistakable signs in their marble facings on the nave side that they also were originally tunnelled in the same manner (compare, for instance, the north-east pier, as seen similarly from across the nave). The secondary piers are similarly tunnelled, as at ground level.

Across all these openings and between the columns of the colonnades there are low marble parapets decorated in relief – mostly with lozenges and crosses – on both faces. These are hidden, when one looks up from below, by outer parapets of timber running around the projecting cornice.

Beyond these differences in plan as compared with the aisles below, there are differences of other kinds that probably have a greater effect on the overall impressions given by the galleries: among them are considerably reduced heights, much ampler natural light, differences in the vaulting and the forms of the supporting columns, the loss of nearly all the vault mosaics, and the poorer preservation of the original marble facings and friezes.

The reduced heights give greater emphasis to the undiminished breadths and so create impressions of greater spaciousness. The ampler light contributes, as does the reduced contrast with the lighting of the nave. The impression is hardly affected by the presence, in the south gallery, of a white marble screen that partly shuts off the central and eastern bays from the remainder.

The vaults of the main bays of the side galleries are more dome-like than those of the aisles, since they are free to rise

above the general level of the roof in the manner that has already been observed on the exterior. And those in the central bays are no longer carried through without a break to the nave colonnades.

The supporting columns within the side galleries all have round shafts of grey-white Proconnesian marble. They are more uniform in size than the taller columns below (to which they answer directly), and there has been no need for separate pedestals to equalize their heights. Their capitals differ considerably from those of the colonnades around the nave. Apart from a slightly anomalous one in the centre bay of the north gallery, their form might now be described as highly compressed Ionic surmounted by an integral and much deeper flared impost

67 The central bay of the south gallery looking westwards

66 The north gallery from the north-east corner. The end column of the exedra colonnade in the centre of the view is half embedded in the whitewashed mass of the pier instead of being free-standing as is the column at the other end near the secondary pier on the left

The church today: exterior and interior   57

68 A capital of an exedra colonnade in the gallery

70 The capital of a free-standing column in the central bay of the south gallery

69 Looking westwards along the central section of the nave colonnade of the south gallery, with the top of the cornice over the aisle at the right

block whose entire surface is decorated with a lace-like 70 pattern of vegetal scrolls.

It is also noticeable that some columns (such as that on the right in the view of the north-east bay in Chapter 4, 134 and that partly visible on the extreme right of the view here of the south-east bay) have a pronounced lean. Closer 65 inspection shows that many lean to some extent. If one steps over the nave parapet and looks along the length of one side, one can also see some inclination at this level in the main piers. The inclinations are, in general, away from 69 the dome, and are the first indication of major forces at work over the years in the load-bearing structure. Other indications are rises and falls in the marble paving of the floor. But there are strange inconsistencies in the inclinations, to which we shall return later.

Apart from fragmentary survivals elsewhere, mosaic 92, 22 decoration of the vaults remains only in the soffits of the 235 arcades that run around the nave and in some closely adjacent areas. That in the soffits has already been noted. 46 That in the vaults behind the nave colonnades in the centre bays consists of stars and other simple geometric forms 116, 2 against a darker ground. The remaining vault surfaces are painted in the same manner as the surfaces of the

71 The Deisis mosaic in the south aisle – see plate 67 for its setting

semidomes over the nave, and are as badly discoloured.

The apparently original marble that remains on the walls is predominantly lighter in colour and is set more simply than that in the narthex and aisles. Above a skirting and a dado of white marble, upright slabs of veined grey marble, set between horizontal bands of veined grey below and red above, extend up to a frieze of cast stucco at the springing level of the vaults. On the faces of the secondary piers that are sharply curved towards the exedrae, and in two positions in the centre bay of the north gallery, up to seven grey slabs with matched veining are set side-by-side. Relief decoration – apart from that of the friezes – is confined to simple mouldings in marble, chiefly at skirting level. Elsewhere the surface is mostly rendered, and then either whitewashed or painted to simulate marble. In a few places though, there are figural mosaics.

Incomparably the finest of the figural mosaics is a superb Deisis in this south gallery. The lower part is lost, but the heads and shoulders of the central Christ and the flanking Virgin and St John are finely preserved. The technique is more painterly than that of other mosaics, with smaller tesserae set more closely, and a soft naturalism in the portrayal of the heads.

The other mosaics are all essentially imperial portraits. Two adjacent panels in the end bay of the south gallery alongside the apse show donor emperors and empresses flanking, in the left-hand panel, a seated Christ and, in the right-hand panel, a standing Virgin holding the Christ Child. Those in the left panel have been identified as Constantine IX and Zoe, and those in the right panel as John II and Irene together with the young co-emperor Alexius. The third portrait is of the emperor Alexander, shown standing in full ceremonial dress. It is set high up on the east face of the main north-west pier, where it is barely visible at the end of the tunnel vault behind the nave arcade.

The western gallery is vaulted by a simple barrel running from end to end. The long rectangular space is lit by large windows along the west side, set between whitewashed piers. In place of the central doorways from narthex to nave there are three linked arched openings carried on paired shafts of *verde antico*, each pair with a single capital. Set in the slabs of the parapet that runs between them are shorter colonettes to support candelabra. Looking over the parapet, one has one of the most comprehensive views of the whole nave.

72 The west gallery looking northwards

73 The central openings to the nave in the west gallery (see also plate 74)

At the south end of this gallery is a doorway leading to two of the 'south rooms'. The first room corresponds exactly in plan to the south vestibule of the narthex, and stands upon its vault. It is spanned by a barrel vault and two slightly domed cross vaults. Opening off it to the east is the second room, which stands above the modified head of the south-west ramp, and is of irregular shape on account of the need to accommodate the flight of steps that now terminates this ramp.[5] Both rooms preserve the remains of mosaics on their walls and vaults. The surface elsewhere is now bare brickwork, and the south walls show clear signs of blocked windows, that of the room over the ramp having had three lights with slightly pointed heads.

The other rooms that must be mentioned are a little further east, within the bulky lower buttress that stands outside the church proper, in line with the main south-west buttress. This lower buttress is far from being as solid as it seems. Within it is the only existing direct ascent from aisle to gallery other than the north-east ramp, though its stairway is not now in use for this purpose. The stairway is entered at ground level through a door in the original outer wall of the church, at the end of a passage through the main buttress pier. The exit to the gallery is through a second passageway above the first. A continuation of the passageway leads, in the opposite direction, to the rooms in the top storey of the buttress. Again there are two rooms, the second entered through the first.[6] The first is cruciform in plan, with a central dome and partly preserved mosaics. The second is roughly rectangular, and contains the remains of frescoes. Both appear to have been chapels, but they are partly filled with debris and await clearance and full exploration.

The upper cornice

An upper cornice runs around the entire nave just below the semidomes, pendentives and principal arches. Like the gallery cornice it projects almost 1 m from the faces of the piers and the spandrels of the arcades below, and it follows similarly the curves of the exedrae, the projections of the piers, and the setbacks below the springings of the pendentives. It differs only in that it continues also round the semicircle of the apse, whereas the gallery cornice stops short at the eastern ends of the side galleries. The circuit is protected by a timber parapet, like that at gallery level, though this has been replaced by light guard-rails or cables where it would otherwise obscure mosaics.

The only access is – and seemingly always has been – from the gallery roofs. Today it is at the extreme west, through a door roughly cut into the southernmost of a row of marble panels at the foot of the great west window. This door is reached by a passageway under the sloping roof of the west gallery. Previously there were two entries slightly further east – near the western ends of the next short sections of cornice at the springings of the western barrel vault. Stairs which are now blocked descended to these points from doorways cut into the outsides of the

74 The central openings to the nave in the west gallery (see also plate 73)

two western secondary piers, in positions just below the two circular turrets that flank the great window (one of which may be seen towards the left of the illustration).

Walking around the cornice, one gets much closer views of the semidomes, pendentives and great tympana, and of their surviving mosaic decoration. One also becomes aware of some other effects of the forces that have acted on the structure in the past.

The Virgin and Christ Child in the semidome of the apse have already been mentioned. In the barrel vault to the right is an equally fine and well-preserved large standing figure of an archangel wearing imperial vestments – presumably Gabriel. Fragments only remain of the wings of a corresponding figure on the facing side of the vault, but there are more extensive remains of geometric and floral borders.

75 The Virgin and Child in the apse semidome

76 The figures of St John Chrysostom and St Ignatius Theophorus on the north tympanum

Barely visible from the nave floor in some of the shallow niches at the foot of the north tympanum are three standing figures of bishops, and fragments of a fourth. These are no more than life-size on account of the limited height of the niches. Those well preserved are St Ignatius of Constantinople (Patriarch 847–58 and 867–77; seen at the foot of the illustration in Chapter 3), and Sts John Chrysostom and Ignatius Theophorus of Antioch. Other areas of purely decorative mosaic have been uncovered alongside the niches and on the soffits of the arches which enclose the tympana.

The actions of forces pressing down from above or generated by past earthquakes are particularly noticeable in the exedrae, where there are signs of major cracks at the bases of the semidomes, and of displacements of the large marble blocks of the cornice itself, alongside these cracks. In the south-west exedra, where the cracks and displacements are worst, there are long iron ties which must have been added in an attempt to halt the movements. The ties can have been effective for only a limited period, because the easternmost one is now sprung out of its end anchorage, and lies well clear of the chase cut for it in the last cornice block.

In the central sections of the cornice, beneath the great north and south tympana, there is, at first sight, less evidence of this kind. At one point, however, there has long been a clear hint of some major reconstruction or repair. This takes the form of a chase cut into two adjacent blocks to receive another tie. The tie is no longer there, and, more significantly, the two halves of the chase no longer line up, as they must have done when they were cut. Since the cornice blocks themselves now line up, one block must have been seriously displaced when the tie was inserted, and subsequently restored to its original place.

Looking up, one sees other irregularities that hint at major forces at work, or partial reconstructions. Most conspicuous is a major jog in the surface of the north-east pendentive. Rather less conspicuous but more typical are slight forward displacements, increasing towards the crowns, of the free forward edges of the semidomes. The greatest displacement relative to the span is seen in the semidome of the apse.

The highest levels

To climb higher it is necessary to return to the gallery roofs and to walk across the roofs to stairs within one of the buttress piers.

These stairs are of the same general character in each buttress, climbing anticlockwise around a north-south spine wall. But they differ considerably in detail and in their present starting points. Those on the south side start below gallery level. That at the south east seems unaltered at the foot, and must originally have communicated there

77 A tie on the upper cornice of the south-west exedra sprung out of its chase on account of past structural movements

78 The misaligned halves of a chase for an earlier tie on the upper cornice below the south tympanum. The nearer parts of the cornice and tympanum (to the left of the superimposed broken line) have been reconstructed as described in Chapter 4, and shown at position A on the right of plate 120. Note that the niche in the centre was formed in the new brickwork of the reconstructed part, but has had to be completed by cutting into the original brickwork at the right

79 Looking up to the north-east pendentive and the forward edge of the main eastern semidome

80 Looking towards the stairs in the north-east buttress pier, from within the lower room formed by walls carried over the gallery roof by the arches seen at the left and right. The back of the north-east pendentive is behind the camera position

with an external stair through a door that is now blocked by the later outer buttress. That at the south west may originally have been almost identical, but has since been modified to furnish the final ascent from a later outer stair, as already described, and this modification has interrupted its continuation to the gallery roof. The two northern stairs seem never to have extended this far down, and that at the north west is today accessible only from the gallery roof.

The buttress piers themselves are linked to the upward extensions of the main piers by pairs of parallel walls to create the seemingly solid buttress arms that are such a conspicuous feature of the distant view. Just above the gallery roofs, the walls are carried by arches spanning over the roofs rather than resting directly on the linking arches and barrel vaults below. Somewhat narrowed openings under these arches provide both a continuous path around the roofs and access to the internal spaces that lead to the buttress stairs. The internal spaces are spanned transversely at two levels by barrel vaults which have clearly been reconstructed at some time, because they show no pronounced deformations, whereas major deformations are visible in the exposed brickwork of the inner faces of the walls and their supporting arches. 239 230

All four stairs terminate at the top of the buttress piers. In the corners of the square dome-base opposite their exits are arched openings leading to further ascending stairs, each now blocked near the top of its second flight. Today the climb must be completed by an external ladder. A low 3

door under a window at the south east then gives access to the interior of the dome.

The dome is less than a full hemisphere. It subtends an angle of only about 162 degrees, so that its centre of curvature is appreciably below cornice level. The marble blocks of the cornice slope inwards towards this centre at an angle of about 9 degrees, unlike the blocks of the lower cornices which are, of course, set horizontally. Close inspection of the blocks shows a number of differences between those at the north and south, and those at the east and west. These differences will be referred to later.

From the cornice rise the forty ribs. Their lines and curvatures, seen from close quarters, show considerable departures from geometric regularity, and there is a further irregularity at the north east, echoing the jog in the surface of the pendentive below. Their surfaces are decorated with geometrically patterned mosaic. Between them are the arched reveals in which the windows are set – except in two positions over the western pendentives where pairs of previously existing windows have been blocked. In the western section also, the top of the main west arch projects well above the cornice, passing slightly in front of the two westernmost ribs and across several window-reveals. Nothing is similarly visible of the other main supporting arches. 109, 113 82 87

Looking down from this cornice, one gets a more dramatic and strongly foreshortened view of the whole internal space of the nave, and a vivid impression of the magnitude of the task that faced the builders of the church. 81

81 Looking down in a north-westerly direction from the dome cornice

CHAPTER 3

The church today:
materials and structural systems

IN THE LAST CHAPTER, questions about what lies behind the visible skins of marble and mosiac and holds up the high vaults were largely set aside, though evidence was noted of some of the forces at work within the masonry. We must now turn to these questions, partly for their intrinsic interest but also as a basis for understanding the structural behaviour of the church, and, through this, clarifying some aspects of its structural history.

The answers cannot all be definitive. Little is visible today of even the outer faces of the working masonry, and there are only limited and mostly inadequate records of what has been seen in the past. Still less is known for certain about conditions within the thickness. Since the available information here relates only to a few small areas, it is necessary to draw sometimes on the evidence provided by comparable structures elsewhere, assuming a reasonable consistency of construction-practice.

Least is known about the characteristic strengths and other physical properties of the materials – essential data for some types of structural analysis – and about the nature of the ground on which the structure stands. A large number of tests on suitable samples extracted from within the thicknesses of the masonry would be necessary to establish reliably the properties of the main materials used, and very few such tests have been made. Bore-hole tests in the immediate vicinity of the church would similarly be necessary to establish the precise ground-conditions, and none has been made.[1]

These latter shortcomings are, however, less important than they might seem. More direct indications of the actual structural behaviour obviate the need for the types of analysis just referred to, and make other types of analysis more revealing for the purpose of clarifying the history. Also it is clear from the present state of the structure that there have not been significantly greater settlements under the more heavily loaded foundations, and it can reasonably be concluded from this and from the other available evidence that the ground conditions have not led to magnified movements of the structure during earthquakes.

Materials

Stone, bricks, and mortar make up all the main elements of the above-ground structure – the piers and columns, and the arches, vaults, and dome.[2] Substantial but far smaller amounts of iron and timber are found as cramps and ties. There are limited internal uses of lead, and a

greater external use as the covering of the vaults. The uses of these materials are summarized in plans A2 to A8 (pp. 271–7), and are considered further in what follows.

Structural uses of stone and marble

Stone is used chiefly in the piers. It is either limestone or greenstone – a local granite. Sometimes the two are found together, apparently used indiscriminately. The blocks vary somewhat in depth, averaging about 0.45 m, with individual blocks sometimes exceeding 1 m in length. They were dressed to fit closely, at least on the surface. The masonry at the outside foot of the south-west buttress pier is seen near the bottom of the illustration.   84

The regular alternation of one or more courses of stone with a number of courses of brick, such as is found in much Byzantine work and is seen in the lower storeys of the skeuophylakion, does not occur in the church itself except 162 in some relatively minor Turkish consolidations of the buttress piers. Single courses of stone are, however, found in some parts of the structure where the construction is otherwise in brick. They occur at several lower levels in the buttress piers, including the springing levels of the barrel vaults that link these piers to the main piers. Examples may be seen at a higher level in the view of the outside of the south-west buttress pier, and at the upper 84 right of the view of an internal stair. They also occur as the 83 three cornices of Proconnesian marble which are carried round the whole nave above the ground and gallery colonnades, and round the tops of the pendentives at the base of the dome. The two lower cornices are formed of huge blocks about 0.6 m thick and up to 5 m long.   85

The remaining structural use of stone is seen in the marble columns of the nave colonnades and in the aisles and galleries. With the possible exception of some of the porphyry shafts in the exedrae (which have more than the usual two bronze collars at head and foot), all the shafts are monoliths. They have necessarily been set up contrary to the natural bedding of the stone, which introduces a risk of splitting or local spalling under load, especially if for any reason the distribution of pressure is not uniform. Reinforcement against this risk must be one reason for the use of bronze collars at head and foot, possibly with horizontal sheets of lead inserted behind them to give more even bearing. The collars also took the place of the projecting necking cut at the ends of the shaft itself in classical columns, thereby permitting some economy in marble.

83 The foot of the stair within the south-east buttress pier, looking inwards towards the aisle

84 Looking towards the outside face of the south-west buttress pier from within the added outer buttress. The face of the pier is seen to the right of centre, from a little above ground level to near the level of the gallery floor

85 The south gallery cornice looking eastwards

Brickwork

Examples of exposed original brickwork may also be seen in the two views of the southern buttress piers. As far as can be ascertained, it is all regularly coursed throughout the thickness, as can be seen more readily in the ruins of roughly contemporary structures elsewhere. Cut or broken bricks were used where this was necessary for bonding purposes, or where salvaged material was used in repairs. But there is no evidence of a fill of roughly coursed loose fragments in walls or piers, such as is seen in some late Roman buildings like the Baths of Caracalla, and the proportion of broken bricks used merely for economy in the original construction appears to have been small. Still less is the face brickwork merely a skin for a much thicker concrete core, as in many earlier Roman buildings.

In most parts of the original structure the face dimensions of the bricks average about 0.375 m square.

Typical thicknesses are 40 to 50 mm. Later the face dimensions become smaller and the thicknesses increase. Only one instance of the use of bricks of a significantly different size has been established. It was apparently considered prudent to use the largest obtainable bricks in the great arches that span between the main piers to carry the dome. Some of these bricks, re-used in a reconstruction, may be seen today where the western arch rises above the dome cornice: they are up to 0.7 m square.[3] A mineralogical examination has shown that they could not have been made from local clays, as apparently were other bricks in the structure. No support has been found, however, for the claim in the *Narratio* that they were much less dense than the normal brick.[4] They appear to be of normal density. They are similar to Roman *bipedales*, and were probably taken from earlier structures elsewhere and re-used.

Of rather more importance structurally, the mortar bed-joints are substantially thicker than the bricks themselves. Typical bed-joint thicknesses are 50 to 60 mm. Thus there is substantially more mortar than brick in the whole mass. This means that the strengths and stiffnesses of the brickwork and the rates at which these developed would have been highly dependent on the characteristics of the mortar.

The mortar that was used was basically a lime mortar made from slaked lime and sand. But it always contains, in addition to the sand, a substantial proportion of crushed brick. This brick ranges from fine dust up to fragments 10 mm and more in size. The larger fragments would have served merely to economize in sand and lime. The fine dust imparts a pinkish colour and, more importantly, it may have given the mortar hydraulic properties similar to those given by the natural pozzolanas used around Naples and Rome.

The great merit of a hydraulic mortar for use in thick masses of brickwork is that its strength can develop by means of an internal chemical reaction that is independent of contact with the air. The strength of a pure lime-sand mortar, on the other hand, depends on carbonation of the lime for which contact with the air is essential. At best this carbonation occurs very slowly, and it may occur to only a limited extent over many centuries in the heart of a thick wall or pier.

Good firing of the brick before it is crushed tends, however, to make it chemically inert,[5] and no specimens of the mortar from within the thickness of walls or piers have yet been available for the critical tests on the remaining free lime, and on the final strength. The only

86 Fallen vault masonry of Justinian's church of St John at Ephesus. The large block is the one seen in the right foreground of plate 214

indications, therefore, come from mineralogical and chemical analyses of representative small samples of mortar taken from near the surface. Since these suggest that the source of the finer particles was usually the discarded underfired brick from the outsides of the firing clamps, it seems likely that these particles did impart significant hydraulic properties to the mortar.

Not all the mortar is identical, of course. Differences can be observed in both precise constitution and colour. They seem largely to stem from the usual slow changes in technique over a period of time and thus serve as rough indications of date, where this cannot be independently established.

The pink colouration becomes more noticeable in later work, including precisely datable work of the tenth and fourteenth centuries. It correlates with higher proportions of soluble silica indicated by the chemical analyses. Turkish mortar, datable to restorations in the last century, is the deepest pink, but has not been subject to the same detailed study as the Byzantine mortars.

Nearly all the brickwork joints are pointed with a different, finer mix, even where they were not intended to remain visible. This pointing is of no structural value. It is nevertheless of interest because slow changes in the technique of pointing sometimes provide another and more immediate rough indication of the date of the brickwork. Sixth-century pointing was always smoothly concave in section, recessed a little behind the edges of the bricks. Later, the face was usually flat – sometimes flush with the wall-face and tending to overlap slightly the brick edges, and sometimes slanted downwards and outwards, starting appreciably behind the edge of the upper brick. 83

Iron cramps and iron and timber ties

Two uses of iron can be readily seen. One is in the form of cramps between adjacent blocks of stone in the cornices. The other is in the form of longer bars, some set in chases on the cornices below the semidomes of the western exedrae, and most spanning freely across the springings of arches and vaults, or between the walls of the buttress piers above the gallery roofs. Visible end-anchorages betray the presence of further long bars beneath the gallery floors. The iron appears generally to be of high quality, with little visible corrosion.

The cramps are mostly of inverted-U form. They vary considerably in size, and the pattern of use is far from regular. It therefore seems likely that most, if not all, have been added after construction. But there is also evidence of earlier buried cramps. 121 93

The longer iron tie bars vary in cross-section, and in the way in which their ends are anchored. Among the largest are those on the upper cornices of the western exedrae, which are about 40 mm by 50 mm in cross-section and up to 3.7 m long, and some of those in the central bays of the side aisles. 77, 93 215

87 Detail of the main western arch where it rises above the dome cornice

Visible anchorages usually take the form of pins driven through eyes in the ends of the bars. In what appear to be the earlier ties – including the bars on the upper cornices just referred to – these pins are usually short lengths of round bar. In later ties – including the largest in the side aisles – they are typically longer, and sword-shaped. There are also invisible underfloor ties in the west gallery which are anchored by being first cranked down to cornice level over the step below the marble parapet, and then cranked down again into the cornice.

The corresponding free-spanning timber members are nearly all relatively short, and, as Choisy long ago pointed out,[6] are equally well fitted to serve as struts, and should sometimes be so regarded. What is normally seen of them is not, however, the true structural member. It is a decorated open-topped timber casing. Inside this, the member proper is some 120 to 150 mm wide and deep. It is

doubtful whether there are many original wooden tie bars still in place and in good condition.

Facings and external vault coverings

The marble facing of the piers and walls consists of sheets only about 20 to 30 mm thick, which are held a slight distance in front of the working masonry by iron nails. The marble paving slabs on the floors are probably much more variable in thickness.

The lead sheet that covers the top surfaces of all the upper vaults to provide an external weathering surface has been seen to follow them closely where they rise above the general level. But, for good drainage, it maintains a continuous fall to the outside of the roof over intervening dips in the vaults. The present covering here appears to be laid over timbers which rest either directly on the vaults or on an earth fill.

The church today: materials and structural systems 71

Structural systems

Recognizing that, in normal circumstances, all weights act downwards and must somehow reach the ground through the solid masonry, we can form some initial idea of their likely paths. Knowledge of the relative strengths and stiffnesses of alternative paths derived from what we have just seen of the materials used helps to clarify the picture, and suggests a distinction between a primary system that carries the principal loads, and secondary systems that support just themselves, perhaps with some help from the primary system.

These systems roughly parallel the principal architectural components: the primary space of the nave and the enveloping secondary spaces of narthexes, aisles and galleries. But the parallel is incomplete because we must consider as integral parts of the primary system those elements which sustain the high vaults over the nave, but rise within the overall boundaries of the aisles and side galleries.

Sustaining the dome and other high vaults over the nave are chiefly the main piers, the secondary piers and the buttress piers – all outside the nave space – and groups of arches spanning between these piers. The primary 88 structural system certainly comprises all of these, as well as the dome and vaults themselves. If, as seems desirable, we include in it the semidomes over the apse and the exedrae, we must also include the apse wall and the exedrae colonnades beneath these. There is no similar reason for including the side colonnades. But the possible roles of the cornices and some of the ties between the columns in restraining outward movements of the main piers must be considered.

The secondary systems might be defined as comprising all other structural elements of the church-proper. They 89 thus include the arches and vaults of the narthexes, and the main bays of the aisles and galleries, and all their supporting walls and columns that are not part of the primary system. They also include the great tympana below the main north and south arches, and the walls of the projecting access ramps.

If defined solely in this way, the secondary systems would not, of course, be self-sufficient, because their vaults rely for support also on the piers of the primary system, and on all the colonnades around the nave. The colonnades are perhaps best regarded as parts of both systems – the side colonnades belonging chiefly to the secondary system. But it would be less reasonable to think in the same way of the piers. It is better here to recognize a dependence of the secondary system on the primary one.

Later outer buttresses are best regarded as supplementary elements of either the primary or the secondary system, according to whether they abut the first or the second. They will be largely ignored in what follows.

AA, CC	main arches
BB	upper north and south arches
DD	east and west barrel vaults
EE	exedrae semidome arches
FF	exedrae semidomes (cut away at the top)
G	main eastern semidome (western counterpart cut away to show better the structure behind)
HHH	pendentives (western ones cut away to show structure behind)
aaaa	pier projections (see text)

secondary pier

88 The primary structural system, with the secondary systems cut away and with further cuts at the west and south to show more clearly the forms of the arches, the buttress piers, and the connections between these piers and the main piers

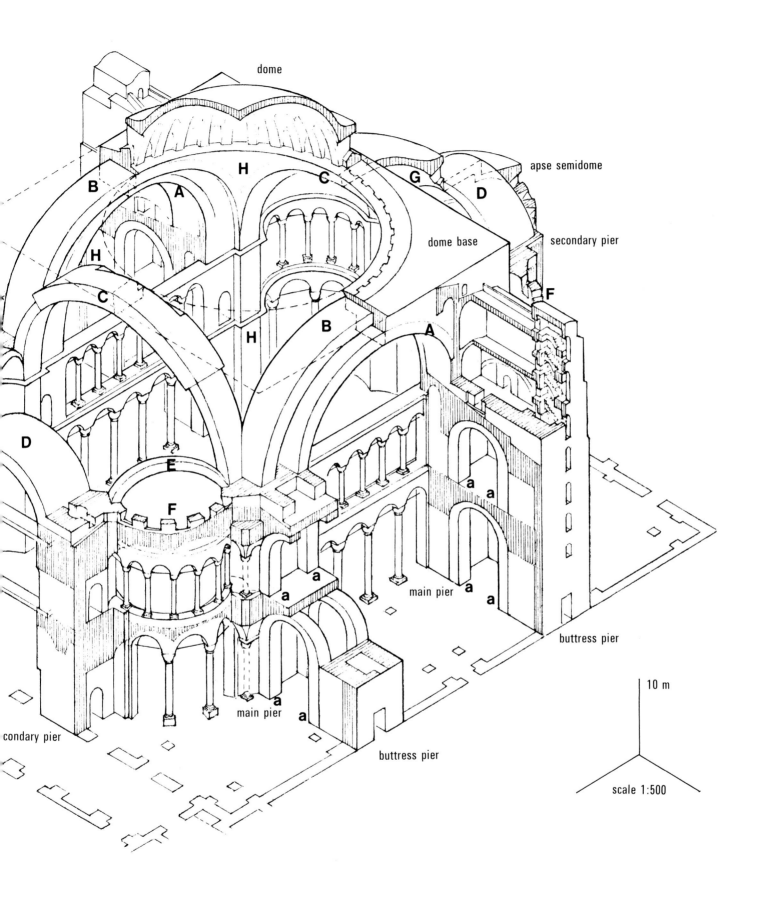

dome

apse semidome

secondary pier

dome base

F

B A H C G D

H

C

H B A

D

E

F

a a

main pier

a

a a

a

condary pier

a

main pier a

buttress pier

buttress pier

10 m

scale 1:500

Piers

The four main piers and the four secondary piers were constructed of stone, at least up to the springings of the gallery vaults. The four buttress piers were similarly constructed at the foot, but only to the level of the springings of the aisle vaults.

Even at ground level, however, none of the piers is a single mass of bonded masonry over the whole of the present cross-section. The pairs of facing projections, almost square in plan, that jut from the main and buttress piers into the aisles (aaaa in the illustration) are unbonded to the main masses of these piers and simply butt against them. And, as will be seen from plan A2, both the secondary and buttress piers are penetrated by vaulted passageways. These are of considerable height. In the north-west buttress pier it can be seen that there were originally further openings, now filled, which penetrated the pier from west to east.

At gallery level the situation is even more complex. The buttress piers were here constructed almost entirely of brick, and, since the projections into the aisles are again of stone on both sides, stone now butts against brick on the buttress side. In addition to vaulted passageways (as at ground level) through the secondary and buttress piers, there are the similar openings that originally penetrated all the main piers from north to south. That at the north west remains open, as we have seen, while the other three now have unbonded fillings. Finally, there are further unbonded additions to all these piers, filling what were originally the first open bays of the exedrae colonnades.

All these discontinuities – whether simple lacks of bond between parts of a pier that are merely butted against one another, or the separations introduced by open passageways or other openings – reduce the total resistances of the piers to horizontal loads, while the potential overall resistances of the main and buttress piers to side-loads were reduced even further by the wider openings that were left between them to provide continuous aisles.

To see how far the resistances were reduced, we must also look at the ways in which the openings were bridged.

The most effective bridging is that of the open passageways in those parts of the piers that are built in stone. Here, it takes the form of stone barrel vaults constructed of voussoir-shaped blocks, above which the normal stone masonry was carried across with full normal bond. If we ignore the projections marked aaaa in the illustration, bridging over the aisles between the main and buttress piers takes the much weaker form of brick barrel vaults only about 0.6 m thick, filled up to the gallery floor over the haunches, but with little or no fill over the crown. But these brick vaults are underpinned, and the interconnections stiffened, by lower and deeper bracing arches of stone spanning between the projections.

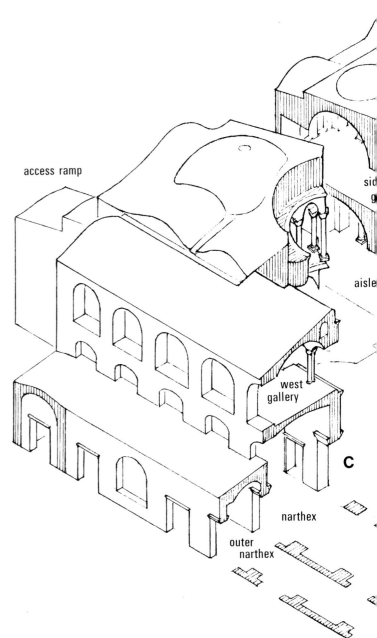

89 The five secondary structural systems, A, A, B, B, C, cut free from the piers of the primary system and with parts of B and C at the south west drawn only in plan to show more clearly the remaining forms

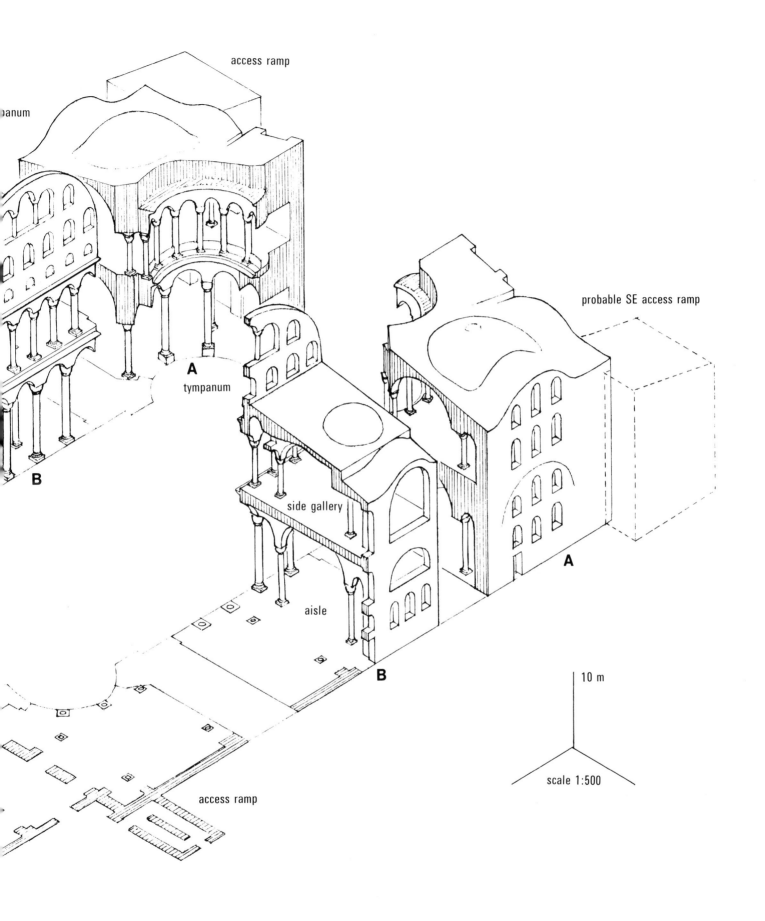

access ramp

panum

tympanum

A

B

tympanum

side gallery

aisle

B

probable SE access ramp

A

access ramp

10 m

scale 1:500

Above the springing level of the gallery vaults all piers seem to have been built of brick, apart from the single course of stone that juts out to form the upper cornice. All also change somewhat in form, as do the interconnections between the main and buttress piers.

The secondary piers are truncated not far above the cornice level, continuing only far enough to buttress the haunches of the barrel vaults that spring from them across the east and west ends of the nave.

The main piers continue without, today, any further penetrations, but there are indications of filled earlier vaulted penetrations, of unknown depth. These were vertically above the vaulted passageways at gallery level, and at a height well above the springing levels of the main arches over the nave.

Finally, the buttress piers continue as stair towers, now mostly substantially modified internally from their original forms. Window openings – originally larger than they now are – in their outermost walls make their east and west walls their principal elements. Thus the stair-landings are carried on transverse arches notched into these walls,

and then carry the main flights by means of other steeply inclined ramping arches alongside them. The walls continue to the outer faces of the main piers without any break in bond over the galleries. But they then simply butt against these faces. In the upper storey, the wall-thickness is considerably reduced.

Colonnades and cornices

The monolithic column shafts are the one type of structural element whose character is plainly visible, and whose function is openly expressed.

Because the columns of the galleries do not stand directly above those at ground level, the arcades and cornices over the ground colonnades have to redistribute the vertical loads coming from above. The upper arcades perform the more usual task of collecting the distributed loads from a higher level and passing them to the gallery columns. The arches of the upper arcades are constructed of brick, with soffit widths of almost 1.2 m. The arches of the lower arcades are wider – about 1.6 m. They are probably also of brick. But this has not been confirmed.

90, ◖

◁ 90 Looking up in the south-east exedra

91 Looking up at the south side of the nave

Architecturally, the cornices are merely the visible projecting bands of marble, with richly carved undersurfaces. Structurally, they should be thought of as having the full widths of the marble blocks of which they are composed. Over the colonnades these blocks extend back to the rear faces of the arcades on which they rest (as may be seen at the foot of the illustration), giving them overall widths of some 1.8 m and 2.2 m. Since they continue without interruption across the faces of the piers, they are well placed to serve as cross ties between the main piers, and as peripheral ties around the exedrae.

Unfortunately, little is known for certain about the original cramping together of the marble blocks, to fit them to serve in this way. All cramps visible on the exposed upper surfaces seem to have been added later, including the long bars on the upper cornice in the western exedrae. But it was a long-standing practice in comparable situations to cramp all the blocks together during construction, and to do so in places where the cramps would subsequently be covered and protected by what was built above. And the disclosure by an open crack of one cramp on the upper cornice of the semidome of the south-west exedra strongly suggests that all blocks were originally so joined. The cramp is about 30 mm square in cross-section and about 50 mm behind the face of the sixth-century brickwork.

Below the cornices, it is possible that there are continuous iron ties running between the piers. Long iron bars span freely in continuous lines across the springings of the arches carried by the colonnades. These bars are about 50 mm square in cross-section with free lengths of 3 m in the ground colonnades. In the gallery colonnades they have slightly reduced cross-sections and free lengths of a little more than 2 m. Their ends are embedded in the springings of the arches, and the emerging bars are accommodated by the marble or mosaic facings of the arch soffits or in the tops of the capitals in such a way that they cannot be later insertions. But the end-anchorages are not visible, so it is not known to what extent they do effectively form – or originally formed – continuous chains.

124

93

90, 91

45, 56
68, 286

Arches, vaults, semidomes, pendentives and dome base

The arches, vaults, semidomes and pendentives that span between the piers high above the nave are all constructed of brick.

Most of those whose springing levels can be easily seen from inside the church spring almost directly from the upper cornice. Only the pendentives appear to spring from appreciably higher.

There are also two lower arches on the north and south sides which have no visible soffits inside, since their inner faces merge with those of the tympanum walls. These are the broad arches whose faces and soffits project prominently on the outside. They spring from the east or west inside faces of the main piers at roughly the level of the gallery roof, and underpin and stiffen the wider-spanning arches that frame the tympana internally on these sides.

These last arches (AA in the drawing) are the most substantial of all, on account of their great soffit-widths of about 4.5 m. They consist of two rings, each about 0.8 m deep, and built of the largest size of brick. Alongside the lowest range of tympanum windows they are bonded into the original brickwork of the tympanum walls, and are even horizontally coursed there on their inside faces, as shown by Salzenberg's nineteenth-century elevation. The fact that this elevation also shows a non-existent course of stone immediately above the cornice indicates that it is not wholly reliable; but its accuracy in relation to the coursing of the brickwork is confirmed by the shadowy outlines of the bricks that can be seen there today, thanks to accumulations of dirt on the undulating surface of the thin plaster.

Much less is known of the upper arches on the north and south sides (BB in the drawing) because their outer faces are hidden within the mass of the dome base, and even their inner faces are obscured by Fossati plaster. Salzenberg shows a single-brick voussoir ring slightly more than 1 m deep. Those parts of their soffits which project inwards from the tympanum walls now increase in width as they rise, but the overall widths are indeterminate. These widths are, however, of less importance than the solidity and continuity of the brickwork that extends from the tops of the lower arches up to the height of the dome cornice.

The approximate forms of the upper parts of the main east and west arches (CC in the drawing) can be deduced from what is visible on the dome cornice, and from indications on the east and west faces of the dome base. These arches differ considerably, having been rebuilt at widely different times. The east arch is about 1.6 m deep and probably of the same two-ring construction as the main north and south arches. It is about 3.5 m wide. The west arch is substantially deeper – about 2.8 m where it projects above the dome cornice – and has an overall width of about 4 m. But its faces are not continuous over the whole width and depth. The upper part of the arch is set back so that it does not excessively impede the walkway around the cornice, and there are corresponding jogs in the soffit and the upper surface. But what survives of the original arch nearer the springings is presumably similar to the east arch.

Behind these arches the main semidomes have minimum thicknesses of a little less than 0.8 m, probably made up of two normal bricks.

Facing page

92 Detail of the west face of the western stone bracing-arch between the south-east main and buttress piers in the gallery – see plate 235 for the position

93 Ties on the upper cornice of the south-west exedra. At the foot is part of the long bar seen in plate 77. Behind this, through the crack in the brickwork and looking very black, can be seen part of an original cramp

94 (*Above*) Interior elevation (partly conjectural) of the south tympanum, with the facings and later narrowings of the window openings removed. (From Salzenberg)

95 (*Right*) View of the west end of the north tympanum today

88 At the east and west ends are the barrel vaults (DD in the drawing) that span between the secondary piers. These are also a little more than 1 m deep at their crowns, and their haunches are buttressed by extensions of the piers somewhat above the cornice from which they spring. The east vault has the apse semidome built against its east edge, but not rising quite as high. This appears to be one normal brick in thickness at the crown – less than 0.4 m excluding plaster and outer covering.

88 Less again is known about the diagonal arches (EE in the drawing) shown as spanning over the exedrae between the secondary piers and the adjacent main piers. Indeed there is no direct evidence of their independent existence, for their soffits and inside faces are covered with Fossati plaster and are continuous (respectively) with the inside surfaces of the exedrae semidomes and the large semidomes into which these open. With no visible jogs in the surfaces there are no indications of either depth or width. It is reasonable nevertheless to assume their presence since some arch-like thickenings of the forward edges of the exedrae semidomes would have been desirable for construction purposes at least – perhaps to a depth similar to that of the

94 east and west barrel vaults. In his elevation Salzenberg shows them – rightly or wrongly – as considerably deeper. Whatever their width, it was absorbed in the drum-like thickenings of the bases of the large semidomes at a slightly later stage of construction.

The exedrae semidomes themselves appear to be of the same minimal single-brick thickness at the crown as the apse semidome.

Least is known about the precise construction of the four pendentives. They presumably have inner skins, at least in their upper parts, constructed in a similar manner to the large semidomes, though there is probably some local thickening of the skin of the north-east one where it prominently bulges inwards, and there may also be more general thickening of the rebuilt parts of the two western ones. But they are all today filled out at the back to the almost semi-cubic form of the dome base, each corner of which is really the topmost part of one of the main piers.

We have already seen that there are still external stairs in each of these corners at the top, and that there is evidence of filled former penetrations a little lower down. Evidence of further arched penetrations has also been seen on the east face of the dome base. But the original depth of these is unknown. All that can be said with certainty is that the dome base is not as solid or continuous as it looks from the outside, and that it was once less solid. The known penetrations and discontinuities are all, however, well above the feet of the pendentives. It seems reasonable to assume a solid construction for about half the total height above the upper cornice.

Dome
Over the crowns of the main arches and around the tops of the pendentives runs the highest cornice, which serves as the springing course for the dome. As we have seen, the marble blocks of which it is composed are not (except at the west) laid with their top surfaces level.

At their feet, the ribs of the dome average about 1.2 m wide and a little over 2 m deep except at the west where the depth was substantially increased in the tenth-century rebuilding. Since they continue vertically on the exterior to the full height of the windows, they become progressively deeper until they are cut back at this height. They are constructed of bricks laid not quite radially in relation to the centres of curvature, but slightly flatter. Falls of mosaic and plaster have shown that, in some at least, thin slabs of marble were inserted as springers for the window arches.

96 There are low breast-walls below the windows. Above them, at the height at which the ribs are cut back externally, the continuous shell of the dome commences. As far as is known, the webs were constructed integrally with the ribs and using the same bricks. They are about 0.7 m thick, except again at the west where, like the ribs, they are thicker. The inward projection of the ribs gradually dies out and disappears well before the crown – perhaps to provide a smooth surface for the central portion of the mosaic decoration.

Though no ties remain today across the window openings, there is clear evidence that timber ties about 100 mm square were built into the ribs during construction at the springing level of their arches. Sometimes this evidence takes the form of square plaster patches in the mosaic, but elsewhere, as seen in the illustration, the lead-lined holes remaining after the timber largely rotted away can still be seen.

96 The extent to which the blocks of the cornice were cramped together beneath the ribs and breast-walls is unknown. But it seems highly likely that, at least in the very carefully constructed earliest sections at the north and south where there are no cramps on the exposed surfaces, the blocks were cramped as in the lower cornices. The later sections are much less regularly constructed, with a good many re-used blocks. They have many visible cramps, and there are presumably others like them under the ribs and breast-walls.

Other ties at this level, added only in the nineteenth and twentieth centuries, will be referred to in the next chapter.

Secondary systems
The secondary systems are not, as we have seen, independent of the primary system. They share with this system the colonnades around the nave and derive some further support from the piers. There are five secondary systems. Two at each side (AB, AB in the drawing) form 89 respectively the eastern and central bays of the aisles and side galleries, being separated from one another by the eastern main piers and buttress piers. The fifth system (C in 89 the drawing), separated from the others by the western main piers and buttress piers, forms the western bays of the aisles and side galleries plus the connecting narthexes and west gallery.

96 Detail of a window reveal in the tenth-century portion of the dome, showing a marble block serving as springer for the window arch and, immediately above this, the lead-lined hole for a timber strut-tie across this arch

All systems include one or more lengths of the nave colonnades and sections of the original outer wall. All except the central bays of the aisles and side galleries on each side also include (or must originally have included) one or two of the projecting access ramps. To the central bays at each side must be added the tympana carried by the side colonnades of the nave, since these are merely infilling screens and not supports for the main north or south arches.

It is unnecessary to describe the construction of each system in detail. We have already seen that the form of some of the vaults is complex and not geometrically regular, because of the need to adapt to the curves, in plan, of the exedrae colonnades, and because all the nave colonnades rise considerably higher than the springing levels of the aisle vaults. It will be sufficient to look at typical details of the vaults and their supports, and at the ways in which ties are incorporated, and then, briefly, at the tympana.

Vaults
Like the high vaults over the nave, all the vaults were almost certainly constructed of brick. It is unlikely that the vaulting-shell is anywhere more than one normal brick in thickness, though it is to be expected that there are solid fills over the shells, especially where they rise steeply, near their springings. These fills must extend over large parts of the aisle and inner narthex vaults to bring these up to the level surfaces required for the gallery floors, though they are less extensive over the gallery vaults.

Falls of plaster from some of the more dome-like gallery vaults, and surface markings on the plaster, show 67 that the bricks of these vaults were laid in circumferential rings (as in a dome) from a height not far above the springings. This is the same manner of construction as can be seen in the larger but otherwise very similar western dome of Hagia Irene. In the flatter groined vaults in the 97 aisles, the bricks were probably laid in the same way as in the similarly shaped vaults (which are now largely bare of plaster) in the large room that opens directly off the south 98 end of the west gallery.

Supporting walls and columns
The original outer walls, and the walls that separate, respectively, the narthex from the nave and aisles and the west gallery from the side galleries, were also constructed almost entirely of brick, as far as can be seen.

The latter walls pass by the west faces of the western secondary piers without interruption, and apparently without any bond, and the east wall passes similarly by the east faces of the eastern secondary piers (plans A2, A3 and *Survey*, plates 9, 11, 17, 19). At the north and south, where the buttress piers extend as far as the outer faces of the boundary walls, there are similarly unbonded junctions with these piers. Thus there is, in these respects, a clear division between primary and secondary systems.

At ground level the east and west walls are thicker and less weakened by openings than the north and south walls. In fact, the latter were originally little more than window-filled screens. At gallery level there is less difference, because the outer sections of the east wall are also largely filled by windows.

97 Looking up into the western dome of Hagia Irene

The other supports for the vaults, apart from the support provided by the nave colonnades and the piers, are the free-standing columns within the aisles and side galleries. If these columns were the only supports and were completely free standing, they would easily have been pushed aside by the principal vaults. Each column is, however, steadied against the thrust of the vault by being connected just above the capital to the adjacent piers, or to pilaster responds on the outer walls.

In the end bays nearly all columns that stand near one or more of the walls are connected to pilaster responds by 55, 63, 66 short arches or half-arches and timber ties. Similarly, those that stand against the main or buttress piers, but are not now partly embedded in them, are linked above their capitals to these piers – in the aisles by marble architraves 41, 57, 59 like extended impost blocks and in the galleries by short 134, 137 half-arches and timber struts – though the struts no longer exist above some columns. Thus all these columns act

virtually as extensions of the answering pilasters or the adjacent piers, and are themselves called upon to take only the vertical load for which they are better fitted.

In the centre bays the paired columns in the aisles are braced together by timber struts, well above the capitals, or show evidence of having once been thus braced. On the 53, 2 corresponding columns in the galleries there remain the stumps of other bracing timbers, as well as shorter timbers 70, 1 at a higher level.

Ties

In these centre bays at both levels there are, in addition, extensive systems of iron ties, mostly running across the widths of the bays to assist in resisting the transverse outward thrusts of the vaults. There are also similar ties across the west gallery.

Most of these ties span freely between the springings of the vaults. In the aisles and side galleries they usually pass

98 Vaults of the main south-west room opening off the gallery

through the springings just above the column capitals and are visibly anchored on the other side, usually by pins driven through eyes in the ends of the bars. The longest have free spans of about 9.5 m and, in the aisles, cross-sections of about 70 by 100 mm. But these are evidently not original, because the surrounding mosaic has been disturbed by their insertion. Those that connect with the taller columns of the main ground-level colonnade are anchored to these columns by hinged forged rings that encircle the shafts. In the west gallery the ties span about 8 m across the width of the barrel vault. At one end they are anchored on the outer face of the west wall, and at the other, they penetrate the east wall, two of them being anchored within the vaulted penetrations of the western secondary piers.

The other ties run beneath the marble paving-slabs of the galleries. The only indications of their presence are their projecting end-enchorages, and, where they are later

insertions, long, narrow patches in the disturbed marble paving. They do not seem to equal in cross-section the largest of the freely spanning ties, but some of them must be more than 50 mm square. In the side galleries they are 20 m in overall length, though each probably consists of two or more bars joined together. In the west gallery they are concentrated in the central part, where there are no ties at the springing level of the vault.

Tympana

Like the other outer walls, the tympana were constructed almost entirely of brick. Stone was used only for the obviously late narrowings of the window openings, and for the columns between the original large central windows at the top. The other principal feature of note is a diminution in thickness of each wall towards the top, which roughly corresponds with the broadening of the exposed soffit of the framing arch inside.

CHAPTER 4

Looking back

LOOKING BACK FROM some two or three centuries later, the unknown author of the *Narratio* gave the most complete, though circumstantial, account of the construction of Justinian's church that we now have. We read in it of two teams of five thousand workmen, each team under fifty masters, building the two sides of the church in competition with one another; of the revelation to Justinian of the plan of the church by an angel; and of further angelic interventions such as that (on a Wednesday at the fifth hour) which settled a point of doubt about the windows of the apse. We also read of mortar for the foundations being made, not with water, but with a broth of barley and the bark of elm; and of the making, on the island of Rhodes, of special large bricks for the main arches and the dome. These bricks were said to be so light that twelve of them weighed no more than one normal brick. And, between every group of twelve bricks in the dome, relics of saints were inserted, to the accompaniment of prayers for the church. It is in this account, also, that details are given of the acquisition of additional land for the church, and of the great porphyry columns for the exedrae.

To understand the sixth-century achievement and to set it in the context of what had gone before, we now must look back over a much longer period, and must do so more circumspectly, and without the advantage of having in front of us, virtually unchanged, the church as Justinian finally knew it.

The first requisite is to identify the changes that have taken place since the church was first completed, and thereby to reach some picture of the sixth-century forms.

There have been three principal types of structural change: partial reconstructions, additions, and losses. Some of them have markedly changed the appearance of the exterior or the interior; others have had little visible effect, and could easily pass unnoticed, but should still be taken into account. There has also been one attempt, without further reconstruction, to return to an upright position columns whose inclinations may have been giving cause for concern.

The other principal changes have been in the surface finishes of marble and mosaic and in the furnishings.

We shall now consider in turn each of these types of change except the last, looking back as far as 537. Full consideration of the early furnishings will be deferred until Chapter 9, and of the earlier history, until the next chapter.

Evidence of changes

With one major and one minor exception, the written record does no more than indicate that, at certain times, certain parts of the structure were rebuilt or certain additions or consolidations were undertaken. It is necessary to look to the surviving structure itself for evidence of what was done. Indeed the surviving structure provides the only evidence of further changes of which there is now no record.

In many structures, changes are betrayed by unmistakable differences in the character of the forms and in some of their details. Where most or all of the working masonry is visible – either because it was never obscured or as a result of the later loss of facings and renderings – further evidence may be provided by differences in the character of this masonry and by structural discontinuities.

In Hagia Sophia, some changes, and certainly some additions, are clearly apparent. This is true of nearly all Turkish additions and of most of the later Byzantine ones. It is also true, for instance, of the tenth- and fourteenth-century reconstructions of the main semidomes and the western and eastern parts of the dome. But other changes are much less obvious. Partly because of the nature of the original structure, they introduced no very notable changes in form, and the structural discontinuities and differences in the character of the working masonry that might otherwise have betrayed the later work are hidden beneath the vast areas of surface rendering, marble revetment, or mosaic. Some of this, especially the mosaic decoration, may indeed show differences in style, technique or subject matter. But this does not necessarily indicate a different date for the underlying structure. The most we can say is that this structure cannot anywhere be later than an undisturbed surface. And with some types of surface such as marble revetment, it may even be difficult to establish, simply by inspection, that there has been no disturbance.

Fortunately there is one other type of evidence available. This is the evidence of the major deformations that the structure has undergone, some of which – such as the backward leans of the main piers and the forward movements of the semidome arches – have been referred to already in Chapter 2. The fact that they are, in part at least, true deformations that have taken place after construction is shown most obviously by the presence of major cracks and dislocations where the working masonry of the upper cornice and high-level walls is exposed. 77–8, 100 229, 230

100 Jog in the upper cornice of the south-west exedra caused by structural movement, seen between two arches of the gallery arcade. This jog corresponds to the crack seen at the foot of the exedra semidome in plate 93

101 Looking westwards along the south edge of the dome base

102 Looking northwards along the east edge of the dome base, the eastern semidome being seen to the right

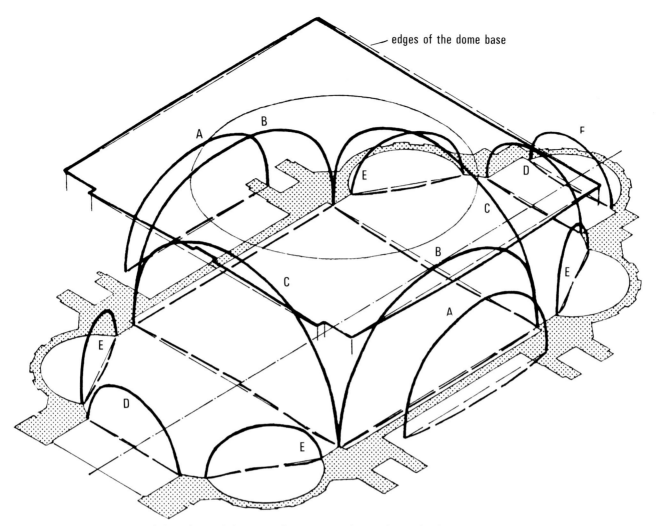

edges of the dome base

103 Isometric representation of the edges of the dome base and the forward edges of all the arches over the nave, arches A to E being lettered as in plate 88. Each edge is shown in heavy full line with its present horizontal deformations and displacements due to tilting of the piers magnified two times. The edges of the arches are also projected down to the horizontal planes through their springings, and shown thus as heavy broken lines. To the right of the centre-line, they are projected vertically to show the total displacements. To the left of the centre-line, the angles of projection correspond to the inclinations of the supporting piers, so that the divergences of the projected curves from the straight lines joining the springings show only the full extent of lateral bowing of the arches. (Scale 1:500)

The evidence provided by structural deformations

The value of such evidence stems from the fact that the deformations developed progressively throughout the history of the church. They began, for each element, from the time at which the relevant forces began to act upon it. Thus, if two adjacent or corresponding elements would have been acted upon by similar forces with similar results if they had been built together, yet one shows significantly less deformation than the other, it cannot have become part of the structure until later.

Of course, the precise deformations cannot be measured directly. They can only be deduced from the present forms on the basis of assumptions about the initial setting-out. And it cannot be assumed *a priori* that the faces of the piers, for instance, were given no outward inclination – Goodyear's 'widening refinement'[1] – at the time of construction; or that the major arches were not deliberately given non-circular profiles, as other scholars have previously assumed.[2]

The overall three-dimensional character of the present precise geometry does, nevertheless, strongly suggest that all original faces of the working masonry of the piers and arches were indeed vertical when built, that all cornices and colonnades were set out in straight lines, or following circular arcs around the great hemicycles and the exedrae, and that the soffits of all major arches were set out as circular arcs. Furthermore that, when additions were made or partial reconstructions undertaken, similar procedures were followed except to the extent that it was necessary to depart from them to adjust the new work to the old. Compare, for instance, the present horizontal bows of the main arches carrying the dome, and of the forward edges of the exedrae semidomes, with those that would be expected to result from the forces acting upon them (as shown in the diagram in Chapter 7) if they were set out originally without any bows.

79, 101–3 192

To build upright faces as nearly vertical as possible has, moreover, always been normal practice. And it is easily

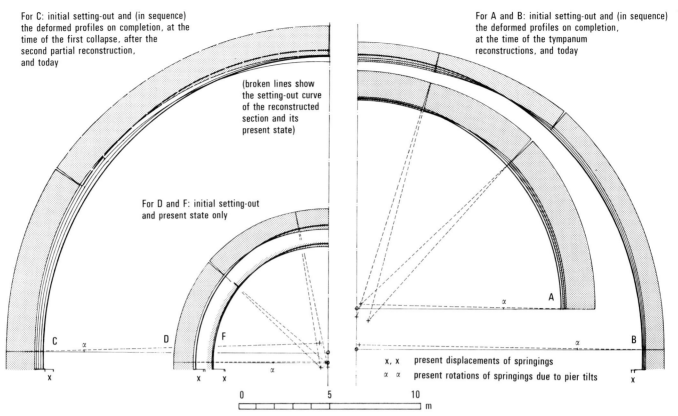

For C: initial setting-out and (in sequence) the deformed profiles on completion, at the time of the first collapse, after the second partial reconstruction, and today

(broken lines show the setting-out curve of the reconstructed section and its present state)

For D and F: initial setting-out and present state only

For A and B: initial setting-out and (in sequence) the deformed profiles on completion, at the time of the tympanum reconstructions, and today

x, x present displacements of springings
α α present rotations of springings due to pier tilts

104 Semi-profiles of some of the same arches as originally set out, and as subsequently deformed. These are averaged curves except for C, which is for the eastern arch only, on account of the different histories of the eastern and western arches. For all except F, the full depths of the arches are shown for the present states to show the manner of deformation: for the initial and intermediate states, only the soffits are shown. Centres for setting-out the initial complete semicircular profiles are ringed, and these profiles are shown in heavier line. Subsequent tilting of piers, displacements of the springings, and separation of the arches into four or five sections have displaced the centres, displacing them differently for different sections of each arch. Typical present positions are marked by crosses. The profiles of the exedrae arches E were analysed similarly. But, unlike those shown here, the deformations are not symmetrical on account of the tilting of both supporting piers of each arch in the same direction. Those at the west also show a greater asymmetry on account of the greater tilting of the western secondary piers in the east-west direction. (Scale 1:200)

demonstrated that, if the arches were sprung from initially vertical piers, those lower parts of their profiles which must have remained undeformed are not only circular arcs, but are the lower parts of semicircular arcs of diameters equal to the original spans. It is merely necessary, for this purpose, to eliminate inevitable minor departures in actual construction from the intended profiles. This was done by averaging the present profiles of similar arches, namely the pairs of upper and lower main arches at north and south, the two pairs of exedrae semidome arches, and the groups of four and eight similar arches that span between the main and buttress piers over aisles, galleries and gallery roofs.

These, then, were the assumptions made. As a final rigorous check of their validity, the complete histories of progressive deformation of all the major arches and vaults and their supporting piers were followed through. This was done taking into account all that was otherwise known of the structural history, and taking care to admit only those types of deformation which were consistent with the type of construction and with the forces that would have been acting and for which there was also visible evidence (in the form of cracks, splayed or slipped joints, or other dislocations), or directly comparable evidence from other structures.

That final check, from which the representative plots 104, are reproduced, is relevant to the elucidation of a number of aspects of the structural history that will be discussed later.

The deformations that are of most immediate interest here are the tilts of certain major elements due largely to the outward thrusts of the arches, vaults and dome.

On the basis of certain known partial reconstructions – in particular the well-documented first major reconstruction of the dome in 558–62 referred to below – and of other known events, it was possible to establish roughly how far the tilts of undoubtedly original elements like the main piers had progressed at different times. Approximate graphs of their progress could then be constructed, to help identify subsequent additions, and provisionally date them. The diagram reproduces the most important one. 105

These graphs were of greatest value for identifying additions made during the initial construction and soon afterwards, to which the character of the masonry gives virtually no clues, even when visible. Such was the rate of growth of the deformations, then, that their relative magnitudes could even serve to distinguish between the work of successive years. This early history will, however, be considered in Chapter 8.

Subsequently the rate of growth slowed down so much in relation to the margins of error inherent in the measurements that only very approximate indications of possible dates could be expected. But these indications were sometimes still invaluable in providing the first clues to other largely undocumented changes, and in suggesting where to explore beneath the surface for confirmation and more precise identification. Other evidence – documentary, epigraphic, or the *termini ante* or *post quem* furnished by the surface treatment or by C14 or similar tests[3] – could then be sought for closer dating.

Byzantine reconstructions

Three major Byzantine reconstructions are clearly documented, each embracing the whole or part of the dome, part of one of the main semidomes and part of the associated main arch. Each was made necessary by a partial collapse, which was hastened, if not immediately precipitated, by an earthquake. In addition there was a reconstruction, poorly documented, of the great north and south tympana and the gallery colonnades beneath them.

Reconstructions of the dome and supporting arches and semidomes
Part of the dome first fell on 7 May 558 after an earthquake in December 557, together with part of the eastern

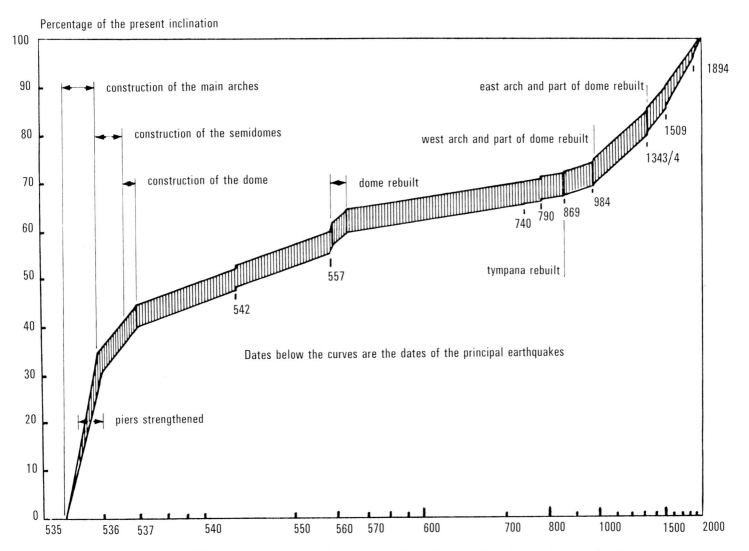

105 A representative history of the progress of structural deformation. The deformation shown is the average inclination in the north-south direction of the main piers between the gallery and upper cornices, expressed as a percentage of the present average inclination. It is shown as a band whose width corresponds to the limits of confidence in the estimates. Note that the horizontal scale is a logarithmic one of elapsed time, which allows the early deformations to be shown in as much detail as the later ones. The apparent quickening pace in recent centuries stems only from this contraction of the scale towards the right

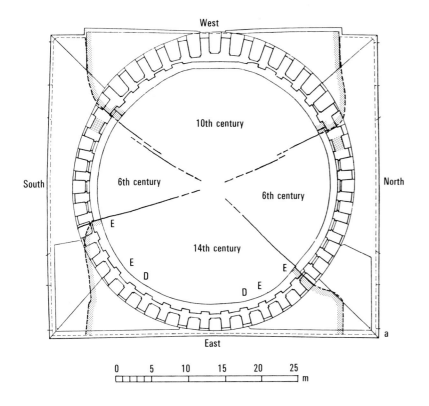

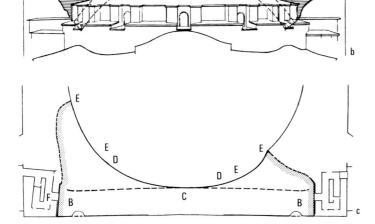

106 **a** Plan of the base of the dome showing the limits of successive reconstructions. **b** and **c** East elevation and plan at a slightly lower level of the eastern half, showing the limits of the fourteenth-century reconstruction. The depression of the crown of the arch at A is accompanied by dips of about 1 in 30 of the brickwork above it (shown only conventionally in the drawing), and by separations at B, B (where the fourteenth-century work was originally butted close against that of the sixth century), which become noticeably wider towards the top. The inward bowing C of the arch is similarly accompanied by a widening of these separations towards the outside, and by splayed gaps between the blocks of the dome cornice which suggest that its curvature has diminished over the distance DD and increased at EE, EE. For F, see plate 110

semidome and main eastern arch. On this occasion the entire dome was rebuilt to a raised profile, after the necessary reconstruction of the semidome and arch and some remodelling of the upper main arches to north and south and the pendentives.

The fullest and most reliable contemporary account of what was done is that by Agathius:

> Through the earthquake the church had lost the most central portion of its roof, that part which was higher than the rest. The Emperor restored it, strengthened it and gave it greater height. Although Anthemius was then dead, Isidorus the younger and the other architects considered the previous design, and by that which remained they judged of what had fallen, made out its structure and its weakness. At the east and west they left the great arches in place as they had been. At the north and south they took the construction on the curve and caused it to project inward more, making it gently wider to correspond better to the others and make the equilateral harmony more perfect, thus reducing the distortion of the void, stealing off a little of its extent to make the plan rectangular. Then they rebuilt the crowning middle part – orb, hemisphere, or what you will – and this became more nearly perfect, well turned, and everywhere true to line, narrower and steep in profile. It did not astonish the observers as before, but it was much more securely set.[4]

The surviving (probably incomplete) text of Malalas, the only other contemporary chronicler, briefly tells much the same story, misleadingly referring to additional rather than widened arches at the north and south, but adding information about the increase in height of the rebuilt dome:

> The rest [of the dome] was taken down, plus the arches themselves. The same was rebuilt and made 20 feet higher. . . . and they also made two additional arches at the north and south.[5]

The accounts of Theophanes and Cedrenus add other details, perhaps ultimately derived from the complete original Malalas. But they are clearly less reliable, because the references to new piers and new ramps rising to the height of the dome cannot be taken at their face value: they do not tally with what can be deduced from the structure itself.

According to Theophanes:

> The designers were censured because, to avoid expense, they had not made the supports secure below, but had left openings in the piers that carried the dome, for which reason they had not held fast. Having realized this, the most pious Emperor erected new piers to support the dome, and so it was rebuilt and made more than 20 feet higher than the previous structure.[6]

107 Looking up to the dome, with the west at the top

And according to Cedrenus:

> Seeing [the damage] the Emperor erected new piers to support the dome, which was made more than 20 feet higher than the previous structure. Outside the church he also erected, from the ground up to the dome, four spiral stair towers opposite the interior piers to buttress the arches and vaults.[7]

The subsequent collapses, on 26 October 989 and 19 May 1346, were of similar extent, first of the corresponding parts at the west and then again at the east.[8] On each of these occasions the rebuilding was confined to making good the loss and repairing the worst adjacent damage. There is no mention in the chronicles of further changes in form, so the only evidence of these is that which can be seen in the present structure.

Dome

The present dome consists of two sections at the north and south that date from the first reconstruction, a section at the west that dates from the second, and a section at the east that dates from the third.[9] The joins between these sections are, for the most part, clearly visible – some even from the nave floor – as irregularities in the dome surfaces. They are most sharply defined on the dome cornice.

In the two sixth-century sections the cornice blocks have a uniform inward slope corresponding to the angle at which the ribs begin to rise, and they are regularly laid with a single block beneath each rib, radial joints, and no visible cramps. Cut with a chisel into the upper surfaces of the blocks are setting lines for the forward edges of the ribs. Their own forward edges are cut to a smooth continuous curve. There is no protrusion of the supporting arches below.

106a
107
108

In the fourteenth-century section, rebuilt between 1346 and 1353 by Astras and the Italian Giovanni Peralta, there is again no continuous setting line for the ribs and no regularity in the spacing of the blocks, so that some ribs again straddle a joint. All blocks seem to be cramped together in line with the forward edges of the ribs. They slope inwards, as at the north and south, and now dip slightly below the level there. There is no projection of the supporting arch, as at the west, and hence no need for a straight section of the lip. But the curvature of this is far from uniform at the northern extremity over the north-east pendentive, where there is a pronounced reverse curve corresponding to the equally pronounced irregularity in the surface of the pendentive.

In the tenth-century section of the dome itself, the heavier construction of the rebuilt supporting arch that resulted in its rising above the cornice is matched by the greater depth given to all the rebuilt ribs. They are about 3 m deep at the foot, as compared with about 2 m in the sixth-century sections. In addition, two window openings adjacent to remaining sixth-century ribs were filled in at each end of the reconstruction. At the extremities of the collapse, above the level of the windows, the edges of the sixth-century ribs were apparently cut back to near-vertical faces, against which the new work was then butted.

In the fourteenth-century section there are no obvious differences between the rebuilt ribs and those alongside of the sixth century. Little or no cutting back seems to have been undertaken at the extremities of the collapse, so that the joins above the level of the windows tend to follow irregular lines up the webs between the ribs. There is also a marked convexity of the rebuilt ribs towards the interior at about mid-height.

These principal distinguishing characteristics are matched by typical differences in the brickwork and pointing, and in the mosaic decoration. The bricks in the fourteenth-century section, for instance, are considerably smaller than those in the earlier sections, and the pointing in the tenth-century section is characteristically different from that in the sixth-century section.

Close inspection, bearing these differences in mind, reveals, however, some local tenth-century repair of the sixth-century section over the north-east pendentive. And in the tenth-century section there is a not unexpected re-use, in the reconstructed supporting arch, of salvaged extra-large bricks from the fallen sixth-century arch. A similar re-use in the eastern arch, though with fewer whole bricks salvaged, was observed when part of the outer face of this arch was last laid bare.

The overall impression is of purposeful care and precision in the sixth-century reconstruction, no doubt with a very strong sense of the need to avoid a repetition of failure that had so soon overtaken the original dome; of great caution in the tenth century; and of either much greater confidence or less care, coupled with a desire to minimize the cost, in the fourteenth century.

109 (*Above*) The join between the fourteenth-century reconstruction of the dome (on the left) and surviving sixth-century work (on the right), above the west tip of the south-east pendentive. Compare the lines of the ribs in the two sections and note the pronounced irregularity of the fourteenth-century work at the top

In the tenth-century section, rebuilt between 989 and 994/5 by the Armenian architect Trdat, everything is different. Most obviously, as we have seen, the western arch now rises above the cornice in front of the four westernmost ribs, necessitating a straight lip to the cornice here, in order to give room for passage. In this region the blocks have virtually no inward slope, and are almost 0.5 m higher than at the north and south. Their spacing is irregular, frequently resulting in a rib straddling a joint. Joints are not all strictly radial, and there are many visible cramps across them. There is no continuous setting-line for the forward edges of the ribs – only a line near the lip over the south-west pendentive, which probably served the same purpose, and was intended finally to guide the cutting of the lip. It is clear, though, that there must have been considerable re-use of salvaged material.

Since nothing remains of the first dome, no similar direct comparisons are possible. The most important recorded change was the increase in height, already referred to.

Semidomes, main east and west arches, and adjacent parts of the pendentives

The necessary making good of the collapsed parts of the west and east arches and semidomes, and adjacent parts of the pendentives, means that the upper parts of these elements in the present structure date from the tenth and fourteenth centuries, the lower parts only belonging to the original structure. It is also possible that something remains from the first reconstruction at the east, if the fourteenth-century collapse was less extensive than this reconstruction.

Since, in recent years, the working masonry has remained hidden in most of the relevant areas, both inside and outside, the precise limits of the reconstructions are not fully known. The lateral limits are today visible chiefly in the stairways in the corners of the dome base, and – more conspicuously but at the west only – in the bringing forward by 1 m of that part of the west face of the dome base which rises directly above the thickened main arch. There is no obvious evidence of reconstruction of the barrel vaults at the extreme west and east, or of any of the

110 (*Above*) Detail of the recess lettered F in plate 106c (part of an earlier vaulted passageway) opening off the stairway in the surviving sixth-century south-east corner of the dome base. One edge of the fourteenth-century reconstruction forms the back of the recess

111 The west end of the church seen from the south-west minaret

exedrae semidomes, so it seems probable that both lower limits were approximately at the heads of the rings of windows at about mid-height of the main semidomes. The same conclusion is suggested by present profiles of the main east and west arches.

At the west, one of these windows was blocked and a heightened drum-like ring was built against the semidome to buttress its springings. Construction then continued almost vertically in the more westerly part, well beyond the level at which the main arch started to close in towards the crown. Finally, it was therefore necessary to move inwards almost horizontally to close the gap at the top, leading to the heavy, high-shouldered external profile as seen from the direction of the Mosque of Ahmet or Hagia Irene (*Survey*, plates 7, 34; see also 43).

At the same time the western main arch was given the greater width and depth that have already been noted, presumably to provide a more secure abutment to the inward thrust of the semidome, before the fallen part of the dome was reconstructed. Nevertheless, the crown did move markedly inwards. It now leans inwards by almost 0.2 m in relation to its springings, if no addition is made for the backward-lean of the piers. In profile, it was made as nearly semicircular as the surviving outward-leaning haunches of the original arch allowed, though its crown is now again depressed. It survived the earthquakes of 1343 and 1344 which preceded the collapse of the eastern arch,

and suffered only relatively light damage in the last serious earthquake of 1894.

At the east, it seems likely that the previous form was followed much more closely, because the rebuilt semidome closely resembles the smaller exedrae semidomes, and the arch does not visibly protrude anywhere, either below the soffit of the semidome or above the cornice or the roof of the dome base. The chief irregularity here is that in the northern pendentive. The eastern half of this was clearly rebuilt, while the northern half was retained to give continued support to the undamaged part of the dome, and this led to a problem in smoothly reconciling the curve of the rebuilt half to that of the existing half.

As at the west, the crown of the arch has moved inwards and dropped. The thrust from the semidome that caused the movement would have been less on account of the different profile. But it is known from contemporary records that the reconstruction took place in two stages separated by a pause of about six years – first the semidome and possibly a start on the dome as far as the inward convexity referred to above, then the completion of the dome.[10] Throughout the pause, the thrust would have acted with only limited restraint from the opposite thrust of the incomplete dome. Also, the arch lacks the extra stiffness given to the western one. So the movements at the east are slightly greater than at the west.

112 The upper levels of the church seen from Hagia Irene

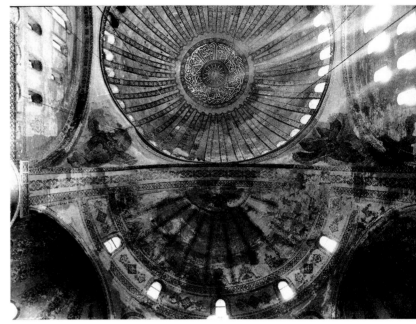

113 (*Left*) Looking up at the north-east pendentive

114 Looking up vertically at the main eastern arch

Thanks partly to a previous exposure of the working masonry on the east face of the dome base, the whole three-dimensional pattern of the movement here can be traced. Direct evidence of the dropping of the crown was provided by marked dips of the horizontal courses of brickwork above the arch, and by tapered separations of the reconstruction from the remaining sixth-century structure at each side. The picture is completed by the evidence already referred to, and by confirmatory indications of movements of the dome cornice given by the present gaps between adjacent blocks – movements which are consistent only with the assumed horizontal bowing of the arch.

106b

North and south arches and adjacent parts of the pendentives
Because of the greater combined depths and widths of the upper and lower arches at the north and south, the smaller clear spans of the lower arches between the piers, and the smaller outward movements of the piers in the direction of the spans, these arches survived all three partial collapses, and have never been rebuilt like the east and west arches. And, despite the contrary statement in the surviving text of Malalas, no new arches were added after the first collapse.

What happened then, as Agathias makes clear in the passage quoted above, was that additions were made to the upper arches to make them progressively wider towards the top. If these arches, like the lower ones, were built with their faces initially vertical, their exposed soffits would originally have been of uniform width. Yet we have seen that they do now indeed become 'gently wider' as they rise – their width increasing from about 0.94 m at the level of the feet of the pendentives to about 1.32 m at the crowns (*Survey*, plates 4, 30, 36). As they were widened, the upper parts of the pendentives must have been rebuilt.

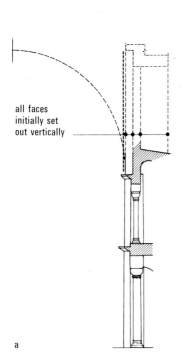

all faces
initially set
out vertically

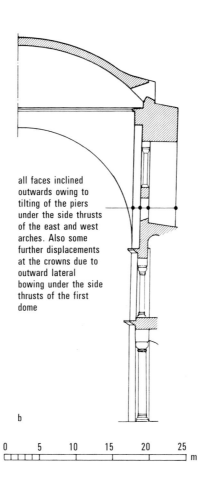

all faces inclined
outwards owing to
tilting of the piers
under the side thrusts
of the east and west
arches. Also some
further displacements
at the crowns due to
outward lateral
bowing under the side
thrusts of the first
dome

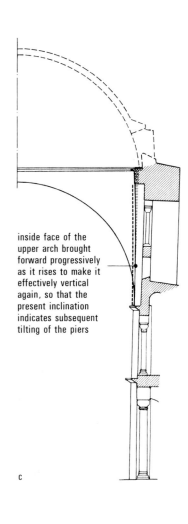

inside face of the
upper arch brought
forward progressively
as it rises to make it
effectively vertical
again, so that the
present inclination
indicates subsequent
tilting of the piers

a   b   c

0   5   10   15   20   25
⌷⌷⌷⌷⌷ ⌷ ⌷ ⌷ ⌷ m

115 Partial transverse cross-sections of the church looking east, showing the principal arches at the south: **a** as initially set out, **b** in 557 before the collapse of the eastern arch, and **c** in about 560 after preparatory work for rebuilding the dome. (Scale 1:500)

Today it is this part of the sixth-century reconstruction that provides the single most direct indication of the amount of structural deformation that had taken place up to 558. Assuming that the objective of the widening was to make the faces of the upper arches vertical again, the present backward-leans of the reconstructed faces are measures of the tilting of the piers in the north-south direction after 558, while the backward-leans of the untouched faces of the lower arches (and hence of the tympanum walls where they meet the upper arches) are measures of the total tilting since the pier were built. It is merely necessary to remember that the present displacements of the crowns of the arches are not solely due to leans of the piers at their springings: they also result partly from the lateral bowing of the arches, for which allowance must be made.

This is the basis of the estimate that about 60 per cent of the north-south tilting of the main piers had taken place by 558, the remainder being subsequent movement.

Dome base

Agathius makes no mention of any change to the dome base. Nevertheless it is clear from measurements of the inclinations of the brick courses and other indications that the upper corners of the present square base with their internal stairs, and the squinch arches that connect the buttress arms to points above the haunches of the north and south arches, also date from near the time of the sixth-century reconstruction. We shall return to this in Chapter 8.

The only substantial later change occurred in the tenth-century reconstruction. This was the addition of the projecting mass on the west face, needed to accommodate the greater depth and width given to the rebuilt part of the main west arch.

There is no hint of any further change in the form of the base in the fourteenth century, except for the introduction of the shallow, arched niches to each side of the main semidome on the east face.

116 The colonnade supporting the south tympanum, seen from the gallery

*Reconstructions of the north and south tympana
and supporting gallery colonnades*

A limited reconstruction of the structure beneath the north and south arches became necessary during the initial building because of the early settlement of the crowns of the arches. This will be referred to later. Here we need only consider the subsequent reconstrucion of everything down to the gallery floor.

Up to 1966, the only hints of the likelihood of such a reconstruction to have been noted were at gallery level.[11] Among these signs were the setting of the bases of the columns of the side colonnades in straight lines rather than on their original setting-marks which follow the present inward curves of the gallery cornices, the poor fit of the seemingly original *opus sectile* panels on the spandrels of the arches above these colonnades, and the apparent replacement, in all the soffits of the same arches, of original mosaics matching those which still survive in the corresponding soffits in the exedrae.

Indications that the date of the reconstruction was later than was originally suggested, and confirmation that it did extend down to the gallery floor, were furnished initially by measures of the present outward-leans of those parts of the tympanum walls which could have been rebuilt with the customary vertical faces, measures of the present inclinations of the columns below, and measures of the present horizontal curves of the upper cornices.[12] Considering all these together (necessary because the tympana and colonnades are only infillings to the primary structure, and are therefore subjected to more complex combinations of forces than the main piers), it appeared that the present deformations were consistent only with a rebuilding when the leans of the main piers had increased by roughly a further 10 per cent since 558. A test to determine the extent of open cracking along the length of the base of the south tympanum in relation to the estimated spreads at different times in the east-west direction led to a similar, though less precise, conclusion.

117 The north tympanum

118 Detail of the foot of the north colonnade showing the bases of the columns now set well back from their original setting marks. On the south side (seen in plate 85) a similar setting back is shown by a different type of setting mark, indicating only the intended centre-lines

By uncovering short lengths of all the joins between the original sixth-century masonry and that of the recon- 120– struction, it was finally confirmed that virtually the whole of each tympanum was rebuilt after the colonnades below had been dismantled to the gallery floor and re-erected (or, just possibly, moved back into upright alignment without complete dismantling), and that this must have happened well after 558. A telling illustration of the extent of the deformation of the upper cornice before the reconstruction is given by the present misalignment of the two halves of a chase in the upper cornice on the south side. 78 This chase must have been cut to receive a cramp in an earlier attempt to halt further movement.

For more precise dating it was necessary to turn to the evidence furnished by the character of the exposed masonry; to C14 tests on embedded timbers; to the limited historical record; to the fact that the niches at the feet of the tympana that frame the mosaics of church fathers were shown to have been introduced for the first time in the reconstruction; and lastly to the nineteenth-century record of an inscription that previously ran across the heads of both tympana. It was concluded that the reconstruction was most probably the one referred to in that inscription. This was undertaken by Basil I in about 869. Though there was an earthquake on 9 January of that year – the first after that of 557 which is said to have damaged Hagia Sophia – the inscription referred only to the structure having suffered from the effects of time. This is entirely consistent with the likely progressive growth in deformations after the tympana were completed.

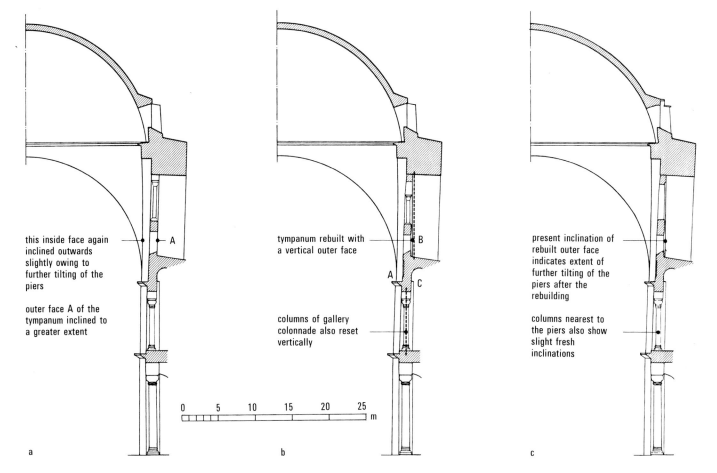

this inside face again inclined outwards slightly owing to further tilting of the piers

outer face A of the tympanum inclined to a greater extent

tympanum rebuilt with a vertical outer face

columns of gallery colonnade also reset vertically

present inclination of rebuilt outer face indicates extent of further tilting of the piers after the rebuilding

columns nearest to the piers also show slight fresh inclinations

0 5 10 15 20 25 m

a   b   c

119 Further partial transverse cross-sections of the church looking east, showing the tympana: **a** as in 562, **b** as subsequently reconstructed, and **c** today. In b, A, B and C identify the locations of details shown in plates 120 to 125. (Scale 1:500)

120 Internal elevation of the south tympanum with superimposed details of its rear at CC and of the exterior of the north tympanum at BB, showing the limits of the ninth-century reconstruction and the subsequent narrowings of the window openings (stippled). The main difference observed between north and south was that less of the original work survived in positions AA at the north. (Scale 1:200)

0 5 10 m

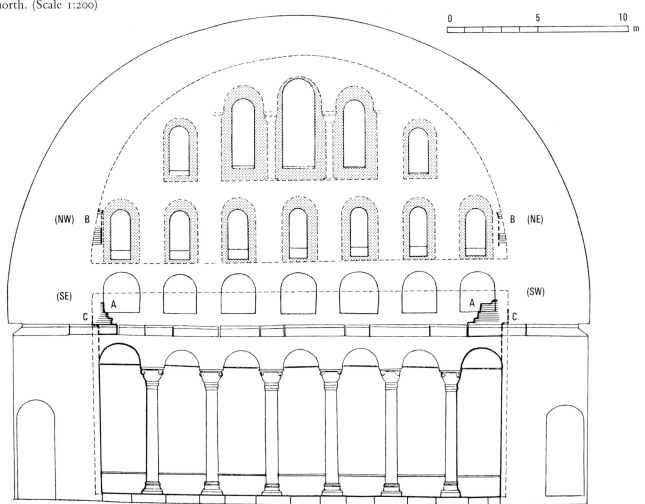

(NW) B   B (NE)

(SE)   (SW)

121 Detail on the upper cornice of the western limit of the reconstruction of the north tympanum (position A in 119 and corresponding to A on the left of 120). The reconstruction is at the right with a new cramp inserted to tie in the reset block of the cornice beneath it

122 The westernmost window of the north tympanum, showing what was retained of the original construction on the right (position B in plate 119 and on the left of plate 120). The junction here between original and reconstructed masonry is the reveal of the original window. The later filling of the opening is seen to the left

123 Detail of the springing of the head arch of
the original window seen in plate 122, showing
(below and to the right of the superimposed
broken line) how the face of the bricks was cut
back to conform to the new outside vertical face
of the reconstruction (seen at the upper left)

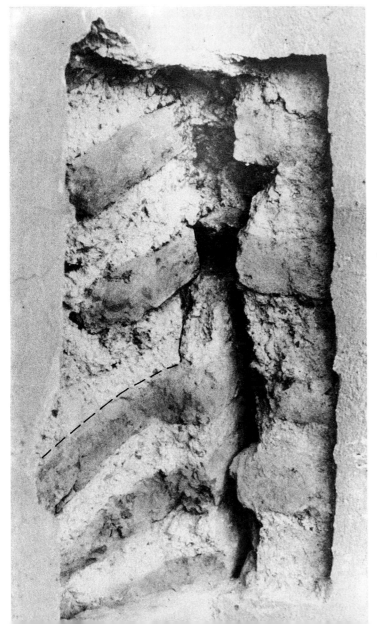

124 Detail of the join between the original
construction and the reconstruction immediately
above the truncated pilaster of the north-east pier
(position C in plate 119 and corresponding to C
on the right of plate 120). The reconstruction
here is to the right of the irregular line of the
join running from top left to bottom right of the
view. The block of marble at the foot caps the
pilaster and extends beneath the tympanum to
form part of the upper nave cornice

125 The church from the south-west in 1847 (Fossati, plate 25)

Byzantine and Ottoman additions and consolidations

While the Byzantine reconstructions just described have altered the form of the church in several ways, the numerous buttresses and other external additions have had a much greater effect on both its appearance and its structural anatomy. In the past there were other additions which are now lost, including most of the buildings of the patriarchal palace.

Alongside the surviving additions we must also consider a number of other consolidation measures, mostly inside the church. These included the filling of openings in the main piers at gallery level and the incorporation of new ties.

Three main phases of structural repair and strengthening are recorded, apart from works associated with the major reconstructions that have already been considered. The first phase was initiated in 1317 in the reign of Andronicus Palaeologus; the second in 1573 under the architect Sinan; and the third in 1847 under the Swiss architect Gaspare Fossati, assisted by his brother Giuseppe.

The principal work undertaken in 1317 was the construction of new buttresses. In 1573, the mandate to Sinan was a general one to undertake all repairs that seemed necessary, though it did include a specific command to build a new minaret in place of one that was to be demolished.[13] In 1847, the mandate was again fairly wide in scope. The actual work undertaken included the rectification of a number of columns in the gallery exedrae, the installation of new ties in several places, and several changes at the level of the dome base.[14] There could have been further work on other parts of the structure at the time of any of the four major reconstructions, particularly the three earlier ones.

Buttresses

We have seen that the present buttresses are, broadly speaking, of three types. First, there are the continuations of the buttress piers above the gallery roofs with their connections to the backs of the main piers to form the broad arms which frame the main arches to north and south of the dome. Then, outside the church and below the level of the gallery roofs, there are lower buttresses of two other types (plans A9–10): flying buttresses like those commonly associated in the West with Gothic church architecture, and the heavier-looking, broad projecting masses of masonry with battered outer faces and sloping roofs.

The upward continuations of the buttress piers and their connections with the main piers date back to the original construction. They have, however, to an extent varying from buttress to buttress, been repaired and consolidated subsequently in various ways. The principal repairs have been renewals of the barrel vaults that span between the connecting walls. The principal consolidations have taken the form of stone pilasters built against the walls, iron ties inserted between the connecting walls, and narrowings of the arched openings that give passage through these walls at gallery-roof level. The major work appears to have been done under Sinan. But there is also evidence of earlier work in about the tenth century; and some further work, including the remodelling of the aedicules at the heads of the internal stairs, was done by Fossati. In addition, small flying buttresses were erected at an indeterminate date over the squinch-like arches between the buttress arms and the dome base. They were removed by Fossati.

The identification of the buttresses due to Andronicus, the dating of the remainder, and the identification of possible earlier forms of some of them, are all more difficult. Nicephorus Gregoras refers to the buttresses of Andronicus as follows:

> For he [Andronicus], hearing from the experienced architects that two sides of it [Hagia Sophia], the south and the east, were in imminent danger of collapse from the effects of age if nothing was done speedily to avert

this, gave, as we have said, thousands of gold pieces . . . for constructing pyramids from the foundations . . .[15]

The term 'pyramids' can only refer to some of the broad masses with battered outer faces. But to how many of these?

The danger of collapse was said to have been at the south and east. This is consistent with the very obvious outward-leans today of the walls and outermost column of the south-east bay of the gallery (*Survey*, plate 41).

The one major difference in the present buttressing of the corners of the church is indeed to be seen at the south east. In all other corners the buttressing is provided by the original access ramps, by adjoining porches or similar structures, and by separate bases for the minarets which appear to have been constructed at the same time as the minarets. In the south east there is now a seemingly solid mass of masonry on the east side corresponding to the access ramp at the north east, and there is a similar mass against the south wall. If, as seems likely, there was originally an access ramp on the east side, it must have been destroyed or filled. Also, this must have happened well before the construction of the minaret that now stands here, because the stairway leading up to its foot is accommodated in a later addition set in the angle between the two masses, instead of rising directly from ground level through the supporting mass as do the stairways of the other minarets. Thus there is good reason for attributing these two south-eastern buttresses largely to Andronicus.

126 The church from the west

127 Detail of the western flying buttresses

128 The central outer buttress on the north side

But there are other broad masses on the south and east, and it will have been noted that Gregoras did not state that the 'pyramids' were built on these sides only. Some of the other masses, including, perhaps, some of those on the north but excluding that against the original south-west buttress pier and those against the central bays of the aisles on both north and south, may well also be due partly or wholly to Andronicus.

More positive identification is greatly hindered at present by the limited knowledge of their construction, except, chiefly, where there are accessible internal spaces. Where something can be seen of the construction, there is sometimes evidence of several successive phases. The complex forms and skew alignments of the two largest masses at the north also suggest piecemeal construction, with earlier forms incorporated in the present ones, either by Andronicus or at some later date.

The flying buttresses at the west are almost certainly of 126– earlier date. It has previously been suggested that they were the work of Crusaders during the Latin occupation in the early or mid-thirteenth century, and that they were originally part of a comprehensive series on all sides erected at this time in an unrecorded campaign of repair and strengthening of a much weakened fabric – the others having later been incorporated by Andronicus in his buttresses. It was argued that, since the flying buttress had been invented in the West just a little earlier, only the Crusaders could have brought knowledge of it to Constantinople. Moreover, only they would have had the skill to devise and execute such an efficient scheme.[16]

This reasoning is doubly suspect. The earliest securely dated flying buttresses of this type are not necessarily the first to have been built anywhere. And, if the Crusaders did undertake an extensive programme of buttressing in the early or mid-thirteenth century, there should have been no need for a further major campaign in the early fourteenth century.

What was most significant about the flying buttress in Gothic architecture was its exploitation as an integral and essential part of a total structural and architectural concept, rather than its initial use as an expedient to overcome an evident but unforeseen weakness. There seems no reason why others should not have independently adopted a similar expedient in case of need, or why they should not have done so in Constantinople at some date before the need arose in the Ile de France. On the basis of the record, the most likely date for a need for support to have suggested itself at the west end of the church is either in the ninth century when the tympana were reconstructed, or in the tenth century at the time of the partial reconstruction of the dome and of the western semidome.

A similar date is possible for the original buttresses in the centres of the north and south sides. These buttresses have never been filled solid. They now consist essentially of pairs of walls answering to the pairs of columns in the centre bays of the aisles and galleries. These walls are bridged by barrel vaults, and the spaces so roofed are also

129 Flying buttresses and porch
at the south east

130 (*Below right*) The north-
west main pier at gallery level

closed in at the ends. The likelihood of a similar original
date stems from the fact that the exposed masonry of the
east wall of the northern buttress incorporates strong
ramping arches of brick, as if the wall (and presumably the
128 west wall also) could have been originally a flying buttress
like those at the west.

129 The very different proportions of the pair of flying
buttresses at the east suggest that they are later, and
probably contemporary with the rebuilt porch alongside
one of them. This porch does not look earlier than the
thirteenth century, but its dating is made difficult by the
re-use of earlier columns and capitals. In their present form
these buttresses look Ottoman, as does the more massive
buttress to the north of the apse. But they could all date
originally from work undertaken by Andronicus.

*Fillings of north-south penetrations of the main piers
at gallery level*

The chief objective of all these added buttresses was clearly
to halt the progressive outward movements that were
occurring as a result of the outward thrusts of the high
vaults. The making good of some of the original
reductions in cross-section of the main piers at gallery
level, as compared with their cross-sections at ground
level, must have been seen as another way in which this
objective might be achieved.

131 View of the nave in 1710 looking north (Loos drawing)

The principal fillings are those of the vaulted penetrations running from north to south through the piers (AAA in plan A10).

130   We have seen that the penetration in the north-west pier is, surprisingly, still open. It shows very clearly the original form and, if allowance is made for the marble facings, the total deformation undergone since construction of the pier. In contrast to the outward tilts of the north and south faces of the piers themselves, the fillings of the other three piers have faces that are still almost vertical. This suggests a date within the Ottoman period. The character of the masonry is similarly suggestive. The limestone blocks are considerably smaller than in the original masonry of the piers, more roughly cut, and with wider joints.

The likelihood that the filling was undertaken by Sinan is supported by the limited graphic evidence. In particular, the drawings of the two sides of the church made by the Swedish artist Cornelius Loos in 1710 show all the
131   penetrations already filled, except that at the north west.

Fillings of the main piers adjacent to the exedrae at gallery level

132a   The other fillings (BBBB in plan A10) extend the piers into what would otherwise be the open end-bays of the exedrae colonnades, partly embracing their end columns and embracing also the columns that stand a little further back to carry the vaults of the end-bays of the side galleries. The justification for regarding them also as fillings of the piers, and not merely as partial fillings of these gallery bays, is that they make good a reduction in cross-section of the piers in relation not only to the cross-section at ground level but also to that above the upper   132b
cornice.

The history of these fillings is probably complex, and cannot now be elucidated fully without making deeper exploratory borings than have yet been practicable. Their most recent history, however, is clear. Their final form can only be the work of Fossati. Not only do they have the near-vertical faces to be expected of work as recent as this, but the mortar used is like that of Fossati's other work; and the column of the exedra colonnnade that is partly embedded in the filling at the south west is one of those which was cut from its base and reset in a vertical position by Fossati (page 110).

But how extensive were Fossati's fillings?

At first sight the meticulously drawn earlier views of Loos already mentioned show the spaces now occupied by   131
the fills completely open, as are the corresponding spaces

at the outer ends of the exedrae colonnades. Closer inspection leaves no doubt, however, that the spaces are actually out of sight on account of the angles of view from positions close to the gallery parapets and on the transverse axis of the nave, while another of his views does show what appears to be a partial fill in the north-east exedra.

This limited graphic evidence is consistent with that of the limited tests so far made beneath the present plaster-surfaces. These also suggest Fossati did not add much to the size of the piers as he found them in 1847.

Unfortunately the later graphic evidence is not consistent and must be interpreted with care. Texier shows more than one form, having presumably had to complete his drawings away from the building, and never having destroyed some of the earlier attempts to reconcile somewhat inadequate measurements and notes. Salzenberg shows an imagined original form; as, finally, does Fossati also in some of his views.

Among this disconcerting plethora, Texier's *plan definitif*, signed and dated 1834,[17] accords best with the evidence of the tests that have been made, with the otherwise more convincing of his sectional elevations and with the view by Loos that shows the north-east pier. It therefore seems decisive. It shows a form for each pier closely following that at ground level, but set back from the curve of the exedra by about half the width of the colonnade over a length matching the final opening at the other end of the colonnade. In this way, half the soffit of the arch that is now only outlined in the *opus sectile* decoration of the face of the pier is revealed, thus giving the exedrae, as seen from the nave, more of the symmetry which the illusionistic painting of the Fossati filling tried in vain to recreate.

If this is correct, Fossati added less than 0.75 m of new masonry.

But was his the first addition? In the absence of further evidence we can only speculate on the basis of probabilities. For two reasons it seems likely that it was not; and that the original form of the piers mirrored exactly that of the secondary piers across the exedrae, as apparently assumed by Fossati.

The first of these reasons is that, with any other original form, we should have here a lack of symmetry of a kind that existed nowhere else in the original structure. In particular, the forms of the main and secondary piers do closely mirror one another across the exedrae, both at ground level and above the upper cornice. The second is that we should have an attempt to mask this lack of symmetry by semi-illusionistic means that would also be entirely without parallel.

132 Typical plans of the main and secondary piers. **a** Main piers today at gallery level showing the limits of the Fossati fillings (stippled) and original form as far as hitherto ascertained. **b** and **c** main piers and secondary piers at ground level (vertical hatching) and upper cornice (horizontal hatching) compared with their forms today at gallery level (heavy outline only). **d** Earlier forms of the main piers at gallery level as shown by Texier (*plan definitif* of 1834), Fossati (plate 14), and Salzenberg. **e** probable original form of the main piers at gallery level, first fillings (lightly stippled) and additional Fossati filling (heavily stippled). (Scale 1:200)

133 The north gallery looking west (detail of a Loos drawing)

If this also is correct we may hazard a guess that the first filling was done by Sinan at the same time as the filling of three of the penetrations. This would be consistent with the lack of any indication of marble revetment to the filling of the north-east pier in the drawing by Loos of the whole north-east bay. But that evidence is far from conclusive because there has been enough known disturbance of the marble revetments in the galleries to show that an earlier revetment in this relatively inconspicuous position might well have been taken away in order to use the marble elsewhere.

Other fillings

Other fillings call for only brief mention. The most numerous were fillings or narrowings of original window- and door-openings. Some have been mentioned already, for instance the filling of four windows in the dome and the narrowing of all the windows of the present tympana, the first at the time of the tenth-century reconstruction and the second probably by Sinan. They included also considerable narrowings of the openings that

originally lighted the stairs in the buttress piers. All are fairly easily identified, many of the blocked windows now being represented inside by Fossati paint.

Other important fillings were the partial closing of voids in the dome base above the main arches and pendentives, probably at the time of the sixth-century reconstruction of the dome.

Ties

The insertion of new ties was another means adopted to halt deformations. It would have called for more skill than the construction of heavy buttresses, if it were to be effective, but it would have been speedier, less costly, and less obtrusive. For this reason it was probably often the first expedient adopted. Where the ties are fully exposed, it also provides telling insights into some of the problems faced by those in charge of the safety of the structure.

Probably the earliest additions were the two series of long bars that run the whole lengths of the upper cornices of the two western exedrae. These will be referred to again in Chapter 8.

134 The same view today

The insertion of the single cramp to retain an already badly displaced block of the same cornice below the south tympanum must have been later, possibly not much earlier than the reconstruction of the tympana. The transverse ties under the floor of the west gallery, if not original, may have been inserted at about the same time. They were certainly inserted before the flying buttresses were built, since some of their outer anchorages are partly embedded in the arched struts of the buttresses.

The corresponding ties under the floors of the central bays of the side galleries were more likely inserted by Sinan, as were the largest ties between the central columns of these bays in both aisles and galleries, and the ties between the walls of the upper buttress piers.

Further iron ties were inserted by Fossati, notably one at the foot of the dome itself and another embedded in a slightly projecting cornice around the dome base. Yet another tie, this time of reinforced concrete, was placed at the foot of the dome in 1926. Unfortunately records of its precise form are lost, and its present condition is not known.

Rectifications

Part of the structural work undertaken in 1847 was of a different nature. This was the rectification – or setting upright – of some of the columns in the galleries. The extent to which they may have then been leaning can be appreciated from the present leans of some of those which were left as they were. It is more precisely indicated by the original setting-marks for the bases of those which were rectified, where these marks are visible. That the leans may have caused some apprehension is also understandable. But, since their elimination would do virtually nothing to improve stability of the structural system in the future and did involve some risks, it is difficult to see quite why it was attempted, and preferable to consider it under a separate heading.

The facts are reasonably clear. Examination of the columns in the exedrae colonnades shows that each of those which is now vertical, or nearly so, is distinguished by having been cut free from its base at the original integral torus moulding and reset on a separate, more sharply curved torus (as seen in most of the photographs of 66, 134, 284

these colonnades – the foreground columns in the view
137
here of the north-west colonnade being undisturbed).
There are twelve which are so distinguished, three in each
of the northern exedrae, four in the south-western, and
two in the south-eastern (marked R on plan A10). Since
this total tallies with the number given by Fossati in a
lecture delivered shortly after the official inauguration
that marked the completion of the whole restoration,[18]
these must be the columns that were moved. The mention
of thirteen in an earlier draft report[19] was presumably an
error. (In this draft, dated 1848, it is stated that the thirteen
columns were rectified 'to persuade the government to
allow me full discretion in the work that I was about to
do'.)

Some evidence of the structure's past was, unfortunately and unnecessarily, destroyed, and the fact that
some columns were left untouched may indicate that
Fossati himself had second thoughts. He clearly had
difficulty in moving the column adjacent to the south-west pier, which appears to have been damaged in the

135 Trial hole in the south-east pier in the position ringed at
the left of plate 132a showing the Fossati filling on the right,
the masonry of the pier projection on the left, that of the
original pier in the depth of the opening at the bottom, and
the impression of earlier marble revetment in the upper part
of the opening

move. This damage may well account for the decision to
add to the existing filling behind it, and, subsequently, to
add to the fillings of the other piers instead of moving their
adjacent columns.

Other additions

The additions described so far are those that were made
primarily to sustain the structure. Other additions
associated more with its use were made in both Byzantine
and Ottoman times. These were the buildings of the
Byzantine patriarchal palace, the belfry, various other
Byzantine structures along the east and north of the
church, and then the minarets, mausoleums, fountains,
imaret, and medresse which were their Ottoman
successors. Most of the Byzantine additions were later
swept away, or have been embedded in later structures.
Here we shall concentrate on what has survived, or
survived for long enough for its form to have been
recorded in the exterior views of Grelot and Fossati.

The earliest, and for our present purpose the most
important, additions, though they have survived only in
part, were the buildings of the patriarchal palace. At one
time these probably extended along much of the south side
of the church, with most of the principal rooms at the
upper levels. The stairway outside the south-west buttress
and the chapels to which it leads may have been linked
with this palace, though they were probably more directly
associated with the related use of the eastern part of the
south gallery, to which we shall return later. The
indisputable remains are grouped around the south-west
corner of the church adjacent to the south-west porch, or
built over the porch and the south-west ramp.[20]

To the west of the porch is what has been indentified as
the *horologion* or clock building[21] (at the left of the view of
this corner). Above it, and above the ramp, are the two 22
rooms that open off the south end of the west gallery.
These have been identified as the great and small *sekreton*,
essentially reception rooms and places for resting and for
ecclesiastical meetings[22]. The south-west ramp served as
the principal entrance to them, and for communication
with the ground-level entrances to the church.

All these indisputable remains appear to be of sixth-century date, but all – except perhaps the horologion in its
original form – are definitely additions and not part of the
original design. This is clear from the alterations in the
head of the ramp that were necessary to allow the
construction of the room over it, and from several
indications that the south-west porch was originally an
open space between the horologion and the ramp. The
changes and additions were probably made in the reign of
Justin II (565–78).

Little is known of the structures at the east of the church,
and still less about those at the north. The present porch to
the south of the apse presumably replaces an original 129
porch, corresponding to that which survives in part to the
north. Both these porches are likely to have been part of
the original construction. At least by the ninth century, the

136 The east bay of the south gallery showing, at the right, an imagined earlier form of the main pier (Fossati, plate 14)

137 (*Below*) The corresponding view today of the west bay of the north gallery

138 (*Left*) The church from the north-west in 1680 (Grelot)   139 (*Above*) The church from the south-west in 1680 (Grelot)

relic of the Holy Well is known to have been placed near the south porch, and perhaps in the porch.[23] It was certainly placed in a large room with four entrances, one from the easternmost bay of the south aisle, one from a colonnaded passageway running southwards towards the imperial palace, and the others from a second passageway running in the opposite direction past the apse and from an imperial dining room probably situated on the far side of the ramp. Behind the apse and opening off the second passageway was a chapel of St Nicholas, which was perhaps a survival from before Justinian rather than an addition. At the north east, to the north of the ramp, there were other rooms which may have been for the deaconesses attached to the church.

138–9 A belfry is shown by Grelot as standing between the middle pair of piers of the flying buttresses at the west. It may have been built only of timber, since no substantial foundations were encountered in Schneider's excavations.[24] It must have been later in date than the buttresses and, since bells were not usual in the Eastern church, it

may well have been added during the Latin occupation. It had disappeared by the nineteenth century.

142

Of the present four minarets, that at the south east is the oldest. It was constructed before 1481 by Mehmet the Conqueror, and was heightened in the nineteenth century by Fossati, to match the others. But it does not appear to have been the first purpose-built one to have replaced the belfry when the church was converted to use as a mosque. This has been shown to have been erected over the original southern stair-turret flanking the great west window.[25] The north-east minaret was erected by Beyazit II between 1481 and 1512, and the western pair were started in 1573 by Selim II, and completed by his successor Murad III under Sinan's direction.

By 1573 some of the Byzantine buildings had already been destroyed, and others taken over by squatters who had to be evicted to make way for the necessary repairs and other works commenced in that year. With new building under way, the surroundings were beginning to acquire their present character.

Looking back   113

140 Interior of the baptistery as a mausoleum

141 The north façade of the baptistery today, showing the screened porch, the raising of the internal floor level, and (seen between the two columns) the font removed to the porch

Shortly afterwards, on the death of Selim II, Sinan began the construction of his mausoleum.[26] This is the central one of the present group, square at the base and becoming octagonal externally below the circular dome (lower left in the illustration). The second imperial mausoleum – that of Murad III, hexagonal in plan (upper left in the illustration) – was added about 1595, and the third large one – that of Mehmet III – was completed in 1608. There is also the smaller mausoleum of the crown princes alongside that of Murad III. After 1608, no more were built. But, for the burial of Mustafa I, the nearby baptistery (upper right in the illustration) was converted to serve as one.[27] This involved, among other changes, the removal of the font and raising of the floor level.

By about 1675, when Grelot visited Constantinople, the atrium had been turned into a garden, the mausoleums stood in another walled garden to the south, and there was a further garden to the north between the mosque and the imaret, or charitable kitchen. The area to the south west was an open court. The primary school and ablution fountain which now stand there were built in the middle of the next century (top right in the illustration). By the nineteenth century a medresse or theological college had been constructed on the site of the atrium and several other structures had been added, including the sultan's entrance outside the old north-east porch (bottom right in the illustration) – the Ottoman counterpart to the entrance from the Byzantine palace past the Holy Well and through the south-east door.

Losses

Numerous losses have already been referred to in reviewing the restorations and additions, or are implicit in the review. Two more must be added. One is that of most of the sixth-century atrium, though its plan was retrieved by Schneider's excavation in 1935. The other is that of the Great Baptistery, which is referred to as having existed on the north side of the church.

Changes in revetments, pavings, mosaics, furnishing and lighting

Marble revetments and pavings, and plaster cornices

Externally, a few pieces of marble revetment have survived on the west front, and there are fixings for more. The rendering of all other original wall-surfaces is recent. So is the lead sheathing of the roofs, though there is no reason to suppose that this does not correspond to the original covering.

Internally, most of the original marble revetment of the walls remains in place at ground level, without evident signs of disturbance.

A considerable part of it remains at gallery level also, but with indications of later disturbance in many places. Much also has been lost here, some of the losses now being made good in Fossati paint. As was noted above, there are also signs of disturbance of the original *opus sectile* decoration of the arch spandrels above the side colonnades.

142 The site of the atrium in 1847 (Fossati, plate 16).

143 Iconoclastic mosaic decoration in the second of the rooms opening off the south end of the west gallery

The floor pavings – which we have seen are of marble throughout, rather than mosaic as in many earlier churches – have suffered extensive changes, especially in those parts of the nave where considerable damage must have been caused by the collapses of the high vaults. The large Cosmati-like panel near the south-east pier cannot, for instance, be earlier, in its present form, than the repair after the fourteenth-century collapse. There are also obvious limited replacements in the galleries, where slabs have been lifted for the purpose of inserting ties beneath the floor. But there is no reason to think that the original pavings differed much from that we now see.

Of the principal cornices which encircle the nave, the gallery one is unchanged, and the next has suffered only minor change from the dismantling and resetting of the lengths beneath the tympana. Only the dome cornice has suffered substantial change, as we have already seen.

The secondary cornices at the springing levels of the arches and vaults of the narthex, aisles and galleries are, on the other hand, recent replacements. They are Fossati plaster casts. The only surviving sixth-century sections (not in the church itself) were modelled *in situ* in wet plaster.[28]

250

144 The Emperor Alexander in the north gallery

145 (*Facing page*) Detail of the mosaic of the Emperor John II and the Empress Irene in the south gallery

Mosaics

Most of the original non-figural mosaic decoration of the vaults has, like the marble revetments, remained intact at ground level, though much of it is partly obscured by Fossati paint. The tesserae are characteristically cut from glass, with gold leaf or other colour applied to the back.

Only a little of this original decoration remains at gallery level and above, the best-preserved being on the sharply curved soffits of the arches above the exedrae colonnades. There are more fragmentary remains on some other similarly curved surfaces, and near the feet of vertical wall-surfaces. Later non-figural mosaics include some from the iconoclastic period in the south-west rooms opening off the west gallery.[29]   143

All surviving figural mosaics are of later date, as is some of the non-figural decoration in the galleries and above – distinguished partly by a much greater use of tesserae cut from natural stones or terracotta. The survivals are, however, only a small fraction of what was once there.[30]

The earliest figural mosaics were introduced in the latter part of the ninth century, after the end of the iconoclastic period. The first was the Virgin and Child in the apse.[31]   75 The other surviving (or partly surviving) high-level mosaics – the archangels in the arch over the bema, the   11 seraphim in the pendentives, and the Church Fathers in the   113 shallow niches at the feet of the tympana – followed soon   76 afterwards.[32] So, probably, did the mosaic over the Imperial door in the narthex, showing, in the centre,   35 Christ seated on a lyre-backed throne and, at his feet, a prostrate emperor.[33]

In common with near-contemporary schemes that survive more completely in a number of smaller churches, this early figural scheme was probably conceived as a whole, if not all at once. It was certainly once much more extensive, as we know from the records preserved by Fossati and Salzenberg, from earlier descriptions, and from other drawings by Loos. In particular it included a number of more narrative subjects such as the Baptism and Pentecost in the main vaults of the middle bays of the side   146 galleries, as well as other mosaics in the upper parts of the tympana and on the faces of the main east and west arches. Though there are also records of a Pantocrator in the centre of the dome, it is probable that this dated at the earliest from the completion of the tenth-century restoration, and it must have been either completely or partly remade in the fourteenth century.

The other figural mosaics were added at various later dates, for a variety of reasons. The date and purpose of the mosaic over the door in the south-west vestibule are not   30 yet established.[34] Of the three panels in the galleries, which are primarily imperial portraits, that of the Emperor Alexander high on the eastern face of the north-west pier   144, is the earliest, either late ninth or early tenth century. The two larger panels on the east wall of the eastern bay of the south gallery were added in the early eleventh and early   145 twelfth centuries.[35] The last addition was the largest and   71, 1 finest, the great Deisis in a well-lit position in the central bay of the south gallery.[36]

146, 147 The south gallery looking west in 1710 (detail of a
Loos drawing), compared (*below*) with the corresponding
view today

Facing page
148 Detail of the Christ of the Deisis panel

149 Reconstruction of the exterior as in 562. Some details are hypothetical, and there is no evidence for the precise forms, at this time, of those elements shown only in broken outline. No attempt has been made to show the outer courts or the precise external ground levels, notably a likely fall at the west end of the atrium

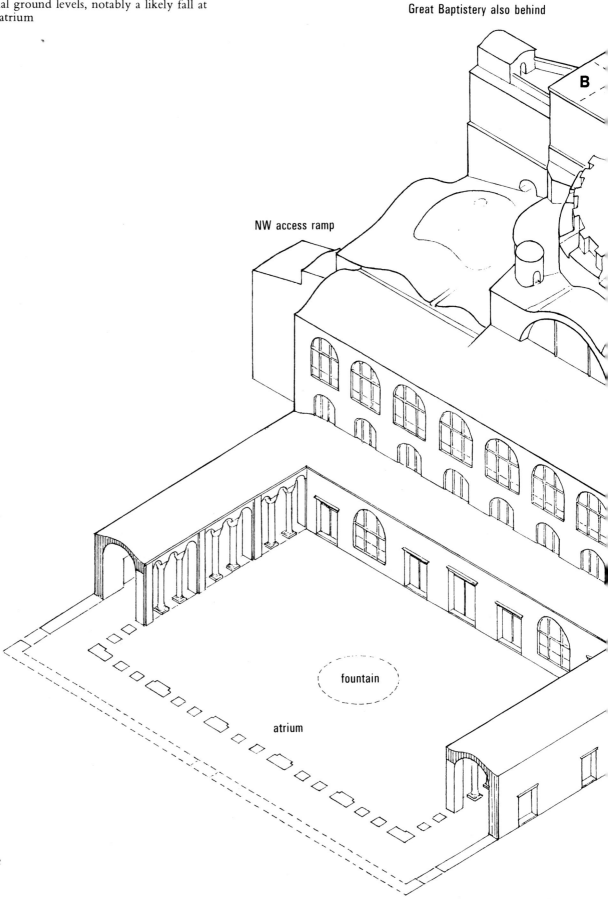

skeuophylakion

Great Baptistery also behind

B

NW access ramp

fountain

atrium

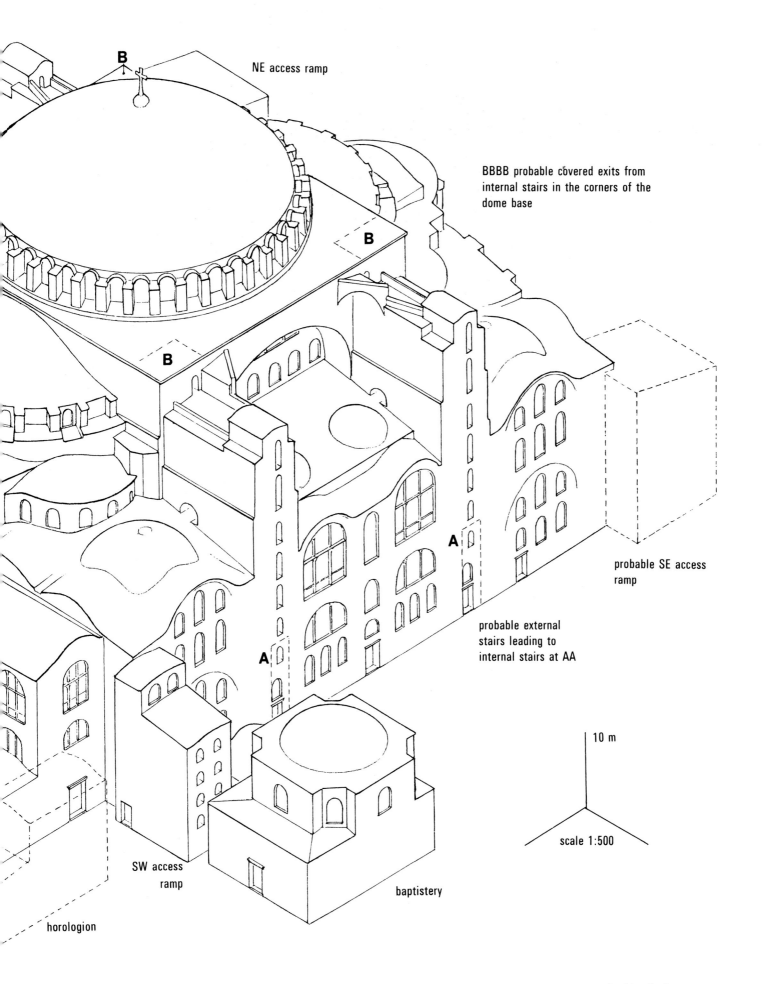

B

NE access ramp

BBBB probable covered exits from internal stairs in the corners of the dome base

B

B

probable SE access ramp

A

probable external stairs leading to internal stairs at AA

A

10 m

scale 1:500

SW access ramp

baptistery

horologion

Ottoman changes

The loss of so much of the figural mosaic cannot be blamed on Muslim religious zeal. The late seventeenth- and early eighteenth-century views of Grelot and Loos show everything except the tympanum mosaics and the Pantocrator in the dome still unobscured. The tympanum mosaics were probably covered when Sinan narrowed the window openings; other mosaics not until the mid-eighteenth century, to await re-exposure by Fossati only a century later.

The fact that losses have occurred very largely in the galleries and above, and especially on flat wall-surfaces, shows that they must be attributed chiefly to loosening of the plaster setting-beds as a result of water seepage, shaking during earthquakes, and long-term structural movements.

Ottoman redecoration was largely confined, until Fossati's restoration, to the usual introduction of Islamic texts. Loos shows large seventeenth-century rectangular plaques suspended in front of the piers. These were replaced during the restoration by the present circular plaques inscribed by Izzet Efendi, who was also responsible for the inscription now in the centre of the dome. As well as considerable work on the marble revetments in the galleries and the insertion of the stained-glass windows in the apse, the restoration finally included the painting-over of all the surviving mosaics and all bare surfaces in crude imitations of marble and of the original non-figural mosaics.[37]

Furnishings

The original altar, screen, and ambo were badly damaged in the first collapse, and rebuilt in the subsequent restoration. In view of changes in liturgical furnishings elsewhere it would be surprising if there were none in Hagia Sophia during the centuries that intervened before the depredations of the Crusaders. Further damage must have been done by the fourteenth-century collapse, and all the Christian furnishings were swept away after the Ottoman conquest.

The present Islamic furnishings are of various dates. The present mihrab, set at a slightly skew angle in the apse, the mimbar set against the south-east secondary pier, the principal tribunes, and the large marble urns in the western exedrae, were all constructed or brought to the church – now a mosque – in the reign of Murad III, probably during Sinan's restoration. The one major addition by Fossati was the large sultan's loge which now occupies much of the north-east exedra.

Lighting

The story of the provisions for artificial lighting of the interior is broadly similar. Nothing remains of the Byzantine fittings. The present wooden lamp-hoops also date only from the Fossati restoration, those in the nave having replaced an earlier single suspended lamp-frame consisting of three huge concentric octagons.

The church in 562

On the basis of this review of the changes that the structure has undergone, it is possible to arrive at a partial idea of the form of the church at the time of its second consecration in 562. The descriptions left by Procopius and Paulus Silentarius and others, and the excavations on the site of the atrium, help to fill in some details of what has been lost, and provide a basis for tentative reconstructions.

Surroundings and entrances

It is necessary first to remove virtually all that now stands outside the main rectangle occupied by nave, aisles, narthex and outer narthex, except for the surviving access ramps at the south west, north west and north east, the apse that projects from the east end, and – both standing a little apart – the baptistery and skeuophylakion. The relatively minor structure of the horologion might also have been completed, and there must have been a palace for the patriarch somewhere near. But there would have been nothing yet of what now survives of the palace, no outer buttresses, no minarets, and none of the other present free-standing structures.

On the other hand, the way in which the structure is now surrounded by gardens or courts on all sides but the east does preserve something of the character of the original surroundings, and more of it was perhaps preserved in the more open gardens depicted by Grelot. According to Silentarius:

> On the west of the church you will see a court surrounded by four stoas or colonnaded walks; one is joined to the narthex and the others open, and various paths lead to them. At the centre of the court stands a spacious fountain cut from Iasian peaks; from it a burbling stream of water . . . leaps into the air . . .
>
> And outside the church you may see everywhere many other open courts around its sides and other extremities. These have been beautifully contrived to make the sacred building appear flooded all round with the bright light of day.[38]

The western court or atrium was shown by Schneider's excavations in 1935 to have extended westward from the present outer narthex for about 42 m, much as does the present garden (plan A2).[39] Owing to the steeply sloping ground, the western walk had to be raised some 7 m above the natural level by vaulted brick substructures. Along the courtyard side of this walk and of the two side walks, pairs of columns alternated with piers – twelve piers in all with twenty-six columns – to support an arcade and either a timber or, more likely, a brick-vaulted roof. In the outer walls at each side there were three doorways, and there was probably at least one other in the west wall, though a steep flight of steps would have been necessary to approach this. The doorways at the south, opening from the square of the Augusteon, were probably the principal entrances.

To visualize the original form of the outer narthex, it is necessary not only to remove the present projecting piers

150 The nave looking east in 1672 (Grelot)

151 The east end of the north aisle in 1849
showing, at the right, the new Sultan's loge
constructed by Fossati (Fossati, plate 9)

of the flying buttresses, but also to discount certain changes in the fillings of the bays. The doorways at the two ends (not now in use) seem original, and would have communicated with the two side walks. The three doorways at the centre also seem original. But the same is true of only one of the windows – that to the immediate right of the central group of doors (and to the left of the tree in the view). Remains of a threshold beneath the far-left window suggest that originally there were two doorways at each end, and only a single window between each of these pairs of doors and the central group.

Thus the east side of the atrium has always been an enclosed outer narthex rather than a fourth open walk – though this does not exclude the possibility that it was originally planned as an open walk like the other three.

To complete the picture of this side, it is probably necessary to visualize the whole façades of both outer and inner narthexes and west gallery as being sheathed in marble, on the evidence of the pieces that still remain in place between some of the windows of the gallery.

There is no similar basis for expanding the brief description by Silentarius of the courts on other sides. But it is important to remember that there were more entrances to the church than are now open and in use. In particular there were two entrances flanking the apse, where entrances were not found in later churches. Also, the main narthex was entered directly at each end, rather than, as now, through a porch.

At the north, the skeuophylakion must have stood higher in relation to the original ground-level than it now does, but without its outer buttressing. Near by, as we know from Silentarius, there was a second baptistery of which no trace now remains.[40] In the *Book of Ceremonies* of Constantine Porphyrogenitus it is referred to as the Great Baptistery, distinguishing it from the Little Baptistery that still stands at the south west.[41] No positive evidence of its location has yet been found. It presumably stood somewhere in the area now occupied by the great buttresses built against the north flank of the church.

The Little Baptistery has recently been restored to something nearer to its original condition by the reopening of the door leading to its northern porch. But a seventeenth-century window (centre bottom of the illustration) still blocks the entrance door of its western narthex, the court in front of the northern porch remains closed off by the added buttress stair outside the south-west buttress, and the font remains outside, while the interior remains essentially that of the later mausoleum. Its immediate surroundings in 562 are not fully known.

Structure and internal access

Structurally, apart from the absence of later buttresses, infillings and internal ties, the chief differences from today would have been seen at the highest levels of the building.

The dome would have been more regular in form, with a smaller difference between its north-south and east-west diameters, no blocked windows, and the same thicknesses of ribs and intermediate webs at the north as elsewhere. Similarly, the semidomes and pendentives would have been more regular in form, with the western semidome similar to the present eastern one, and the north-east pendentive similar to the other three.

Externally there would have been minor differences in the form of the corners and west face of the dome base. There must have been small turrets or aedicules of some kind over what are now the blocked heads of the internal stairs in the corners. And the west face would have been similar to the present east face, without the projections necessitated by the greater depth and width given to the main west arch in the tenth-century reconstruction.

The buttress piers would have had larger openings where there are now only narrow slits in their end walls; there would have been none of the later internal fillings; and they would have had slightly different terminations at the top – though there is no evidence of the precise original form here.

Lower down, the main piers at gallery level would all still have been penetrated by vaulted openings running through from nave to gallery. They would have projected less towards the exedrae – thus giving the exedrae, as seen from the nave, a more convincing symmetry than that now ineptly suggested by Fossati paint.

It is more difficult to say at present what additional means of access there would have been to the galleries. The ramp at the south west would have more closely resembled that at the north west, and there would almost certainly have been a fourth ramp at the south east similar to that at the north east, unless there were already other provisions for direct entry to the south-east bay from the palace. There must also have been lower outer stairs connecting the internal stairs in the buttress piers on the south side with the ground. And we cannot exclude the possibility of other means of direct access to the west gallery.

Finally it will be apparent, from what has been said above, that there would already have been large deformations in much of the structure, though only about half those seen today.

Lighting of the interior

Inside the church, the most obvious differences (if we ignore furnishings, which will be considered in Chapter 9) would have been those which have already been briefly mentioned – in lighting and surface character.

Many windows now blocked must be envisaged as open. The outer walls of the central bays of the aisles would, for instance, have been more than half glass, like the corresponding bays of the galleries. And, in the north and south tympana, a different arrangement of windows would have admitted much more light than the present narrowed openings. At the same time the greater expanse of gold mosaic and the polished marble on nearly all other surfaces would have reflected the light, and given a more even illumination and less glare. The glare would

153 The west window

probably have been further reduced by the use of glass which was slightly opaque by present standards.

The original arrangement of windows was completely symmetrical. In each small semidome over the exedrae five windows answered to the central five openings in the gallery colonnade. In each large semidome there were five more, and forty around the foot of the dome. And, according to Silentarius, there were eight in each tympanum:

> Towards the murmuring south wind and the rainless north there rises a mighty wall to the underside of the rounded arch, and it is lit by twice four windows.[42]

Their precise arrangement is less certain, however, because of the almost complete demolition of the tympana before the ninth-century restoration.

The 'twice four' might be taken to refer to two rows of four each, were it not that the explorations of the limits of the reconstruction in 1968 showed, at all extremities, the beginning of an original window arch just inside the soffit of the main arch that frames the tympanum.[43] The positions and approximate diameters of these original arches indicated fairly clearly that there must have been, at the foot of each tympanum, a row of seven windows as now, answering to the openings of the colonnades below in the same way as do the windows of the semidomes of the exedrae.

Thus there can have been only one large window above. Whether this filled the whole available width, like the corresponding later windows in Hagia Sophia in Thessaloniki – though here presumably with six columns and seven lights as suggested by Conant[44] instead of the three and four at Thessaloniki – there is now no means of knowing. The window would almost certainly have been of the same general type as the great west window. But it seems more likely that it filled only the central width, as was normal practice in earlier Roman architecture, and that it had not more than five lights answering to the same number of openings in the colonnade below.

After dark there was a blaze of light from countless oil lamps. Silentarius first describes three rings of lights suspended from the dome:

> For our wise Emperor has stretched from the projecting stone cornice, on which stands the church's lofty dome, long twisted chains of beaten brass . . . They fall from many points . . . But before they reach the floor, their fall is checked and they form a united circling choir. And to each chain he has attached silver discs hanging in the air above the central nave. Thus descending . . . they form a circle above the heads of men. The skilled craftsman has pierced the discs with his iron tool so that they may receive narrow beakers of fire-wrought glass and provide pendent sources of light for men at night.

Yet not from the discs alone does the light shine at night, for in the circle you will see, close to the discs, the symbol of a mighty cross with many eyes, and in its pierced back it holds other lamps. . . .

And in a smaller inner circle you will find a second crown bearing lamps around its rim, while in the very centre another noble disc shines in the air, so that darkness is made to flee.[45]

He continues by describing other lamps in the aisles and around the colonnades and the walls. These also were set in silver vessels, some suspended in mid-air at different heights and some standing on the floor. Those on the lines of the main colonnades must have hung from the iron tie bars that still span between the columns just above the capitals and have holes cut through them for the lamp chains.

Others again formed a high corona of light around the dome cornice, or were ranged along the top of the chancel screen. Stopping short of enumerating them all, Silentarius concludes: 'Countless other lights, hanging on twisted chains . . . illumine the aisles, others the centre or the east or west, and others shed their bright light high up.'[46] And, with this, he likens the total effect to the light of day, or to the light given by the stars to the traveller on a cloudless night.

The effect would certainly have been utterly different from that of harsh modern electric light, as those who have been fortunate enough to see similar illumination by myriads of constantly flickering oil lamps will know. This light is softly diffused, never quite still, and with a complete absence of clearly defined shadow. Multiple reflections from marble and mosaic would have contributed to the diffusion.

Marble and mosaic

Would all the original mosaic have been non-figural, like that which survives on the vaults of the aisles and narthex and in limited areas elsewhere?

The presence of some figural mosaics cannot be wholly excluded, partly because they were common elsewhere at the time and partly because we know that there were figural representations on the rebuilt chancel screen. On the other hand Silentarius, to whom we owe our knowledge of these representations, is completely silent about any others. This would be strange if there were any, particularly since the most likely position (on the basis of the positions of roughly contemporary mosaics elsewhere) would have been the very prominent one now occupied by the Virgin and Child in the apse. His only references to mosaic are to gold:

The ceiling is formed of gilded tesserae set together, from which pour golden rays in an abundant stream striking men's eyes with irresistible force.[47]

and to a cross in the centre of the dome:

At the navel the sign of the cross is depicted in mosaic within a circle so that the Saviour of the world may always protect the church.[48]

Before him, Procopius referred only to gold mosaic. First to that on the high vaults of the nave:

The whole ceiling [of the nave] has been overlaid with pure gold which combines beauty with ostentation . . .[49]

Then to that which still survives on the vaults of the aisles:

They too [the aisles] have vaulted ceilings adorned with gold.[50]

It therefore seems likely that all the mosaic was of this same non-figural character, intended more to contribute to the total effect of the architecture than to make any independent statement.

It is however the marble to which both Silentarius and Procopius paid most attention. Procopius even concluded his reference to the gold mosaic of the nave vaults with these words:

. . . yet the light reflected from the marbles prevails, vying with that of the gold.[51]

Either the original polish reflected far more light than do the present surfaces, or viewers were almost dazzled by the unprecedented profusion and variety of colour. The great expanse of marble is repeatedly likened to a meadow full of flowers.

The church of 537

For the original form we have, as the primary source, the description of Procopius, though this cannot have been written until shortly before the partial collapse in 558.[52] As a further basis for looking back to the time before the reconstruction of 558–62 we have the records of modifications introduced then, and what can be seen of them in the present structure.

The question of how complete the church and surroundings were at the time of the dedication in 537 must be left open, since there is no basis for deciding this. What we shall really be considering are therefore the differences between the church as first completed and as described by Procopius, and the church as it was in 562.

Structure

The chief difference to be taken into account is the recorded increase of some 20 Byzantine feet in the height of the dome at the reconstruction (pp. 90–1).

It has sometimes been suggested that the original dome simply continued the curve of the pendentives.[53] For this to have been so, the rise of the crown above the level of the cornice would have been between 5.5 m and 6 m (depending on the precise form of the original pendentives) as compared with about 14.5 m for the rebuilt dome. With a foot of 0.312 m (p. 177), the difference in height would have been about 28 ft not 20 ft.

Procopius throws a little more light on the possibilities. Having described the four main arches he continues:

Above the arches the structure rises in a circle, rounded in form; it is through this that the first light of day always smiles. Indeed I believe it towers above the whole earth, and it has gaps at short intervals, being intentionally interrupted so that the openings in the masonry are channels for the admission of light in full measure. . . . And rising above this circle is the huge spherical dome which makes the building exceptionally beautiful.[54]

This passage confirms the existence of a cornice around the tops of the pendentives, and a ring of windows around this, both as in the rebuilt dome. Given a cornice, it would be surprising if there were not also, as in this dome, a setback above it wide enough to permit passage around it. But Procopius is silent about this, and leaves open the number of windows and the precise character of the dome.

Starting from this evidence, Antoniades proposed a ribless dome of part-circular profile with forty windows, and with its crown about 8.1 m above the cornice, as called for by a difference in height of the two domes of just over 20 ft.[55] Conant subsequently proposed a ribbed dome with the same number of windows and of the same height, but (in the mistaken belief that similar non-circular or 'functional' profiles had been adopted elsewhere in the building) markedly non-circular in profile, to leave more headroom around the cornice.[56]

With such a low rise, there are indeed difficulties in seeing how it could have been possible to walk around the cornice, even with a stoop, unless the dome was set further back on it, or the cornice itself projected much further out than the present cornice. Conant's profile is, however, so

different from others throughout the building, and contrary to all known earlier and contemporary practice for large domes, that it seems highly unlikely that it would have been adopted for the one element that would have caused greatest concern. It also calls for an excessively flat curvature over the whole central area.

Another possibility is that the 'rounded structure' referred to by Procopius was almost a low drum containing the windows – either rising vertically on the inside or inclined only slightly inwards for the first metre or so above the cornice. But this would still call for a flatter curvature of the dome proper, because it would reduce the rise with little compensating reduction in the span.

We shall consider this last possibility further in Chapter 8, after looking at possible forms of the original pendentives.

There seems no reason to question that the original number of windows was forty, as now. This would, for instance, equal the total number of windows in the semidomes, and the spacing would relate closely to that of the windows at the feet of the tympana.

Each corner of the dome base probably originally terminated in a triangular horizontal shelf at about the springing level of the squinch arch. Vestigial shelves still remain under some of the arches.

Interior

The only significant difference in the character of the interior before the reconstruction, except for possible differences between the original liturgical furnishings and their replacements, would have been that due to the shallower dome. Its surface would have caught more of the light reflected up from the cornice and the sloping window sills, and this would have accentuated the impression of hovering.

155 Old St Peter's. (Ferrabosco after Tasselli)

CHAPTER 5

The church before Justinian

IT IS NOT POSSIBLE TO LOOK BACK in the same way to the churches which stood on the site before Justinian's complete rebuilding. So little physical evidence has survived. And of what does survive beneath the floor of Justinian's church, even less has been brought to light. We must therefore look first at the historical record. Even this furnishes few indisputable facts. They can be summarized very briefly.

A Great Church serving as the cathedral and also called Sophia was dedicated under Constantius in 360. During a riot provoked by the expulsion of St John Chrysostom in 404, this church was set on fire. After a reconstruction it was rededicated under Theodosius II in 415, and the reconstructed church survived until the more serious Nike riot of January 523. It was then, in turn, set alight, and shortly afterwards razed to the ground to make way for Justinian's church.

The extents of the damage caused by the fires are largely unrecorded, as are the manner and extent of the reconstruction after the first fire, and the form of the church before and after this reconstruction. Different sources, moreover, give different dates for the initial foundation. The earlier sources attribute it to Constantius. Some of the later ones attribute it to Constantine. To fill in the picture, it is necessary to look closely and critically at the surviving documents against the wider historical background.

For the understanding of how Justinian's church came to have the form it did, it is of greatest interest to establish, as far as this is possible, the form of the church after the Theodosian reconstruction. But for the understanding of Justinian's objectives, it is worth looking further back to Constantine's re-unification of the Empire, his recognition of Christianity, and his foundation of Constantinople. We shall look first at these and at the early history of the church, and turn to the archaeological evidence and to questions of architectural form only at the end.

The foundation of Constantinople and Constantine's wider aims

Both the choice of Byzantium as the site of a new capital and the official recognition of the Christian Church were, in the end, to have such far reaching results that it is easy to see them as more revolutionary than they would have appeared at the time.

After Diocletian established the Tetrarchy as part of his administrative reforms of the late third century, the co-emperors had resided in and ruled from a variety of new provincial capitals that were more strategically placed than Old Rome in relation to the threatened frontiers – at Milan, Trier and York in the West, at Sirmium and Thessaloniki in the Balkans, and at Nicomedia and Antioch in the East.[1]

As Augustus in the West (or Caesar, as Galerius would have it) from his father's death in 306, Constantine had himself ruled from York and Trier, though he was necessarily continually on the move – as he continued to be to the end of his reign. Only after his defeat of Licinius and his assumption of the mantle of sole emperor in 324 did he choose his own new capital, and only after its formal dedication in 330 did it become his preferred place of residence. Between 324 and 330 he was more frequently in nearby Nicomedia. It is unlikely, moreover, that he intended Constantinople – New Rome though it was – to supplant Old Rome completely as capital of the whole Empire. The senate remained in Old Rome, though shorn of much of its earlier authority. And nothing could compete, in the foreseeable future, with the size and splendour of the old capital or with the ecclesiastical prestige that attached to the see of St Peter.

His official recognition of the Church after his earlier defeat of Maxentius was a greater break with the past, though it came after a long period during which toleration was more the norm than persecution, in spite of the severity of the periodic persecutions in some parts of the Empire.[2] The recognition was backed by substantial material support. Assistance was given in the restitution of church buildings and property, where these had recently been damaged or confiscated, and in the building of new churches and memorial structures. But the policy was linked with – if not subservient to – a desire to strengthen and unify the Empire, as evidenced by Constantine's immediate and direct involvement in attempts to avoid open schism within the Church. So it seems to have been deliberately pursued in such a way as to give minimum offence to those in high places who might not approve.

Thus one of his first acts after the defeat of Maxentius was to give to the bishop of Rome the imperial palace of the Lateran and an adjacent site for a new cathedral. This was built as a large and splendid basilica whose overall plan has largely survived to this day in the nave and transepts of the present Lateran church. But the site chosen was land within his gift on the edge of the city where there was already a substantial Christian minority, and not, more

156 Relief from the pedestal of the obelisk in the Hippodrome, showing the Emperor in his box attending games

provocatively, in the centre near the forum. Later he was similarly responsible for the even larger basilica erected outside the walls over part of the cemetery containing the tomb of St Peter, for several smaller covered cemeteries at other venerated sites near the city, and for the palace church of the Dowager Empress Helena.[3] But the old temples were all left inviolate.

In the East, Christianity was already much more securely established in spite of recent persecution under Licinius, so that there was less need for caution. New churches were sponsored in many of the principal centres. Those described by Eusebius in the *Vita Constantini* include the Golden Octagon in Antioch (probably adjacent to the palace and intended to serve as the cathedral of what was then the chief city in the East), a large new church in Nicomedia (probably also to serve as the cathedral), and several new commemorative churches in the Holy Land.[4] The best known – both through the descriptions given by Eusebius and through recent excavations – are some of the last group in and near Jerusalem commemorating Christ's nativity, crucifixion and resurrection. Like the basilica of St Peter and other new structures outside the walls of Rome, these all reflect an emphasis, in Constantine's approach to Christianity, on the visible manifestations of the deity – earlier counterparts of the vision he had been vouchsafed before his victory over Maxentius at the battle of the Milvian Bridge.

Whatever the chief reason for the choice of Byzantium as site of the new capital, this choice did offer a greater freedom of action than would have existed in better established centres.

The city, as Constantine found it in 324, was a relatively minor one. Its walls enclosed an area little more than a twentieth of that of Old Rome, and sheltered a population proportionately even smaller. Nor did it compare, in these respects, with cities like Antioch and Nicomedia. Before it could become a credible capital, it had to be substantially built anew within walls enclosing a much larger area.[5]

Thus there were initially few of the constraints that counselled caution in Old Rome, though it must have been borne in mind that it would be necessary, in due course, to induce some of the more influential (and predominantly pagan) citizens of the old capital to move to the new city. There was, however, a different type of constraint on the building programme, in that it was necessary to give priority to the essential urban and governmental infrastructure of houses, palace, senate house, baths, and even a larger hippodrome. Most of the surviving sources concentrate on these.

56–7

The first cathedral and the first Hagia Sophia

In this situation, what are Constantine's priorities likely to have been in his attempt to give the city a Christian character? An enlarged population would, of course, require new churches and, in particular, a larger cathedral. But, had all attention been devoted simply to meeting the needs of worshipping congregations, he might nevertheless have thought that the new capital would have lacked something. There would have been nothing like St Peter's in Old Rome or the new churches in the Holy Land to proclaim openly the presence of the deity. So we might also expect to find some counterpart to these.

If we return to the *Vita Constantini* we find two relevant passages. The first is very general, with a strong hint of exaggeration:

Honouring with special favour the city that was named after him, he [Constantine] adorned it with many places of worship and martyrs' shrines of great size and beauty, some in the suburbs and others in the city itself; by which he honoured the memory of the martyrs and dedicated the city to the martyrs' God.[6]

Only the second – which occurs considerably later and may be an addition to the original text – is specific, and it refers not to a cathedral but to the church of the Holy Apostles:

After these things he prepared to build the memorial church in memory of the Apostles . . . Having reared the whole building to a vast height, he made it resplendent with stone of every kind and colour, facing it from foundation to roof with marble, marking the divisions of the ceiling by finely wrought coffers, and covering the whole with gold. . . .[7]

This church was built on a site just inside the new wall, and was destined to serve as Constantine's own mausoleum. But it seems reasonable to identify it also, and perhaps primarily, as the likely desired counterpart to St Peter's and other similar churches. Lacking true relics or associations, it made this good initially with twelve symbolic stelai.

How are we to interpret the lack of specific reference to anything that might have served as the cathedral? Was it just one of the unnamed places of worship?

For specific references to such a church, we must turn to the next available source. Writing almost a century later, Socrates gives a more matter-of-fact account of Constantine's enlargement and transformation of old Byzantium:

After the Synod [of Nicea] the Emperor spent some time in recreation, and after the public celebration of the twentieth anniversary of his accession, he immediately devoted himself to the repair of churches. This he carried out in other cities as well as in the city named after him which, being previously called Byzantium, he enlarged, surrounded with massive walls, and adorned with various edifices; and, having rendered it equal to imperial Rome, he named it Constantinople, establishing by law that it should be called New Rome. This law was engraved on a pillar of stone erected in public view in the Strategium, near the Emperor's equestrian statue. He built also in the same city two churches, one of which he named Irene, and the other the Apostles.[8]

Subsequent references make it clear it was the church of Hagia Irene – and not yet Hagia Sophia – that served as the cathedral.[9]

In it was played out part of the sometimes bloody drama of the conflict between the upholders of Nicean orthodoxy and those who refused to acknowledge the agreements reached at Nicea and continued to support Arius.

Thus, towards the end of Constantine's reign, the bishop Alexander shut himself up at the altar for several days when Arius was called to Constantinople to account for his actions in Alexandria. Next Paul, the successor nominated by Alexander, was consecrated bishop in the church in 340. Shortly afterwards Paul was ejected by Constantine's son and successor, Constantius, and replaced by Eusebius of Nicomedia, a leader of the Arian faction. On the death of Eusebius, Paul returned. But the Arians then ordained Macedonius in another church as a rival bishop, and an uneasy period ensued during which Paul was twice again forcibly ejected on Constantius' orders in favour of Macedonius.

It is after a reference to the second of these occasions that we first read of Hagia Sophia. We are also told here that Constantine's Hagia Irene was not a completely new church but an enlargement of an existing one, which might account for Eusebius' failure to mention it:

About this time [probably in 350 or 351], the Emperor [Constantius] constructed the Great Church now called Sophia, alongside that called Irene which, because it was too small, the Emperor's father had enlarged and beautified. Today both churches are enclosed by a single wall and served by the same clergy.[10]

Only at the time of the enthronement of another bishop in 360 is the dedication of Hagia Sophia recorded, after which it took the place of Hagia Irene as his principal seat:

Eudoxius having been made bishop of the imperial city, the great church called Sophia was at that time dedicated, in the tenth consulate of Constans and the third of Julian Caesar, on the 15th February.[11]

The sequence indicated here by Socrates seems entirely reasonable. By the time of Constantine's death the population may have doubled, approaching a tenth of that of Old Rome. But the important sees in Asia Minor remained those of Antioch and Nicomedia. Thus an enlargement by Constantine of the existing Hagia Irene could easily have met all needs for some time further. By about 350, however, it would be becoming less adequate. The forcible reinstatement of the Arian Macedonius in place of the orthodox Paul in about 350 was, moreover, an assertion of power by Constantius over a somewhat rebellious city – a city which he visited only occasionally from his preferred place of residence, Antioch. The building of a completely new cathedral could have been a way of giving it added emphasis.

There the matter might rest were it not for the confusion introduced by some later writers. This confusion probably stemmed initially from an ambiguity in the early seventh-century *Chronicon Paschale*. In recording the dedication of Hagia Sophia, the chronicle states that it took place almost thirty-four years after a foundation by Constantine.

> At the time of this council of bishops, a few days after Eudoxius had been enthroned as bishop of Constantinople, was celebrated the dedication of the Great Church of that city, more or less thirty-four years after its foundations had been laid by Constantine, the victorious Augustus.[12]

There is only a trivial inconsistency here with other records if the reference is to the laying of the foundations of the city (in November 324), and not of those of the church. The later writers appear, however, to have interpreted it as referring to the foundation of the church, and accordingly attributed this to Constantine. The most notable among them is the eleventh-century Cedrenus, whose record has sometimes been taken as decisive for the early history[13] because it includes details found nowhere else.

Cedrenus attempted to reconcile a foundation of the church by Constantine with Socrates' clear attribution of it to Constantius by assuming that a first church started or built by Constantine later collapsed, and had to be rebuilt by Constantius and reconsecrated by Eudoxius.[14]

Some plausibility is given to this assumption by evidence that not all the new building undertaken by Constantine was as sound as it should have been. There are imperial edicts that indicate a shortage of skilled architects and craftsmen at the time. And we have the allegation by Zosimus in the early fifth century that buildings were constructed over-hastily, with the result that some had to be demolished and rebuilt.[15]

On the other hand, Zosimus makes his allegation immediately after referring to the foundation of Constantinople and the new building there, and as an illustration of Constantine's extravagant spending of public money. Bearing in mind that Zosimus normally displays a strong anti-Christian bias, it is surprising therefore that he does not cite the first Hagia Sophia as a telling example, if it was, in fact, one of the buildings that had been demolished.

In assessing these late sources, it is also necessary to bear in mind their very secondary nature, their unreliability even in relation to events nearer to the time of writing, and certain internal inconsistencies. Cedrenus, for instance, first suggests that the church was completed during Constantine's lifetime by recording the deposit in it of a finely bound copy of the Gospels given by the Emperor.[16] But he then contradicts this suggestion by stating that it was consecrated by Eusebius of Nicomedia after it had been completed by Constantius 'according to the will of Constantine'.[17]

Writers as late as the seventh or eleventh century would, moreover, view a now distant past with faded memories coupled with the sometimes doubtful benefit of hindsight. For them, the growth of Constantinople to be the most important city and centre of power in the civilized world, the full triumph of the Christian Church, and the later importance of Justinian's Hagia Sophia, were all accomplished facts, somehow linked together. Constantine had founded Constantinople and given it his name. In the absence of clear evidence to the contrary, what could have been more natural than to attribute to him also the initial foundation of the church which, after Justinian's rebuilding, had become the city's greatest glory?

In the end it seems safe to dismiss this attribution and accept the unequivocal early record that the first Hagia Sophia was founded in about 350 by Constantius, and dedicated in 360. This leaves open the possibility that, as the city continued to grow, Constantius was merely putting into effect an intention for the future that Constantine had previously discussed with him.

Cedrenus also reports a partial collapse in 361, which was said to have led to the gibe of Julius the Apostate, Constantius' successor:

> See what sort of church the Christians have. If I return there from the Persian war, I shall store hay in the centre and turn the aisles into stables for horses. Then I shall see on what their faith rests.[18]

This collapse is not recorded elsewhere and also seems unlikely.

Whether the church was known from the time of its dedication under the name 'Sophia' or merely as 'the Great Church' – 'Megale Ecclesia' – is less certain. All that is clear is that the name 'Megale Ecclesia' continued to be used throughout the Byzantine period, that the further name 'Sophia' (initially without the prefix 'Hagia') had come

157 Plan of early Constantinople, showing the walls of Constantine and Theodosius, the sites of the principal churches referred to in this and later chapters, and some other features. The alignments of the earlier wall and of the principal thoroughfares are partly conjectural. The present shore is shown in broken line. (Scale 1:40,000)

into use by the early fifth century, and that it referred to Christ and not to any saint of that name. Later fuller forms of the name – of which there were several – show that the reference was to Christ as the Wisdom or Word of God made flesh, and this is confirmed by the fact that the patronal feast was celebrated at Christmas.[19]

Eudoxius, who performed the dedication in 360, had been translated to Constantinople from what had previously been the more important see of Antioch, just as, in 338 or 339, Eusebius had been translated from Nicomedia. These translations were other indications of the growing status of Constantinople. From 360 the see could claim parity of esteem in the East with that of Alexandria. In 381 it claimed supremacy. The third canon of the Council of Constantinople proclaimed that: 'The Bishop of Constantinople shall have pre-eminence after the Bishop of Rome, because Constantinople is New Rome.'[20] Patriarchal status was achieved.

In 397 another priest (though not this time the bishop) was brought from Antioch by the then emperor, Arcadius, to be bishop. He was John Chrysostom. John was consecrated and enthroned in 398. As in Antioch he soon built up a devoted following through his preaching and his care for the poor. But he also aroused opposition in high places through his uncompromising reforming zeal. He was deprived of his see on largely trumped-up charges and exiled, shortly afterwards recalled, and then forcibly exiled again on 9 June 404 after an excessively outspoken sermon against the Empress Eudoxia.[21]

This second expulsion brought to an end the short existence of the first Hagia Sophia. It led to a riot during which the church was set on fire. Accounts of the expulsion and the fire provide the chief literary evidence of the architectural form of the church. But it will be convenient to consider them later, after looking at the equally sparse record of the history of the second church.

From the Theodosian reconstruction to the fire of 532

The extent and manner of the reconstruction after the fire can only be surmised. We do not know whether it was little more than a partial rebuilding to restore the previous form, or a complete reconstruction, retaining only the separate sacristy or skeuophylakion which seems to have survived the fire. The rededication did not take place until 10 October 415, under Theodosius II, which suggests either a lengthy major reconstruction or a considerable delay before the real work was commenced.[22] A hint that the damage may not have been extensive enough to put the whole church out of action for long is given by the recorded deposit of relics of the Prophet Samuel in it in 406.[23]

In this connection it is worth recalling Socrates' statement that Hagia Sophia and Hagia Irene were 'enclosed by a single wall and served by the same clergy'. Thus it would have been relatively easy for Hagia Irene to serve again as the principal church for a time, and this would have reduced the urgency of any major reconstruction. Secondly, there is no recorded major building activity by Arcadius, who may have had little inclination for it. Theodosius II may well have had more, for it was he who was responsible for the construction of a new circuit of walls which roughly doubled the size of the city. The walls were completed in 413. It is therefore possible that the major part of the restoration was undertaken only between 413 and 415, after limited earlier temporary repairs.

The Theodosian church was, in turn, set alight in the much more serious Nike riot of 532. This riot is described in detail by Procopius; also by Malalas and others.[24] Procopius refers to it again, more briefly, in the introduction to his later description of Justinian's church:

> Some men of the common herd, all the rubbish of the city, once rose up against the Emperor Justinian . . . And by way of showing that it was not against the Emperor alone that they had taken up arms, but no less against God himself, unholy wretches that they were, they had the hardihood to fire the church of the Christians, which the people of Byzantium call Sophia . . . ; and God permitted them to accomplish this impiety, foreseeing into what an object of beauty this shrine was destined to be transformed. So the whole church at that time lay a charred mass of ruins.[25]

It appears that a mob set fire to the main entrance to the palace on the adjoining square of the Augusteion on the first evening of the riot, 13 January. This fire spread northward around the square, first to the Senate House situated on the same side as the palace and then to Hagia Sophia. Three days later, another fire spread to the church of Hagia Irene.

The architectural forms of the churches of Constantius and Theodosius

Literary evidence

No description of the form of the original church has survived apart from brief references to it as 'circus-like' or 'oblong'.[26] These are too late to carry conviction by themselves. The silence of the earliest sources on this topic, in contrast to Eusebius' descriptions of the forms of the octagon at Antioch and the Church of the Holy Sepulchre at Jerusalem, may, however, imply that there was nothing special to record – in other words, that the church was indeed a simple rectangular basilica like most others at the time, including the earlier cathedral at Tyre of which a description had been included in the *Historia ecclesiastica*.[27]

A similar conclusion may be drawn, for the Theodosian church, from a comparison of the description by Procopius of Justinian's rebuilding of it with his descriptions of the rebuilding of Hagia Irene and St John at Ephesus. The passage just quoted continues:

> But the Emperor Justinian built not long afterwards a church so finely shaped that if anyone had enquired of the Christians before the burning if it would be their wish that the church should be destroyed and one like this should take its place, showing them some sort of model of the building we now see, it seems to me that they would have prayed that they might see their church destroyed forthwith, in order that the building might be converted to its present form.[28]

The emphasis here on a change of form contrasts sharply with the absence of any mention of the form in the reference to the rebuilding, as a fairly normal basilica, of Hagia Irene. This is said merely to have been rebuilt 'on a large scale'.[29] And it contrasts almost as sharply with what is said of the rebuilding of St John. It is known from excavations that this rebuilding did involve, not only an increase in scale, but also the substitution of a series of masonry domes for the timber roofs of the previous church, and other associated changes. But Procopius is content to liken the size and beauty of the new church to those of the rebuilt Holy Apostles, without any direct mention of the change of form.[30]

This suggests that the change at Hagia Sophia was more substantial than at Hagia Irene or St John, and implies that the Theodosian church was as unremarkable in its form as its predecessor. Since all other congregational churches of the fourth and fifth centuries in Constantinople whose form is definitely known were aisled and timber-roofed basilicas, this form seems the most likely.

A little further evidence is provided by descriptions of the fires and – for the first church only – by references to the preaching of John Chrysostom, by a passing remark in one of his sermons, and by a record in the *Chronicon Paschale* of gifts at the consecration.

In describing the burning of the Theodosian church, the *Chronicon Paschale* and Theophanes refer, in parallel passages, to the toppling of the marble columns.[31] The texts are somewhat contradictory about the precise form of the columns. But both passages are entirely consistent with the assumption of a normal basilican structure. The extent of the damage implies, moreover, a timber roof to fuel the fire – most likely the type of trussed roof, with or without a coffered ceiling, that was then usual in all basilicas.

The description by Palladius of the expulsion of John Chrysostom and the earlier fire of June 404 is, indirectly, a little more informative about the first church.[32] It suggests first that this church was, at least, similarly roofed. It speaks of the fire rising up the lamp-chains to the roof from a pulpit used by John in the centre of the church, and then spreading – presumably from truss to truss – at this top level. When the roof was well alight, burning brands, driven by the wind, carried the fire across the Augusteion to the Senate House and set this also on fire. But the flames spared a small separate building in which the sacred vessels were kept.

Earlier, John is said to have come down to the church from his palace to pray and take leave of the other clergy. He then went to a baptistery known as 'Olympas' to address and dismiss a group of women awaiting him there, and, after sending his mount to the main entrance as a distraction, left quietly through a door at the east. Thus the main entrance was at the west from the start, and not (as in some Constantinian churches) at the east, and there was, from an early date, an adjoining palace for the bishop.

The accounts of these events by Socrates and Sozomen add nothing significant. But these writers do elsewhere confirm John's practice of preaching from the reader's desk (or ambo) in the centre of the church so that he could be better heard, instead of from the bishop's throne in the centre of the apse as was usual.[33]

From a reference to women 'up above' in John's sermon on Psalm 48, we gain the most significant information that the church possessed galleries over the aisles.[34]

Finally, the record of the consecration of the first church in the *Chronicon Paschale* that has already been quoted in part, concludes with this reference to imperial gifts:

> At the dedication the Emperor Constantius Augustus presented many offerings, namely vessels of gold and silver of great size and many covers for the holy altar woven with gold and precious stones, and, furthermore, various golden curtains for the doors of the church and others of gold for the great outer doorways.[35]

The latter doors could perhaps have been the doors of a narthex. But the word used is that also used for the gates of a city, and suggests, rather, the doors of the main entrance to an atrium.

Schneider's excavations

The directly relevant physical evidence is that which was brought to light by Schneider's excavations in 1935 within

158 Schneider's excavations at the west end of the church, showing, at the left, the stylobate of the monumental portico and the flight of steps leading up to it, and, to the right of the fallen architrave blocks, the length of early wall (now topped with several courses of modern masonry)

Justinian's atrium[36], and by a few trial holes dug in 1945 within the present nave,[37] plus that furnished by the surviving structure of the skeuophylakion, and by the local topography of the old acropolis rock across whose crest the church was built.

Schneider excavated a considerable area lying to the west of the present outer narthex. In addition to foundations of parts of Justinian's atrium that have now disappeared, he found substantial remains of a monumental colonnade and entrance portico, approached from the west up a flight of six steps and aligned at an angle of about 3 degrees to the present narthex. A length of wall which he identified as the west wall of the Theodosian church lay about 4 m eastward. The floor between this wall and the colonnade was about 2 m below the floor of the present church, and still retained fragments of mosaic. Westward of the flight of steps were the remains of a paved roadway. Beyond this, the original ground-level dropped sharply, so that it had been necessary to raise the western extremity of Justinian's atrium about 7 m above it by means of tall vaulted substructures.

A1

157

158

159 Schneider's reconstruction of the portico, adapted to show it as leading to an atrium rather than directly into the Theodosian church

Enough of the portico remained to indicate that the entrance was approximately centred on the axis of both the present church and the remains subsequently exposed beneath its floor.

To the north of this centre-line, the colonnade extended at least 3 m beyond the northern extremity of Justinian's narthex and atrium, although the wall lying further eastward could be traced for only part of this distance. To the south, both were largely destroyed. Enough fallen blocks of the architrave and pieces of fallen columns remained to permit a tentative reconstruction of the elevation of the colonnade. The carved detail of the fallen blocks suggested that it was part of the Theodosian rebuilding. The character of the masonry of the wall could indicate an earlier date for this. But the preserved height of only about 1 m and the limited comparative data are insufficient to distinguish between probable mid-fourth- and early fifth-century dates.

The presence of the flight of steps and the roadway, the sharp fall in the ground further westward, and the absence of earlier substructures there preclude the existence of a contemporary atrium to the west of the portico.

Thus, if there was previously an atrium, as all evidence from contemporary churches elsewhere and the reference to 'outer doors' in the *Chronicon Paschale* suggest, it must have been to the east, with the portico serving as a monumental entrance to it. This is not what Schneider thought.[38] He envisaged the portico as corresponding more to the colonnade that forms the eastern boundary of the atrium at the Studios church, with the wall to the east of the colonnade being the west wall of the church, or of its narthex. But it would precisely correspond to the arrangement at Constantine's Church of the Holy Sepulchre in Jerusalem as disclosed by recent excavations, even to the slightly skew alignment of the colonnade along the street in relation to the present front of the church.[39] The length of wall would then have been part of the west wall of the atrium.

Later excavations under the nave floor

The trial holes beneath the present nave floor disclosed three short lengths of wall towards the west end. Those to north and south were aligned almost parallel to the axis of the present church, and about 20 m apart measured between their centre-lines, and the third transversely to it. The walls varied in width from 1.7 m to 2.3 m, and stood on natural rock not far below the present floor level.

There can be little doubt that these lengths of wall are parts of the foundations of one of the earlier churches, most likely of those for the two nave colonnades and for the wall containing the western entrances. Mamboury attributed them to the first church, on the grounds that the west wall of the Theodosian church had already been found further westward in Schneider's excavation. But, now that that identification of Schneider's find no longer seems tenable, it must remain for the present an open question whether they belong to the first church, to the Theodosian church, or to both.

160 The colonnade on the east side of the atrium of the Studios church, with the west wall of the church behind it

The skeuophylakion

The free-standing skeuophylakion is now a three-storey structure that is approximately circular in plan, and shows evidence of considerable modifications over its long existence, and varied uses. The lowest storey is below the present raised ground-level on the north side of the church, and was, until recently, filled up to this level. Entry was through a Turkish doorway cut into a niche at second-storey level. But in 1979 the fill was removed to reveal the original floor level, only slightly above that of the church.[40]

Internally a number of differences are apparent between the two lower storeys and the upper one. The lower storeys are constructed in bands of brickwork of varying depth alternating with bands of three or four courses of stone. Shallow brick-arched niches stand above one another in each storey, and between them is a ring of much smaller brick-arched sockets, presumably to receive consols to support an encircling gallery or an intermediate floor. The top storey is constructed wholly of brick, with niches that are both larger and more uniform in size and spacing. Most niches at all levels are now blind. But, whereas most of those at the lowest level probably always were so, in those at the top level, marble window frames are still partly visible, similar to those in the aisles of the Studios church. One niche at the lowest level – to the west and larger and shallower than all the others – must however have been an original entrance, and there may also have been a slightly narrower entrance at the south

where, instead of a niche, there is an arch now filled flush with the wall-face.

The differences strongly suggest that the two lower storeys are of one date, and the top storey a later modification. Unfortunately the recent removal of the fill and uncovering of the internal wall-faces threw little further light on this. In the fill were a number of carved consols probably of fifth-century date. But it was not established with certainty where they came from. No detailed study of the masonry techniques was reported, and a complete repointing has made further study and comparative analysis difficult. The conclusion reached by Dirimtekin in an earlier study was that the whole structure was probably fifth century.[41] Certainly the techniques, especially in the lower storeys, are markedly different from those seen in the sixth-century masonry of Justinian's church. Independent examination of the evidence visible before the recent works suggested that these lower storeys were probably fourth or early fifth century, but that the top storey could have been added up to a century later.

We shall see in Chapter 9 that this structure was long used as a treasury, and place of preparation of the sacred gifts. Bearing this in mind, it seems reasonable to identify its two lower storeys as the small building that Palladius tells us was miraculously spared by the flames in the fire of 404. There would have been no reason then to rebuild it, and its separation from the Theodosian church would have saved it again in the fire of 532, especially if it then (as now) had a brick dome.

161 The skeuophylakion from the north east

162 Interior of the skeuophylakion, looking to the south

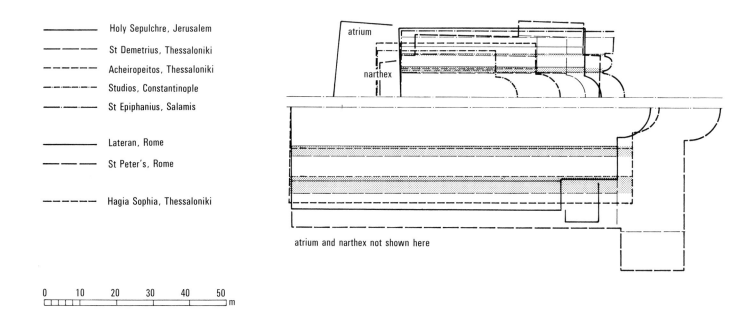

Holy Sepulchre, Jerusalem
St Demetrius, Thessaloniki
Acheiropeitos, Thessaloniki
Studios, Constantinople
St Epiphanius, Salamis

Lateran, Rome
St Peter's, Rome

Hagia Sophia, Thessaloniki

atrium
narthex

atrium and narthex not shown here

0 10 20 30 40 50 m

163 Half-plans of fourth- and fifth-century basilican churches drawn to the same scale of 1:1000, those above being in the Eastern Empire and those below (except for Hagia Sophia, Thessaloniki) in Rome. The centre-lines of the colonnades are shown in light line and the insides of the outer walls in heavier line. The stippled bands denote the limits within which the inner and outer colonnades lie

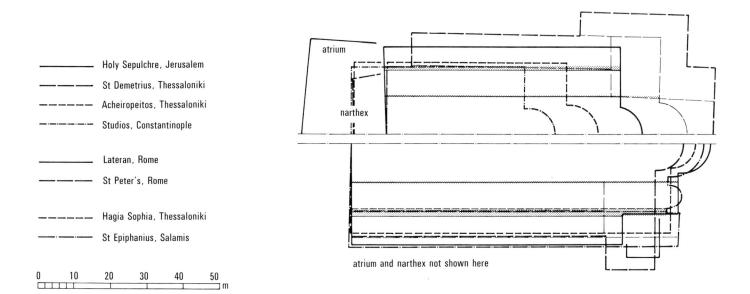

Holy Sepulchre, Jerusalem
St Demetrius, Thessaloniki
Acheiropeitos, Thessaloniki
Studios, Constantinople

Lateran, Rome
St Peter's, Rome

Hagia Sophia, Thessaloniki
St Epiphanius, Salamis

atrium
narthex

atrium and narthex not shown here

0 10 20 30 40 50 m

164 The same plans as in plate 163, redrawn to show (again at 1:1000) a constant 20 m width of the central nave

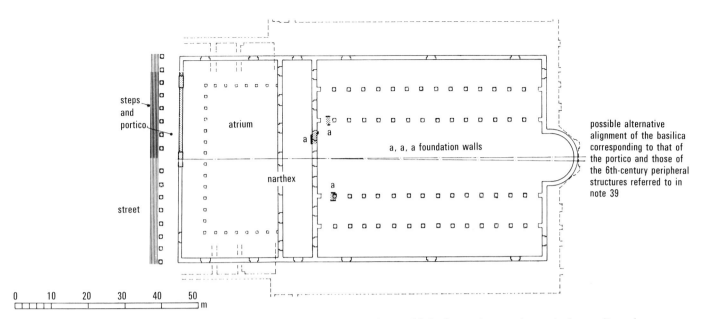

steps and portico

atrium

street

narthex

a a

a

a, a, a foundation walls

a

possible alternative
alignment of the basilica
corresponding to that of
the portico and those of
the 6th-century peripheral
structures referred to in
note 39

0 10 20 30 40 50
m

165 A tentative reconstruction of the Theodosian Hagia
Sophia, based on a scaling-up of the plans of the Church of
the Holy Sepulchre in Jerusalem and other related structures.

The established remains are shown in heavy line, the
tentative reconstruction in lighter full line, and the outline of
Justinian's church (for comparison) in light broken line

The chief significance of this survival in relation to the
forms of the churches is that it suggests that the apse was
always in roughly its present position. The skeuophylakion is unlikely to have been further east than the apse,
and a more easterly position of the apse itself is rendered
unlikely by the fall of the ground on this side also, and by
the apparent absence of old projecting substructures.

A tentative reconstruction of the Theodosian church
All previous attempts to reconstruct the plan of the
Theodosian church have assumed that it was an aisled
timber-roofed basilica. We shall make the same
assumption here, on the basis of the literary evidence.

The best starting point seems to be to test the suggested
identification of the three lengths of wall beneath the
present nave floor against the evidence brought to light by
Schneider, and what is known of other comparable
fourth- and fifth-century churches. If these lengths of wall
were indeed foundations for the nave colonnades and west
wall of the church, and if the apse was indeed in
approximately the same position as now, the plan of the
nave is virtually established, and Schneider's finds then
establish the space available for atrium and narthex. The
siting of the skeuophylakion does no more than place an
outer limit on the width of the aisles, but the position of
the northern doorway in Schneider's wall suggests a
possible inner limit.

In terms of overall size, the comparable churches whose
163 plans are known fall into two broad groups. There are the
very large basilicas, best represented by the Constantinian
churches of St Peter's and the Lateran in Rome. And there
are the more numerous smaller basilicas, among which
were many of the principal churches of the period in the
Eastern Empire. As a partial compensation for their

smaller size, many of the latter group had galleries over the
aisles, as the first Hagia Sophia has been seen to have done.

In plan, we may note first that most major churches had
two aisles on each side and a single apse at the end of the
central nave. There were no transepts properly speaking,
the approximations found at St Peter's and St Demetrius
in Thessaloniki being present for special reasons connected
with the use and history of the buildings. It is also very
noticeable that there is much more variation in length than
in width, and that the width of the great Roman basilicas
was exceptional. Only in Old St Peter's and Old St Paul's
were widths approaching 25 m achieved, and in the
Eastern Empire the limit was closer to 20 m. The reason
for this was no doubt a purely practical one – the
increasing difficulty of roofing the nave as its width was
increased. Beyond a certain limit, which must have varied
somewhat according to the available skills and resources,
increased capacity – apart from that provided by outer
aisles and galleries – could be obtained only by increasing
the length.

If attention is concentrated on the cross-section, there is
however a remarkable consistency in the relative widths of
central nave and aisles. This is shown by redrawing all the   164
plans to give a constant width to the central nave. With
few exceptions the aisle-widths are close to 40 per cent of
the nave-width.

The likely nave-width in Hagia Sophia of about 20 m
(as indicated by the centre-line spacing of the exposed
foundations) is only a little less than in the later fifth-
century church of Hagia Sophia in Thessaloniki,[42] and
completely consistent with the general pattern. Taking
this width as the basis, and still working with centre-line
dimensions, twin aisles on each side, each about 8 m wide,
seem likely. This would give an overall width between the

166 St Demetrius, Thessaloniki

outer walls of about 52 m. This width is well within the outer limit set by the siting of the skeuophylakion, and sufficiently in excess of the inner limit suggested by the northern entrance door in the wall of the atrium.

There is less comparative evidence from elsewhere to assist in completing the plan at the west. The most relevant is probably that provided by recent excavations of the Constantinian basilica of the Holy Sepulchre in Jerusalem.

163   Here, also, an atrium in front of the basilica was entered from the street through a monumental portico, the only significant difference being that a flight of steps ascended to the atrium level behind the colonnade instead of in front of it, so that the atrium wall was set slightly further back.

Planning must have been more constrained by the restrictions imposed by the site than it would have been in Constantinople. The basilica is also smaller. If scaled up to the same nave width, its plan nevertheless agrees almost 165 exactly with that suggested for Hagia Sophia. If the atrium is similarly scaled up, its clear depth on the axis of the basilica is a little less than 22 m. No space remained for a narthex.

The corresponding clear depth at Hagia Sophia is about 35 m from the presumed west wall of the church proper to the outer wall of the atrium found by Schneider. Thus there is ample space for a single narthex of a depth slightly greater (as then seems to have been usual) than the aisle-width. There was probably an internal colonnade around the other sides of the atrium, as suggested in the tentative reconstruction.

165

Until more extensive excavation is undertaken, this is possibly as close as we can come to envisaging the plan of the Theodosian church. We have already seen that the first church almost certainly had galleries, as did other major churches in the Eastern Empire. So it is reasonable to assume that the Theodosian church had them also. Its interior probably looked very much like that of St Demetrius in Thessaloniki today, apart from some

166

substantial differences between their liturgical furnishings.

There is, as yet, no physical evidence to help us to decide whether any significant change in plan was introduced in the Theodosian rehabilitation. The absence of any reference in the written record to enlargement or other change, the fact that there is no inconsistency between the earlier record and what has been proposed for the Theodosian church here, and the hint referred to above that the fire damage was not serious enough to put the church wholly out of action, all suggest that there was little fundamental change.

CHAPTER 6

Justinian's church:
his objectives and the architectural brief

AFTER THE SECOND FIRE, Justinian would have had to undertake a further rebuilding of some kind. But the architectural challenge and opportunity that he presented to his architects has few parallels, and calls for some further explanation.

The straightforward course would have been to rebuild again to much the same design. This, we have concluded, is what Theodosius probably did. And it is what was done in two well-documented .more recent instances – the rebuildings of the extra-mural basilica of St Paul in Rome after a fire in 1823,[1] and of St Demetrius in Thessaloniki after a fire in 1917.[2] Contemporary drawings of the first of these churches and photographs of the second give some impression of the likely state of the Theodosian Hagia Sophia after the fire. Brick and stone do not burn. The chief damage is caused by the burning of the roof-timbers. These fall while still alight and, as they continue to burn, generate high temperatures that cause the masonry to expand and to crack and spall, and lose strength. Finally the middle parts of the long colonnades and clerestory walls flanking the nave, thus weakened and deprived also of the lateral support previously given by the fallen roof-timbers, collapse. All that is likely to have differed in the damage to Hagia Sophia is the precise extent of this collapse. It is unlikely that it was as extensive as the *Chronicon Paschale* and Theophanes later suggested,[3] or so extensive as to preclude the retention of part of what had survived the fire.

The actual manner of rebuilding was very different, and is far more reminiscent of that of another early basilica – the Constantinian St Peter's. For the objectives that prompted Nicholas V to embark there upon the replacement of the old church by a far more splendid new one, we have his own statement of aim:

> Only those who have read widely and studied its origin and growth will really understand the authority and highest nature of the Roman Church. To sustain the faith of the unlettered masses there must be something that appeals to the eye or it will wither away. But if authority were visibly displayed in magnificent buildings, imperishable monuments and everlasting witnesses seemingly built by God himself, the belief implanted by doctrine would be confirmed and strengthened. . . . Such works would add greatly to the glory of the Apostolic See.[4]

Would it be unreasonable to assume that Justinian's aim was similar – to proclaim the unity of belief that he sought, and to enhance the authority of the See of Constantinople and his own?

To answer this question in the absence of any similar record, we must first look at his wider aims, and at the overall situation at the time. We can then turn to the type of instructions that may have been given, and to the choice of Anthemius and Isidorus as designers.

City and empire in 527, and Justinian's wider aims

Justinian, though of peasant origins, had been brought to Constantinople at an early age by his uncle, the Emperor Justin I. Justin had reached the throne on the death of the elderly Anastasius by the not unusual path of rising through the ranks in the army. Being himself relatively uneducated, he saw that his protégé was given a good education. Justinian was an apt pupil, taking a keen interest both in affairs of state and in the theological debate that was one of the chief preoccupations of the time. Increasingly he assisted his uncle and made himself the obvious heir presumptive. Four months before Justin's death, on 4 April 527, he was himself crowned, with the equally remarkable Theodora as his consort.[5]

The city he had been brought to was a very different one from that which Constantine had known.[6] It was close to the peak of its prosperity. Its population within the expanded Theodosian walls had grown to around 500,000, which far outstripped that of Old Rome, as well as that of each of its erstwhile rivals in the East, Antioch and Alexandria. And, as both the imperial residence and, now, the sole seat of government, it was the unchallenged capital of the Empire. But if, in this, Constantine's wildest dreams had come true, his vision of a strong Empire united under the protection of the Christian God and ruled from New Rome in partnership with Old Rome, was even further from fulfilment.

Theodosius I had been the last emperor to rule both East and West. Well before his accession, Milan had taken the place of Old Rome as the effective capital of the West. On his death in 395, the Empire was partitioned between his sons Arcadius and Honorius, with the West falling to the very young Honorius.

Thereafter the West was soon subjected to increasing pressure from barbarian tribes to the north. Old Rome was sacked by Alaric in 410, and over the next few decades the whole of the West, including much of North Africa, fell effectively into barbarian hands. Only a semblance of

168 Interior of the extra-mural basilica of St Paul, Rome, looking eastwards after the fire of 1823. (Drawing by Acquaroni)

Roman rule remained, now with a succession of puppet emperors in Ravenna. Even this semblance came formally to an end in 476. Thenceforth, the chief focus of continuity here with the empire of Constantine was provided by the papacy, thanks partly to the early conversion to Christianity of the invaders.

To that extent the Church did serve as a binding force, in the absence of any other save for a sense of tradition. But it was a very questionable one because of deep-seated internal dogmatic differences. The Arian heresy with which Constantine had had to contend had diminished in importance, its only remaining adherents being Germanic settlers in the West. But a new difference had arisen over the nature of Christ. Did he have one nature or two? Was he wholly divine or both human and divine? The former – the monophysite – view had been condemned by a council at Chalcedon in 451, and the decisions of this council were accepted both by the papacy and by the then-dominant party in the East. But they were never truly accepted throughout the East, and were thought by some to have been unreasonably enforced. Even Anastasius had been a monophysite in predominantly Chalcedonian Constantinople, and had favoured the monophysite cause. Egypt remained staunchly monophysite, Syria only slightly less so; and these religious differences served as rallying points for other differences in ways only too familiar today.

The failure to achieve doctrinal unity was all the more serious because out of Constantine's vision had developed a concept of the Empire as the earthly counterpart of the Heavenly Kingdom – as part of the Divine order through which man would be saved and the Kingdom of Heaven attained. The Church was an essential component of this order. If the Divine plan was to be fulfilled, Empire and Church must be at unity in themselves and with one another. Their futures were indissolubly linked.

Justinian passionately believed in this concept, and saw it as his mission to restore to both the unity they lacked.

169 Interior of St Demetrius, Thessaloniki, looking westwards after the fire in 1917. (From Sotiriou, op.cit., note 2)

He prepared the ground by initiating internal reforms for the more efficient running of the State and the provision of the necessary finance. With the assistance of the able lawyer Tribonian and John of Cappadocia, he overhauled the legal system and reformed the civil service.

He then embarked upon a programme of military reconquest of the West. After the eastern frontier had been secured against the ever-present Persian threat, his armies, under Belisarius and Narses, moved to North Africa and then to Italy and Spain.

But he had already recognized that reconquest of the entire Empire would achieve little if the disruptive doctrinal differences could not, at the same time, be bridged, and his authority as Christ's Vicegerent be seen to rest on more than the power of arms.

To this end, and right from the start, he tried in turn all the other means at his disposal.[7] That which concerns us here is his exercise of the traditional imperial responsibility for a wide range of public works.

Nicholas V had not been the first to appreciate the potential propaganda-value of impressive works of architecture. Roman emperors had long used some of the buildings they undertook to enhance their standing and proclaim, as openly as possible, what they stood for. Constantine had done similarly in his principal commissions for new churches as well as in more conventional commissions. And, if Justinian needed any prompting to see the value for himself also, this was provided at the very outset of his reign by the construction in the city of a remarkable new church by a wealthy private citizen, the noble Anicia Juliana.

This new church was St Polyeuctos, built between 523 and 527, and recently excavated close to one of the city's principal new thoroughfares.[8] It was no cathedral, but virtually a private chapel set alongside Anicia Juliana's palace. Yet it equalled the existing Hagia Sophia in size, and, judging by the surviving decorative details which are all that we have of its superstructure, probably exceeded it 167 in magnificence. In an inscription which ran round the nave Anicia Juliana even claimed, as Justinian was said to have done later, to have surpassed Solomon. Why such *hubris* on her part?

In the circumstances it is difficult to escape the conclusion that she was openly asserting a rival claim to the throne, and aiming a challenge directly at Justinian as the probable successor to the upstart Justin.[9] For she was a descendent of Theodosius and Constantine, and her son, married to the daughter of Anastasius, had a better dynastic claim to the throne.

Be this as it may, Justinian certainly took the lesson, even to the extent of later commissioning first Procopius and later Silentarius to celebrate his achievements – much as the Holy See published a splendid celebration of the rebuilding of St Peter's, as this neared completion under Paul V.[10]

The architectural scene in 527

A further stimulus to action – and one more relevant to the likely architectural brief for the new church – would have been the changes that had occurred in the architectural scene elsewhere since Constantine's day.

We have seen that, where the architectural form of Constantine's church foundations is known, it is usually some variant on the rectangular timber-roofed basilica. The most important examples were the basilicas of the Lateran and St Peter in Rome and the Anastasis basilica or Church of the Holy Sepulchre in Jerusalem.[11] Right up to the sixth century, and indeed far beyond this date in the West, this simple form continued to be preferred for churches that were intended primarily for congregational use. It had the triple merits of being easy to build, free of undesirable pagan connotations through prior use as a temple, and almost ideally fitted for the accommodation

170 San Vitale, Ravenna, looking eastwards

of large congregations attending a priestly liturgy. For precisely this last reason, a variant was, in fact, re-introduced in Rome by the Jesuits in the religious revival that followed the Council of Trent; and it is only very recently that centralized plans have been adopted again to encourage greater lay participation in the liturgy.

The only exception among Constantine's foundations (if we exclude purely commemorative structures) was the Golden Octagon in Antioch. Eusebius described it in these words:

> A church unique in size and beauty. . . . surrounded outside with vast enclosures and raised inside to a great height in the form of an octagon surrounded on all sides by two-storeyed spaces and decorated with gold, brass, and other costly materials.[12]

In the absence of any physical remains or fuller descriptions of this Golden Octagon – save for a reference by Evagrius to a timber dome[13] – it is impossible to reconstruct the precise form. But it is clear that the simple, almost barn-like, rectangular basilica was not considered adequately expressive. Apparently setting aside any problems in accommodating a larger congregation, a centralized form was chosen, perhaps having some of the character of the considerably later sixth-century Church 170 of San Vitale in Ravenna.[14]

Hitherto this alternative centralized form had been typical chiefly of palace reception-halls, from the octagon 171 within Nero's Domus Aurea to the free-standing decagon 172 of the so-called Temple of Minerva Medica; and herein lies a clue to its choice. In these halls the emperor would hold court. They were symbolic of his dominion, and a painted heaven on the central vault or dome might have further emphasized this and his quasi-divine status.[15]

For the first Christian emperor, what could be more natural than to carry over this symbolism to the House of the Lord, in what was still, in his time, the principal city in the East as well as the first Christian centre after Jerusalem?[16] This is made all the more likely by the fact that the Golden Octagon appears to have been·built close to the palace, so that the symbolism would operate on two levels.

The next church of similar plan of which much is 173a known is San Lorenzo in Milan. Substantial remains are incorporated in the present church beneath a largely superficial Baroque remodelling. It was built around 375 when Milan was capital of the West, and it was similarly close to the palace. It differed from the Golden Octagon chiefly in two respects. Its central space at the highest level was square, and it was most probably roofed by a brick groined vault.[17] This square was, however, expanded below on all sides by semicircular two-storeyed exedrae, so that the space there was really a tetraconch, and not so very different from the probable octaconch-form of the Golden Octagon.

By the early sixth century the tetraconch – albeit usually on a somewhat smaller scale, and without ousting the

171 Octagonal room, Domus Aurea, Rome

172 The so-called Temple of Minerva Medica, Rome. (Detail of a painting by Klengel, c.1790)

rectangular basilica as the more usual form – had become relatively common for major cathedral churches in the East. Examples well known from excavations or more extensive remains are to be found at Seleucia-Pieria, Bosra, and Apamea.[18] Variants on the form survive (or survived until recently) in the Balkans, though there is some doubt about the original use of the structure set in the courtyard of the Library of Hadrian in Athens.[19]

To these examples of alternative forms must be added certain maverick structures like the circular Church of San Stefano Rotondo in Rome, the conversion of one of the two large palace rotundas in Thessaloniki to use as a church, and the construction of numerous centralized commemorative structures such as the large octagons at Heirapolis and Kalat Siman.[20]

That the forerunners of Justinian's Hagia Sophia, the Great Churches of Constantius and Theodosius, were of the commoner basilican form need not cause surprise. Constantius never made Constantinople his capital, preferring to reside in Antioch and, for a much shorter

period, in Milan. He would not have regarded it as meriting a cathedral church of any special character. And the Theodosian reconstruction took place at a time when Constantinian basilicas were being taken again as models for new churches in Rome, though with a new classicism in their detailed design as befitted the spread of Christianity there among the cultured élite.[21]

But, when Justinian ascended the throne more than a century later, it would indeed have been surprising if he (or his advisers) had not seen the value of replacing the Theodosian church by something more comparable with the Golden Octagon and its successors, and thus more in keeping with his concepts of his role, and his visions of the future.

Preparations for rebuilding

Not only did the rebuilding go far beyond a straightforward making good of the damage caused by the fire. It was begun and completed (according to the

Justinian's church: his objectives and the architectural brief

records) with an alacrity and speed that are hardly credible for such a vast undertaking, and are inconceivable unless there had been considerable earlier planning.

We have seen that Justinian would have had ample reason to contemplate a possible rebuilding well before the fire. So we shall assume that he did so, and that tentative discussions of possibilities had indeed begun. After the riot and the fire the situation would have been changed dramatically. His authority had been challenged and had to be reasserted as quickly and unmistakably as possible. And he was presented with an unexpected opportunity to demolish all that remained of the old church, to clear the site, and even to finance a completely fresh start by confiscating some of the property of those who had sided with the rebels. In late January or early February 532, therefore, the discussions would have been resumed with a new sense of urgency, and the final architectural brief would have been drawn up.

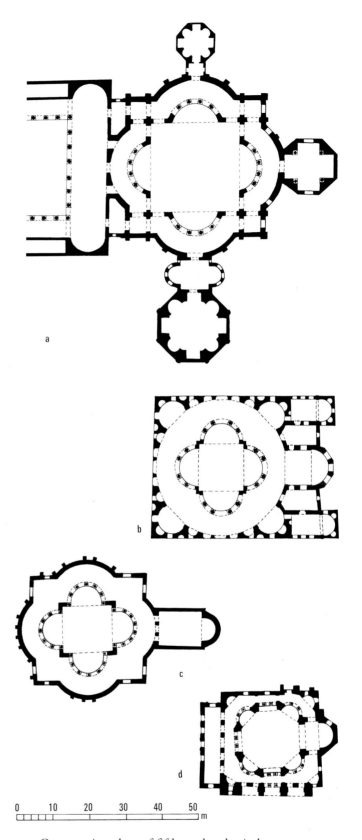

The architectural brief

Two centuries before, Constantine, having decided to raise his commemorative structure over the sites of Golgotha and the Holy Sepulchre, sent instructions for its construction to Bishop Makarios. According to Eusebius, these instructions called for a structure that would 'surpass all others in beauty'. They promised all that was needful to ensure that it was worthily decorated; in particular, whatever columns and marbles were deemed fitting. And, in hinting that the ceiling should be panelled and gilt, they seem to have assumed that it would be timber-roofed. But all else was left to the Bishop and his architect.[22]

This is unlikely to have been the whole story. Today, certainly, architectural briefs usually go much further than a broad statement of the objectives to be met, and the means that will be made available. The best do, nevertheless, allow the architect to use his own skill and creative imagination to the full. Sometimes the statement of objectives includes a fairly precise statement of the uses for which provision must be made. Since, over the life of a building, both users and uses change, and do so partly in response to the building, such a statement should not be too precise or restrictive. Purely abstract statements are difficult to formulate. So it is common to illustrate what is sought by referring to known existing buildings.

We shall never know how much further than Constantine's instructions to Makarios the brief that Justinian finally presented to his architects went; still less what its precise contents were, or how they were arrived at. In the written records that have survived, the closest we can come to it is perhaps in a passage by Agathias written after the first partial collapse of the dome and its rebuilding. Agathias wrote that Justinian, in his earlier rebuilding of the whole church from its foundations, had 'endowed it with great size, beauty of form, and richness of material. He built it of baked brick and mortar, binding it together in many places with iron and using no timber so that it should not easily burn.'[23]

173 Comparative plans of fifth- and early sixth-century centralized churches: **a** San Lorenzo, Milan; **b** Cathedral, Bosra; **c** Cathedral(?), Seleucia-Pieria; **d** Sts Sergius and Bacchus, Constantinople

Although this is an account of what was actually built, most of it could as easily be read as the essence of the brief. The earlier part closely parallels Constantine's corresponding instruction to Makarios, and the additional emphasis on fireproof construction would be a natural response (with many parallels, both before and since) to the recent fire.

It would be surprising, however, if the keen interest on Justinian's part in the actual design that is portrayed in various ways in the sources did not have some more substantial basis than this. Particularly in the earlier exploratory discussions, he is likely to have been an active participant.

At the first meetings to talk, merely, about a possible future rebuilding, we can imagine him stressing mainly his overall objectives, and his desire for a larger, more impressive, more beautiful, and more permanent structure that would stand comparison with anything built in the past, and, if possible, outshine it. Discussion would then turn to some of the existing structures that have been referred to above, and to possible new forms.

After the fire – if not already before it – another group of structures would have been seen to be of further interest because they were essentially fireproof, as well as longer lasting in other respects. These were the great concrete-vaulted structures of Old Rome and their brick-vaulted counterparts in the Eastern Empire. They included a few of the centralized structures already mentioned, such as the so-called Temple of Minerva Medica, the domed rotundas in Thessaloniki, and probably San Lorenzo in Milan. But they also included a much larger number of domed structures like the Roman Pantheon, and other similar, though smaller, rotundas in Constantinople, Pergamon and elsewhere, and large cross-vaulted structures like the Roman Basilica Nova, and the tepidaria of many imperial Roman baths.[24]

174 Martyrium (of St Philip?), Heirapolis

175 Basilica Nova (of Maxentius and Constantine), Rome

The question of the way in which the church would be used must also have been raised. The requirement for a fitting setting for imperial participation in the liturgy on great feasts would already have been implicit in any consideration of earlier centralized churches as possible prototypes. But the clergy are sure to have voiced the wider needs. Though it is impossible to say in what terms they did so, the evidence from later periods suggests a likely emphasis on their own needs and those of the congregation, coupled with a certain conservatism in envisaging how these could be best met. In both the rebuilding of St Peter's, Rome, in the sixteenth century, and St Paul's, London, in the seventeenth century, for instance, fully centralized forms were proposed and strongly advocated, but in both a more conventional long nave was insisted upon by the clergy.

What can be learnt of early sixth-century liturgical practice in Constantinople from the planning of other churches of the period warns, however, against drawing direct parallels with much later situations. As we shall see in Chapter 9, the evidence is consistent with a very different type of liturgy and lay participation, involving, in particular, mass processional entrances into the church and other processional movements through it. This called for multiple entrances and for spaces for the assembly and marshalling of those present. There may also have been requirements for the segregation of different groups – of women on the one hand and catachumens on the other – and for some provision for their independent entry or departure. These requirements were easily met by the aisled and galleried basilica preceded by atrium and narthex. The fully centralized form would be less well suited to them.

This same evidence also indicates that requirements for provisions within the church for the preparation of the gifts of bread and wine for the Eucharist, and for vesting and devesting by the clergy, were unlikely to have arisen at this time, so there is no reason to expect any call for the prothesis and diaconicon that flank the apse in the later church.

176 Pantheon, Rome (Piranesi)   177 (*Facing page*) Frigidarium, Baths of Caracalla, Rome. (Reconstruction drawing by Cockerell)

There is no evidence that the architects were asked in advance to incorporate any particular symbolic references in the design beyond those already inherent in the forms likely to have been suggested as possible prototypes. References such as those in a Syriac hymn describing the cathedral of Edessa as rebuilt soon after 525[25] seem more likely to be interpretations read into the completed structure, or that evolved with the development of the design, than pre-existing ideas to which the design deliberately gave formal expression – though such symbolism runs through so much of contemporary thought that the last possibility cannot be wholly dismissed.

The other chief components of the brief must have been decisions on the size of the structure, and on the means to

be made available. The final decision on the size must have been made soon after the fire at the latest; coupled with some assurances about the means to be made available. No doubt, also, Justinian would have urged on all concerned his desire to see the church completed in the shortest possible time.

Hagia Sophia and Sts Sergius and Bacchus

The chief doubt about the whole planning process relates to the part – if any – that was played in it by the design and construction of the nearby Church of Sts Sergius and Bacchus.[26] Though modest in size compared with the Theodosian Hagia Sophia and St Polyeuctos, this church introduced to the capital the fully centralized form with all   173d
its imperial associations. Its octagonal central space is   178–8

178 The gallery of Sts Sergius and Bacchus

179 Interior of Sts Sergius and Bacchus

expanded by alternately square and semicircular columnar exedrae on all sides except the east, and through these it opens to surrounding ambulatories on two levels. At the east a projecting bema terminates in an apse. Above the central octagon rises a melon-shaped dome, though it is unlikely that the present dome is the original one.

This design is so closely and obviously related to that of Hagia Sophia that it could have served as a vehicle for trying out some of the ideas for the new church. But whether this was possible depends on the precise dates of construction. These are not adequately documented and are still a subject of scholarly argument.[27] We have only a firm *terminus post quem* for the completion of Sts Sergius and Bacchus, which is given by the presence of a priest who served it at a council held in 536. This would make its foundation roughly contemporary with that of Hagia Sophia, at the latest. A date much before 527 (as given for it by Cedrenus) is precluded by the inscription which runs around the frieze of the entablature over the ground-level columns. But we cannot say for certain whether it was before or after the critical date of January 532. On balance, taking into account the other indirect documentary evidence, the more conservative character of the design, the more obvious improvizations in its execution, and the church's siting immediately alongside the Hormisdas Palace which Justinian occupied only before becoming emperor, a foundation in 526 or 527 seems likely, in which case it would certainly have been one of the principal possible prototypes to be considered.

The choice of architects

The brief, of course, is not all. Equally important is the choice of architect to execute it. Since, indeed, the architect may be called upon to assist in clarifying what is feasible and what, within the limits of feasibility, is wanted, this choice may even be the crucial one.

The fact that we know, not merely the names of the architects of Hagia Sophia, but also something about their other activities, is one indication of their importance. Very few names, even, are known for the vast amount of building undertaken at the time. Justinian's choices for the task were Anthemius of Tralles and the elder Isidorus of Miletus.

Equally significantly, they are referred to – first by Procopius and later by Agathias – not as architects (though this term was in common use at the time) but as *mechanikoi* or *mechanopoioi*.[28] These terms suggest engineer rather than architect, but both translations would be misleading, since the professions of both architect and engineer as we now know them – and particularly the latter – have developed far beyond anything that existed in Hellenistic, later Roman and Byzantine times. It has been shown by Downey that the titles denoted those few practitioners of

180 Sts Sergius and Bacchus from the east

the arts of design, whether of buildings or of machines or other works, who were masters of the relevant theory, especially of geometry, and of mechanics as then known.[29] They were not just master-builders who knew from experience what could be done, but people able to bring a fresh theoretic insight to new problems.

What else we know of Anthemius and Isidorus suggests that they may have been primarily academics.[30] Isidorus seems to have beeen a professor of geometry or mechanics, and wrote a commentary on the lost treatise 'On Vaulting' by Heron of Alexandria. Anthemius also appears to have been a teacher, and wrote treatises on mathematics and mechanical devices.

Whether either of them had prior experience of building is, on the other hand, unknown. Procopius merely records that they were called in later by Justinian to advise on a problem that had arisen with the flooding of the eastern frontier city of Dara.[31] One or both may have been associated with the design of Sts Sergius and Bacchus. But there is no direct evidence in support of this. If they did lack practical experience, they would, however, have been in no very different position from Renaissance architects like Brunelleschi, who relied for the practical know-how they lacked on men brought up on the job. In Justinian's time, these were the men known as *architektones*, and we probably have an echo of their contribution in the reference in the late *Narratio* to the fifty masters in charge of the work on each side of the church.[32]

CHAPTER 7

Justinian's church:
the initial development of the design

FOR COMPARABLE LATER STRUCTURES like St Peter's, St Paul's, and the Paris Panthéon it is possible to follow the design and construction processes in considerable detail on the basis of surviving drawings and other records.[1] Whether there was one architect, as at St Paul's, or several in succession over a long period, as at St Peter's, the picture is broadly similar.

At the outset, before construction starts, numerous ideas are explored in varying degrees of detail. Out of them comes the first definitive design, sufficiently detailed to allow work to start at ground-level. Only as construction proceeds are the necessary detailed designs made for the subsequent stages. With these later designs, the initial intentions are not only clarified, but may undergo repeated revision.

St Peter's was exceptional in that new proposals by Michelangelo when he assumed control involved the demolition of a substantial amount of work already completed to the previous design of the younger Sangallo (the outer walls shown in light outline to the left and top of the illustration). Usually the revisions affect only what remains to be built, as when Wren tried one scheme after another for the dome of St Paul's before finally committing himself to allow construction to proceed. Or they call only for additions to what has been built already, as when, more than once, the main piers of St Peter's were substantially increased in cross-section, after the death of Bramante, to give better support to the future dome (heavily shaded parts of these elements in the illustration). But revisions such as these are no less real, and may be just as important, so that it would be a serious misinterpretation to ignore them.

For Hagia Sophia we have far fewer firm data to assist in reconstructing what happened between Justinian's first decision to rebuild and its completion. But it would be contrary to all subsequent experience if the church as it finally took shape was exactly what had been envisaged when construction began; or, indeed, if everything had been worked out at that early stage. It is just as unlikely that the first definitive design, however incomplete, was arrived at without numerous preliminary explorations.

In this chapter we shall consider the evolution of this first design, attempting to reconstruct it as far as possible by looking at likely initial ideas, at some of the problems that they would have presented, at available precedents, and at the evidence furnished by the setting-out of the building itself.

Initial ideas

Designing, like any other creative act, proceeds from the known to the unknown. The more innovative designs usually bring together, for the first time, possibilities inherent in a number of different existing forms.[2]

The exploration of possibilities would have been closely associated with the development of the brief, and with the consideration for this purpose of the prototypes that have already been referred to above, and of others of more conventional basilican character. Early planning would almost certainly have been largely an exercise in two- and three-dimensional geometry, leaving practical problems of construction to be solved later, if it could reasonably be assumed that they would then be soluble.

Centralized possibilities

Starting from earlier centralized churches or from Sts Sergius and Bacchus, the initial objective could have been simply an increase in scale. But, even without a further intention to provide fireproof vaults, the problem of spanning the central space would soon have loomed large. Had this space been equivalent in area to the nave of the design that was finally adopted, it would have had to have a diameter close to that of the largest dome hitherto built – that of the Roman Pantheon. And it would not have been possible to provide the continuous support that the Pantheon dome has, were the space to be open, beneath it, to surrounding aisles or ambulatory as in the prototype churches.

So, prompted also perhaps by resistance on the part of the clergy to a purely centralized plan, means would have had to be sought for expanding the central space longitudinally to obtain some of the desired increase in scale.

Basilican possibilities

The obvious prototype for this expansion would have been the longitudinal plan of the existing church. The need now would have been for a suitably telling central focus. This focus might have been provided by a square tower rising above the general roof level, either over the centre or further eastward.

Prototypes might have been found here in a group of churches built in the latter half of the fifth century, mostly in Cilicia, and all probably timber-roofed. The best preserved today is the east church at Alahan, which had a 181 square tower over the eastern part of the nave. Small

181 East church, Alahan Manastir, looking westwards. The tower rises over the bay immediately beyond the chancel arch seen in the foreground

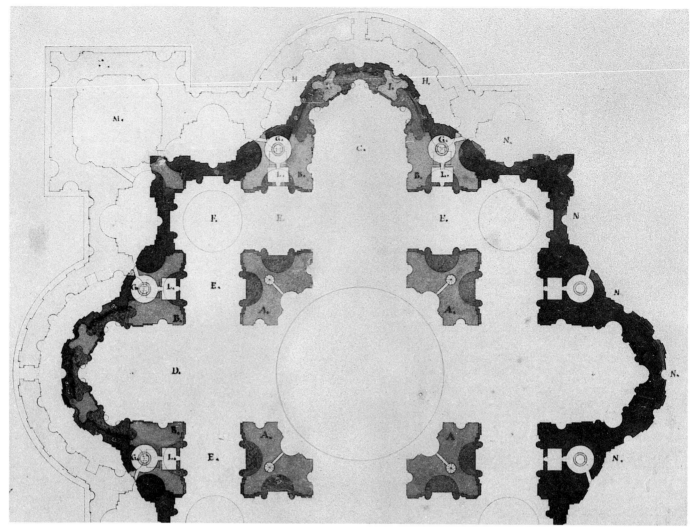

182 Partial plan of St Peter's, Rome, showing changes in the design during construction. (Drawing by Vanvitelli,

Museum of S. Martino, Naples, with accompanying annotation deleted for greater clarity of reproduction)

183 squinch arches spanned the corners of the square at the top of the tower, so that the roof probably had the form of an octagonal pyramid.[3]

St Polyeuktos might have been a later representative of the type. Nothing can be deduced about its superstructure from the surviving massive walls below floor level on either side of its nave: these walls may have been built less as foundations for a particular set of piers and columns than as part of the high podium on which the whole church stood. But some of the architectural fragments bearing the inscription that ran round the nave suggest, by their curvature in plan, the presence of exedrae; and exedrae would not be inconsistent with the presence of a central bay emphasized by a tower.

If the roofing of the new church were of timber, there would, however, have been limitations on the spans. A central span of around 30 m, as actually adopted, would have presented considerable difficulties with the types of timber-framing then in use. Either to permit the span to be increased, or to meet the likely requirement after the fire for a fireproof roof, vaults would have had to be substituted, with necessary increases in cross-section of the

supports to carry the greater weight and resist the greater thrusts.

Centralized basilica

The outcome of some such exploration was the centralized basilican plan.

The starting-point of the basilica is apparent in the longitudinal expansion of the central space, and in the flanking aisles, and we shall see further evidence of it later. But had the basilica been the only starting-point, we should not expect to see the central space expanded quite as it is, by two large hemicycles with smaller semicircular exedrae opening off each.

The chief inspiration for the large hemicycles must have been one or more of the centralized churches, and it is even possible that the complete arrangements at each end, with exedrae as well, were derived from Sts Sergius and Bacchus. But it is equally possible that this final arrangement was reached in two stages. The first stage would have been to add to the central bay the two large hemicycles. These hemicycles are direct counterparts – albeit much larger – of the conches in tetraconch churches

183 Looking up into the tower of the east church, Alahan Manastir

183a, b like San Lorenzo in Milan and the cathedral in Bosra, and they could even have been inspired by similar terminations of some of the halls in earlier imperial baths. Then, to give a more uniform width and a more nearly rectangular overall plan to the nave, the smaller exedrae would have been added, much as they had been added to give a radial expansion of the circular or polygonal central space of many earlier fully centralized structures.

Vaulting possibilities

Earlier practice would have suggested the use of semidomes for roofing the hemicycles. But in developing the whole idea further, it would have been necessary to decide, at least provisionally, how to roof the central bay.

Since the bay would have to be square, or at least rectangular, there was probably only one existing type of vault that would have been directly applicable. This was the groined vault – which seems to have been used in San Lorenzo in Milan. Such a vault would, however, have sat uneasily between the large semidomes, and would have 184 been a poor central feature of no obvious symbolic significance.

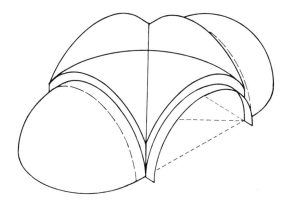

184 A possible idea for vaulting the nave of Hagia Sophia, using a groined vault over the central square

185 Small domes set over square rooms, Haran

186 Approximation to a pendentive, Baths of Caracalla, Rome

A dome would have clearly been preferable, as being more telling in itself and relating better visually to the flanking semidomes. It was therefore probably the preferred choice from an early stage. The problem then would have been to find a way of placing it over a square bay.

Much smaller domes had already been placed over square bays for a long time. The usual technique was essentially to start building the dome in the corners only, so that, as it rose in separate triangular segments, it gradually closed in towards the centres of the sides, and became roughly a full circle in plan when these were reached. Its diameter was the diagonal of the square.

In early stone construction, the blocks were laid in horizontal courses, each successive course oversailing the one below. In early brick construction, the courses were 185 either laid in the same manner or were arched up slightly in the corners to give greater initial stability.

Probably as a development of the former technique, later Roman concrete domes over polygonal rooms were usually constructed by first bridging the corners with ill-defined forms resembling pendentives, though there was usually little or no surface discontinuity where these met the dome. Examples can still be seen in the so-called Temple of Minerva Medica, and in what remains of two large octagonal rooms of the Baths of Caracalla. On a 186 much smaller scale, pendentive-like forms were also sometimes used to bridge the corners of square rooms, or domes were set over such rooms so as to spring directly from the four corners, much as in the earlier prototypes. But there is no evidence here of the use of the true independent pendentive to carry a dome of any size over a square bay.[4]

Probably as a development of the technique of arching the courses of brick in the corners, the arch across the corner became a separate element, known as the squinch. Early examples of this survive in the Sassanian palace of Firuzabad, and later examples in the palace of Sarvistan, in 187 the Baptistery of Soter in Naples, and, as we have just seen, at Alahan.[5] But these were all still on a fairly small scale, and, by themselves, did no more than turn the square into an octagon. The dome must itself be octagonal, as, in its lower part, was the earliest surviving large Roman concrete dome – that of the principal reception room of Nero's Domus Aurea. Or the corners of the octagon must, in turn, be bridged, as they were (by means of pendentive-like forms) at Firuzabad and Sarvistan.

In seeking, inititially, a geometrical solution to the problem as it arose at Hagia Sophia, the practical problems associated with scale could have been temporarily set aside, provided there was no obvious reason to believe them to be insuperable. Thus some of these precedents, if known, could have served as starting points.

The most directly applicable would have been the squinch, since it alone had already been fully developed. But, if it had been used, there would still have been a need for a further transition from octagon to circle, and there was no adequate precedent for this. The later Islamic solution of adding a second tier of smaller squinches, and even a third, is unlikely to have been considered because it would have been so out of character with semidomes to east and west. To geometers like Anthemius and Isidorus, it would have seemed almost as inelegant in the context as the geometrically indeterminate transitions that sufficed at Sarvistan and the Domus Aurea.

Earlier approximations to the pendentive coupled with the forms of the large semidomes, could, however, have served as triggers to their imaginations. If these semidomes were envisaged as being open, as they finally were, to the smaller semidomes over the exedrae and to barrel vaults at the extreme east and west, their lower portions (shown shaded in the illustration) would already have been, in effect, merging pendentives. Once this had been recognized, it would be a short step to seeing the possibility of placing a larger dome directly over the central square, as also shown in this illustration.

187 Squinch, Firuzabad. (From Dieulafoy, *L'art antique de la Perse*)

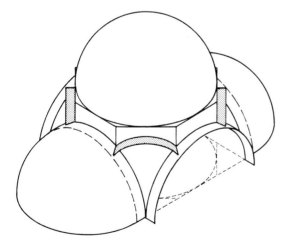

188 A possible alternative idea for vaulting the nave, using squinches (shown stippled) to bridge to corners of the central square

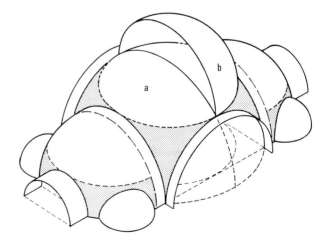

189 The probable development of the final idea for vaulting the central square: **a** with a dome on merging pendentives (shown stippled like the corresponding portions of the semidomes); **b** with a steeper dome rising above the pendentives

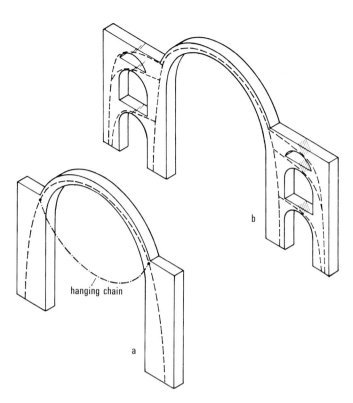

190 Thrust-lines in arches and their supports (dashed lines), compared with the curve assumed by a hanging chain. The shading in **b** indicates possible planes of failure in shear

hanging chain

b

a

Visually, at least, this would have been the ideal culmination to the vaults to east and west. Its appeal would have been immediate, both for its geometric simplicity and for the visual unity that it would give to the whole vaulting system. In no other way could the conflict between requirements for a basilica-like nave and for the central emphasis and symbolic meaning of a crowning dome be so perfectly reconciled.

189b At what stage the further idea arose of separating the dome proper from the pendentives by a cornice and then giving it a different curvature, we cannot say. The history of later comparable buildings suggests that, once one acceptable and seemingly feasible way of proceeding had been found, attention would shift to more immediate problems.

Practical problems to be faced in developing the idea

Before construction could begin, these preliminary ideas would have had to be developed much further. Even for a smaller building there would have been practical problems of various kinds to be faced. The unprecedented scale of Hagia Sophia would have accentuated all these problems, and particularly those associated with the construction of the high arches and vaults, and with the final stability of the whole structural system. While limitations on the available sizes of monolithic marble columns would, for instance, have had to be taken into

account, and a more rigorous setting-out would have been called for than the rather slipshod procedures that seem to have served at Sts Sergius and Bacchus, the chief concern of the planners was probably to ensure final stability. Under normal conditions, with self-weight loading only, the chief threats would arise from the outward thrusts of the arches and vaults. Earthquakes could pose a further threat.

Today, with the benefit of hindsight and a better understanding of the behaviour of arched and vaulted structures, we are better equipped than Anthemius and Isidorus to see what was involved. A brief review may be helpful before we return to the precedents that could have guided them.[6]

The stability of the arch and its supports

The arch is the simplest of the spanning elements. It carries the loads that act upon it by a purely compressive action analogous to the tensile action within a hanging chain, but 190a inverted. Just as the hanging chain changes its curve to support any change in the pattern of loading, or any movement of its supports, so the curving line of compressive thrust within the arch must change if the loading changes or the supports move.

The chief difference is that the hanging chain is inherently stable and can therefore be infinitely flexible to permit the necessary changes, whereas the arch is inherently unstable, and must therefore be deep enough to accommodate safely within its depth any required line of thrust. Just how deep it needs to be depends on how closely the chosen profile conforms to the possible lines of thrust. For a semicircular profile, and with some masonry against the haunches, a minimum depth of about 1/20th of the span is likely to be necessary for the type of loading to be expected in a vaulted masonry structure.

The more troublesome characteristics of the arch are its need for temporary support – known as centering – during construction, and its outward as well as downward thrust on its supports. The flatter the arch for a given span and loading, the greater the outward thrust. This thrust can push the supports apart at the springings, and the safety of the arch is highly dependent on their movement not being excessive.

In principle the movement may be restricted in either of two ways. One is by means of a horizontal tie across the springings to absorb directly the horizontal thrusts, leaving the supports to carry only the vertical load. The other is to give the supports themselves the ability to resist the horizontal thrusts without giving way excessively in doing so, though that ability is called for only from the end supports where a number of similar arches stand directly in line. This second way calls essentially for supports that are stiff enough, massive enough, and deep enough in the direction of the thrusts to direct these down to the ground well within the area of the base. They must, in effect, extend the arch down to the base, as sketched in the illustration.

If it would be inconvenient to provide the whole depth by single solid piers, it is possible to use coupled piers. But the effective combined stiffness will then be highly dependent on the interconnections. With weak interconnections, shearing failures may occur on the shaded sections and the separate piers will then give way to the thrusts more freely.

The dome

The fact that the dome is curved in two directions, and consists of horizontal rings as well as vertical arches, opens up the possibility of a further way of supporting the load. Through this, some or all of the outward thrust can be eliminated, the necessary depth (now more appropriately referred to as the thickness) can be reduced, and it becomes possible in principle to construct it without the temporary support of centering.

Centering can be dispensed with because, during construction, each completed horizontal ring will itself function as a circular arch and prevent the inward collapse of the incomplete vertical arches. The only temporary support that may be called for is that necessary to retain in place the individual bricks or blocks as successive horizontal rings are added.

In the completed hemispherical or part-spherical dome, the constituent vertical arches still tend to drop in the region near the crown. But, lower down, they tend to open out. To resist these movements the horizontal rings still develop internal compressions near the crown, but will now develop internal tensions lower down.

Provided that the strengths of the materials are not exceeded, this sharing of the loads between the vertical arches and horizontal rings means that there is no need for the dome to have a thickness sufficient to accommodate a particular internal line of thrust: the lines of thrust in the constituent arches can simply follow whatever profile is selected. A thickness of a mere 1/100th of the diameter should suffice. It also means that, if the sides are vertical at the foot, as in a complete hemisphere, the lines of thrust can also be vertical, and there need be no outward thrust on the supports. In a shallower dome the thrusts will be tangential to the surface at the foot.

Strengths of the materials are, however, important. In the masonry dome, the tensile strength of the masonry itself will be low. As the scale increases, it is almost certain to be exceeded near the foot in the completed dome because the tensile stress here is proportional to the radius of curvature, irrespective of the thickness. It may also be exceeded even in quite a small dome, simply as a result of thermal expansions or slight movements of the supports.

When this happens, radial cracking ensues in the lower part, and a greater thickness is again called for here. The dome becomes in effect a ring of independent partial arches, all leaning against the uncracked crown region. Like other arches, they will thrust outwards on the supports.

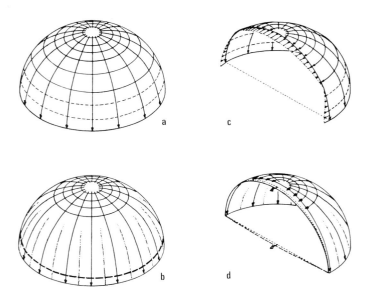

191 Domes and semidomes: **a** and **c** Thrust-lines (here shown in full line) and circumferential tensions (shown in broken line) in the ideal forms with ideal edge support for the semidome. **b** Radial cracking of a dome restrained by a circumferential tie at the foot. **d** Thrust-lines in an actual masonry semidome with a free edge

In principle, the thrust can again be prevented from reaching the supports by means of ties – now circumferential.

The semidome

The semidome is an incomplete dome in which each horizontal ring is rendered partly ineffective by being cut through. It must therefore behave more as a ring of outward-thrusting partial vertical arches, with the further difference that these arches will thrust on the crown region from one side only. If the semidome butts against something else, the crown region will simply pass on that thrust to it. The constituent vertical arches will then be behaving in much the same way as the arched flyers of a flying buttress – though requiring less depth to do so. If there is nothing else to butt against, the crown will be pushed forwards and will drop slightly. Through this forward movement, another arch will be established within the curved surface lying just behind the edge, and this region must be thickened. This arch will carry the thrust downwards and outwards to the springing level.

Problems associated with the construction-process

The chief problem associated with every construction-process is that of ensuring that the incomplete structure will be as stable, at every stage, as the completed structure must be. Sometimes this is easily done, for instance when building a wall or pier simply by placing suitably shaped blocks above one another. At other times, as when building an arch, it calls for the temporary support of centering, as already mentioned.

A second problem arises when some of the materials used gain strength and stiffness only slowly – a characteristic, in particular, of all mortars. Early loading will cause a slow plastic flow and may result in large overall deformations which will subsequently jeopardize stability. Sequence and speed of construction may become critical.

An incidental result of the use of such materials is that early deformations will be frozen into the structure even if the forces that produced them later cease to act. This is because the reverse movement when the load is removed will be smaller if the mortar has hardened in the meantime. Thus if a semidome is built with a free forward edge and only later is something else built that thrusts against this edge, some of the initial outward movement of the edge will persist – evidence of which we have already seen.

103, 114

The structural implications of increased scale

Some implications of increased scale have been referred to already. In general, they arise because the forces associated with self-weight increase at a greater rate than the resistances opposed to them. Double all dimensions, and the forces increase eightfold, while the cross-sections, and hence the resistances, increase only fourfold.

This does not matter much when there are considerable reserves of strength and stiffness. It becomes more important as the reserves diminish. In any masonry structure, reserves diminish first wherever tensile strength is called for. But, in a structure of the size of Hagia Sophia, compressive loading also can cause problems. In pure ashlar construction, the chief risk is of splitting of the stone under high local stresses. In construction with a high proportion of mortar, the risk is more that of excessive squeezing or plastic flow of the mortar before it has fully hardened, leading to excessive overall deformations.

The effect of earthquakes

Earthquakes give rise to rapidly fluctuating additional loads, both vertical and horizontal, whose magnitudes depend both on the magnitudes of the ground-movements and on certain characteristics of the structure – notably its mass, its natural frequencies of vibration, and its ability to absorb the energy fed into it. For a simple structure like a free-standing mast, the dependence is straightforward. For any masonry-arched and -vaulted structure it is far more complex, and can be considered here only in broad outline.

The chief effect of the horizontal loads is alternately to add to and reduce the horizontal thrusts exerted on the supporting piers. The additions may well lead to new cracking, and continued shaking will tend to loosen debris into the cracks to jam them progressively wider open. This will result in permanently increased outward movements.

The direct effect of the vertical loads will be more significant on arches and vaults. But, by alternately adding to and reducing the normal gravitational loading, they will indirectly lead to further fluctuations in the horizontal thrusts exerted on the piers.

The full effect will be that of horizontal and vertical loads fluctuating rapidly together. Much will depend on how they do so, and particularly on how the net horizontal loads on one support of a major arch vary in relation to those on the other. The worst that can happen is that the loads on the two supports will begin to fluctuate exactly out of phase, for this allows the crown of the arch to slip down irreversibly. This cannot happen initially. But since the manner of response of all supports is unlikely to be identical on account of slight differences in foundation-conditions, construction and subsequent cracking, there is a tendency towards it as shaking continues.

The complete vaulting system and its supports: present possibilities

Whether the final design included a central dome continuous with the pendentives or one of reduced radius of curvature, springing afresh from a cornice set above them, it would be feasible today to realize it in more than one way.

If, for instance, it were to be built of reinforced concrete, with some additional ties where they were structurally desirable, the dome, pendentives, and semidomes could all be constructed as thin shells of part-spherical form. They would be suitably reinforced to resist the circumferential tensions in their lower parts, and suitably thickened wherever one element met another in an arch-like form and where the dome (if separate) met the tops of the pendentives. The barrel vaults at the east and west ends would have to be somewhat thicker because they are curved only in the direction of the span, but only the main supporting arches would have to be of substantial depth.

If, then, the supporting piers were allowed to expand outwards only to the slight extent necessary to match the expansions associated with the tensions in the lower parts of the shells, the shells would exert purely vertical loads on them. Outward horizontal thrusts exerted by the two barrel vaults and by all the arches could be resisted by ties spanning directly between the springings, so that they, also, did not press outwards on the piers. The deformations that would otherwise occur during construction could be limited by casting all the shells in a suitable sequence on stiff supporting formwork (temporary moulds) and by some pre-tensioning of the reinforcement and the other ties. Only relatively slender piers would then be necessary, suitably braced to resist the lateral loads that might result from wind (which could be relatively more significant on account of the much reduced weight) or earthquake.

Choices open to Anthemius and Isidorus

Without these techniques, and the analytical ability that is necessary if they are to be used effectively, the possibilities were more limited.

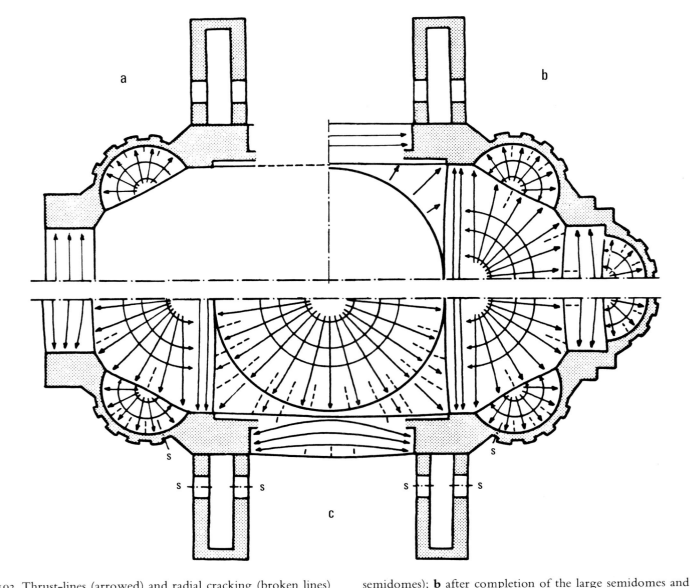

192 Thrust-lines (arrowed) and radial cracking (broken lines) in the vaulting system of Hagia Sophia at successive stages of construction: **a** after completion of the small semidomes (assuming that they were completed before the large semidomes); **b** after completion of the large semidomes and pendentives; **c** after completion of the dome. In the final state there are large shearing actions (similar to those shown in plate 190b) in the positions marked s

It might still have been possible, even using masonry for all the vaults, to absorb the outward thrusts by means of ties. The thrusts of the dome could have been absorbed by a circumferential tie at the level of the tops of the pendentives. Ties could similarly have absorbed the thrusts of all the semidomes, barrel vaults and arches. But it would not have been sufficient for these ties to run only around the cornices. They would also have had to span directly between the feet of the arches, including those at the forward edges of all the semidomes.

The tie-strengths necessary would have depended on the precise forms and weights of the vaults and arches. For the present structure, for example, the circumferential tie around the base of the dome would have had to have a strength in excess of 1 MN. If the tie took the form of a continuous chain of wrought-iron bars, these bars would have had to be at least the equivalent of 100 or 120 mm square in cross-section. Ties of six to eight times this strength and cross-section would have been necessary between the springings of the four main arches beneath the dome. And a tie of considerably greater strength and cross-section than the one called for by the present dome would have been required around the base of the actual original dome, on account of its shallower profile.

Without any such ties, both vaults and arches would have transmitted all their thrusts to the supporting piers. Weaker ties would have assisted by absorbing parts of the thrusts after some initial movement of the piers; but it would have been unwise to place much reliance on them.

In these circumstances, it was really necessary to think largely in terms of providing a system of supporting piers that had sufficient potential strength to resist the entire thrusts and was able to mobilize this strength as soon as it was needed. Taking the thrusts of the vaults of the present structure as a guide once more, it would have been necessary, for instance, for the main piers beneath the dome to be capable of resisting thrusts to north and south of between 7 and 8 MN by the time that construction was completed. This is some twenty times the maximum total lateral load (due to both thrust of the high vault and wind) that is resisted by each pier of a large Gothic cathedral assisted by its flying buttress.

A major part of the problem presented by having to proceed in this way would have been the choice of the necessary proportions of the supporting piers in relation to the method of construction and the time that would be available for mortar to set and strength to develop. Once it had been decided to separate each main pier into a pier-proper to take all the vertical load, and a buttress-pier on the far side of the aisle to assist in resisting the side thrusts, an important part of this choice was to decide how to interconnect the two.

Closely associated choices would have been of the profiles and cross-sections for the arches and vaults, and of the manner in which they were all to be constructed.

All these choices, moreover, would have had to be made without the benefit of the insights and other guidance provided by modern theories of statics and structural behaviour. There is no evidence whatever that the theory available in the sixth century went beyond the simple statics of Archimedes. This suffices for calculating the conditions of balance of vertically acting forces, such as weights on a balance-arm, and for calculating centres of gravity, but it is wholly inadequate for calculating the horizontal thrusts necessary at the foot of an arch to establish equilibrium with the vertical forces acting on it.[7]

Structural precedents

In the absence of the kind of theory that permits the calculation of forces, stresses and required strengths, and of means of estimating the strengths likely to be achieved, it would have been necessary to rely for guidance on the direct evidence of what had been built previously, and on the practical experience and wider tacit understanding derived from this evidence and from other relevant experience.[8]

The direct evidence would have been of two kinds: first the forms, proportions and manner of construction of existing structures, and second, what could be seen of their behaviour under the loadings to which they had been subjected.[9]

Arches and barrel vaults
The arch had long been a common form. Already in the time of Augustus, stone voussoir arches had been built with spans of 30 m and more. Later, in and around Rome, these were copied in brick-faced concrete, divided internally into voussoir-like blocks by other bricks which penetrated the full width. In the Eastern Empire, a parallel development, from an even older tradition using bricks of unfired earth, led to the arch – superficially almost indistinguishable from the Roman concrete one –

193 Detail of the Theatre Gymnasium, Ephesus

194 Arch (originally, supporting a floor vault) in a tower of the Theodosian walls, Constantinople

195 Arch in the substructures of the stadium, Perge

193 composed of flat fired bricks, like the Roman *bipedales*, throughout the thickness. Cut stone was still preferred where maximum strength and durability were desired, or where stone was more readily available, but its use had greatly diminished by the sixth century.

The profiles of these Roman arches were nearly always semicircular. Depths of the arch-rings varied from 1/10th to 1/20th of the span, except where they spanned openings in walls that carried heavy loads from above, when they were relatively deeper. It might be expected that brick arches would be deeper than stone ones in similar situations, because the necessary use of substantial quantities of mortar in brick construction must have led to much greater settlements on removal of the centering than would have occurred with accurately fitting stone voussoirs set without mortar. But there is little evidence of this. The brick-faced concrete barrel vaults spanning 24 m
175 over the side bays of the Basilica Nova in Rome had, for instance, an arch-depth of almost exactly 1/20th of the span.

It must, however, also be noted that the haunches of the arch were always stiffened and weighted with some sort of superimposed fill. This indeed was why depths of 1/20th of the span were possible, right at the limit stated above.

Two types of behaviour would have been observed had the supports spread enough to permit serious distortion. One was the opening of certain joints at top or bottom, with hinge-like relative rotations of the parts of the arch to 194
each side. The other was a relative slip at certain joints, 195
with part of the arch dropping down in relation to another part. It would have been clear that the latter behaviour was potentially more damaging, both because it led to an effective local reduction in the depth of the arch and because it was likely to be irreversible.

If there was no relative vertical movement of the supports, the hinges or slips would usually occur symmetrically on each side of the crown, giving rise to a symmetrical deformation of the arch. But if there was a 194
relative vertical movement, as there could be if the arch formed a connection between two piers that were together subjected to a single side-thrust at a higher level, there would not be the same symmetry, and the overall deformation would be a shearing one. Greater depth in 195
relation to span, or more stiffening from whatever was built above the arch, would then be necessary to avoid failure.

196 Centering for the construction of the arches of Ballochmyle Viaduct, 1847

197 Flying centering for the construction of the principal arches of St Peter's. (From Fontana, *Templum Vaticanum*)

Palmi 107.

Centering

The centering that provides temporary support for an arch or barrel vault during construction needs to be strong and stiff enough to take the changing loading without excessive distortion, and must have the desired profile. There must also be provision – which may be made by incorporating retractable wedges at the main points of support – for easing the centering away gradually as the arch consolidates and settles.

There are, broadly speaking, two types.[10] In one – the ground-supported center – the support given relies largely on struts rising from ground- or floor-level, like that seen rising from the river bed in the illustration. In the other – the flying center, of which a sixteenth-century example is illustrated – the only supports are situated near the springing level, so the center itself must be capable of spanning freely as an arch or beam. The flying center is more economical if the height of the springings above a firm base is comparable with the span, and if it can be re-used on a number of similar spans. It also causes less obstruction. But it calls for more skilful design, and may itself present problems in erection or positioning and subsequent removal.

Few centers of either type eliminate all outward thrusts on the supporting piers while the arch is still under construction. Indeed an arched flying center without an effective horizontal tie will itself exert a thrust before anything is set on it, and the thrust will increase continuously as construction proceeds. Other types will, at best, reduce the thrust while they remain in place.

No representations of early centers survive. But the very existence of numerous wide-spanning arches points to considerable skill in constructing them. On this evidence alone, we might cautiously conclude that at least the simpler ground-supported center was known. There is, however, ample further evidence pointing to the use of flying centers in earlier Roman construction. The more direct evidence takes the form of provisions near the feet of arches for supporting the centers – either projecting ledges or large holes to receive short, stout, cantilevered timbers. Good early examples of the first may be seen in the arches of the Pont du Gard. Indirect supporting evidence, demonstrating the feasibility of constructing the centers, is to be found in records of timber-arched bridges, notably Trajan's Danube bridge, though the designs are unlikely to have been the same because the requirements were not identical.

Domes and dome-like vaults

The dome was another very old form, probably even older than the arch. The earliest large domes had been built of stone in Mycenaean times to roof burial chambers, when their final stability owed a good deal to their being surrounded by broad mounds of earth. The discovery by the Romans of the tenacity of a concrete made with their natural pozzolanas enabled them for the first time to build even larger free-standing domes, though usually leaving

198 A pier of the Pont du Gard showing, a little above the springing of the arch, projecting blocks which must have been supports for flying centering similar to that seen in plate 197

an open eye at the crown and thereby eliminating what would have been the most difficult task of closing it.

176 The largest of all was the Pantheon dome, cast in successive layers with a carefully graded choice of aggregates to reduce weight in the upper layers. It had a span of 43.5 m and a thickness near the open eye of 1.5 m. The brick ring of the eye itself was 1.6 m deep.[11]

But these proportions were heavier than usual, and the manner of construction in horizontally bedded layers was specifically Roman. The earliest dome in the baths at Baia, that of the so-called Temple of Mercury built not later than the early first century, was constructed from small splinters of stone mortared radially in place like voussoirs, and had a diameter of 21.5 m and a thickness near the top of 0.6 m.[12] Several centuries later, the dome of the so-

172 called Temple of Minerva Medica in Rome incorporated an elaborate system of brick ribs within the concrete, and, with a diameter of 25 m, was given a similar thickness near the top.[13] A little later again, the considerably smaller dome over the octagonal Neonian Baptistery in Ravenna was constructed from double-layer spirals of interlocking earthenware tubes that gave an overall thickness of a mere 1/50th of the diameter.[14]

All these domes were hemispherical, and all had survived largely unimpaired. Thus it had been shown, in Italy at least, that for domes of this form a ratio of thickness to diameter of 1:35 or 1:40 in the upper region was quite feasible, and that even smaller thicknesses might be adequate. Lower down, all the domes had been given a greater thickness, akin to the weighting of the haunches of an arch or barrel vault.

Further from Rome, pure brick construction was more usual, or construction similar to that of the dome of the Temple of Mercury at Baia. If the surviving domes of the

199 octagon of Diocletian's Palace in Split (now the cathedral), the northern rotunda of Galerius' palace in Thessaloniki (later the Church of St George) and the two rotundas of the Serapeum in Pergamon may be taken as a guide, hemispherical forms were again preferred, with similar ratios of thicknesses to diameter in the upper region. There was, however, less thickening lower down, and the additional thickness was simply built against the foot of the dome rather than being constructed integrally with it.

The largest of these domes now surviving is the one in Thessaloniki, with a diameter of 27.5 m.[15] Among others of which only substructures now remain, that of the Pantheon-like rotunda in Constantinople, adjacent to the later church of the Myrelaion, must have had a diameter of almost 30 m if it was ever completed.[16] But unfortunately the sources are silent about this.

Some of these domes were certainly constructed without centering.[17] The Roman concrete ones would have called for stiff formwork to support the wet concrete. But it is probable that this was largely strutted up, a lift at a time, from the hardened concrete at a slightly lower level.

A late-fourth-century letter from St Gregory of Nyssa to the Bishop of Iconium (Konya) requesting workmen skilled in constructing vaults without centering confirms that such techniques were also known there.[18] The reference was presumably to smaller brick dome-like vaults, or to vaults similar to those seen in an earlier illust- 98 ration, where the technique would have been analogous.

The most noticeable feature of the structural behaviour of the completed domes must have been the tendency to crack radially in the lower regions, referred to earlier. Evidence of such cracking may be seen today in all the survivors where it is not wholly obscured by recent surface repairs. This bursting outwards can have left no doubt about the tendency of domes to thrust outwards on their supports.

Semidomes

The semidome was probably a Roman innovation, at least as a major structural element. Successes in using concrete to build complete domes could have suggested its possibility. Or perhaps it was demonstrated more directly by partial domes remaining standing when the other parts were demolished or fell. Once introduced, the semidome was widely used over apsidal recesses in basilicas and public baths and other large halls, and then became almost ubiquitous over the sanctuary apses of churches, from the time of Constantine onwards. Even when the rest of the structure was roofed in timber, the apse semidome was usually constructed of brick or stone, following procedures similar to those adopted for domes.

Early concrete semidomes were very thick over most of their height. Often, indeed, like that of the Serapeum of the Villa Adriana at Tivoli, they were thick enough to allow the inner surface to be partly scalloped out. Early semidomes constructed of cut stone were not much thinner.

There is less available information about the thicknesses of surviving semidomes of the fourth and fifth centuries. Those constructed of cut stone, of which there are numerous examples in partly ruined churches in Syria, Turkey, and elsewhere in the East, are still proportionately thicker than most full domes.[19] Brick semidomes, too, tended to be thicker, perhaps not entirely because of an understandably greater caution. Diameters are less, and some of the thicknesses seem to have been simply the minimum that was feasible using bricks or blocks of normal size.

As with the full dome, a tendency would have been observed for radial cracks to develop in the lower part of the semidome. A further characteristic would have been noted, however – the tendency of the crown to move forwards. This would always have been accompanied by the slight depression that was also noted above. Both movements would have been clearly visible in the semidome built from cut stone, because they would have occurred partly by small slips, downwards and forwards, of some of the blocks near the crown. The depression of the crown might have been less noticeable in a brick 200 semidome, particularly if this was plastered internally.

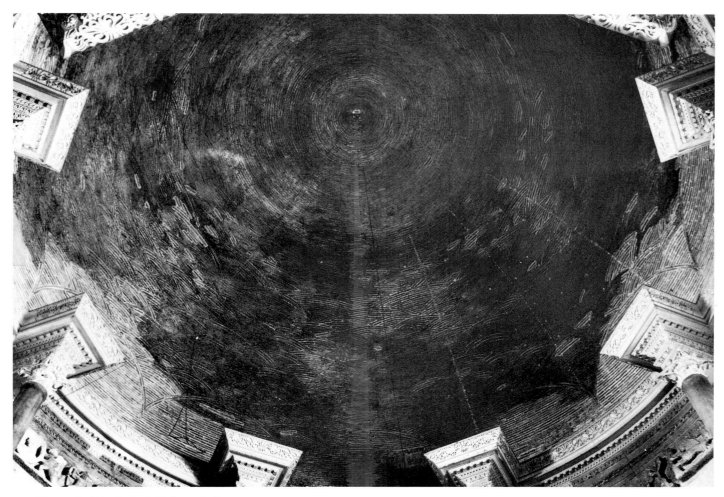

199 Dome in Diocletian's Palace, Split

200 Apse of the church of Kalb Lozeh

Photographic surveys of a representative group of early Italian brick-built apse semidomes in 1967 showed, nevertheless, that forward movements of the crowns of such semidomes of between 1/30th and 1/50th of the span were common.[20] These movements would have provided ample confirmation, if any were needed, of the weakness of a free-standing forward edge, and of the potential value of the semidome as a buttress if it was built against something else.

Piers and walls

More diverse traditions were to be found in the building of walls and piers. The traditions reflected both the importance of these elements as guarantors of stability, and the fact that most of the material usually went into them, so that they offered the greatest scope for economies. Locally available materials were used as far as was possible, and attempts were also made to minimize the labour of shaping and placing them.[21]

One unbroken early tradition was to use, throughout the thickness, blocks of squared stone carefully fitted together with only a sparing use of mortar, or even with

none. The strength and durability of this form of construction, given a suitable stone, is apparent today from many survivals from classical times. The sizes of the blocks and the manner of shaping and bonding them varied with the character of the stone and the skill of the builders. But the principle remained essentially the same, except that in some situations wooden or iron cramps, and sometimes also dowels, were used between the blocks in an attempt to tie them together more securely. This procedure was adopted throughout the masonry of many Doric and Ionic temples, but later was usually reserved for the reinforcement of string courses, cornices, and other critical regions.

A parallel tradition, more economical in labour, was to use squared or roughly squared stone for the faces only. The core was then filled with rubble. Much depended on the bonding of the facings to the fill, and on the character of this fill. Many early defence-walls were built in this way with fillings of little intrinsic strength, relying on overall thickness to make good this deficiency. On the other hand, with a well-compacted fill bound together with a good mortar, strengths similar to those of walls of solid ashlar could be obtained.

The realization that the local natural pozzolana yielded such a mortar led to the development of the brick-faced Roman concrete wall and pier, in which the concrete fill was the real source of strength. Even the heaviest-loaded piers of the later imperial baths, and of structures like the Basilica Nova and the Temple of Minerva Medica, were constructed successfully in this manner. This type of concrete wall and pier was, however, almost confined to Italy, and its use seems to have lapsed after the early fourth century.

Its nearest counterpart in the Eastern Empire (as in Gaul and Britain) was a form of construction in which a weaker rubble fill was faced with roughly dressed small blocks of stone. Fill and facing were laid together in fairly shallow courses, and, after every few courses several through-courses of flat bricks like Roman *bipedales* were laid in order to bond together the whole mass more securely. The strength and durability depended a good deal on the mortar and the workmanship as well as on these bonding courses of brick, and survivals show that both were very variable. But they could approach those of Roman concrete construction when similar properties were imparted to the mortar by the addition of crushed brick to the lime and sand.

In Constantinople this type of construction was adopted for the Theodosian walls, and is also seen in what remains of the inner wall of the propylaeum of the Theodosian Hagia Sophia. But there is no surviving evidence of its use to carry very heavy loads. Foundations and heavily loaded piers continued to be built with solid ashlar – both in Constantinople (as in the rotunda adjacent to the Myrelaion church) and elsewhere (as in the baths at Ephesus and the rotunda of the Temple of Asklepius at Pergamon). By the sixth century, moreover, mortared rubble seems largely to have fallen out of use.

201 Base courses of the rotunda of the Temple of Asklepius, Pergamon

Another alternative to solid ashlar had, however, made its appearance at least by the start of the third century. This was pure mortared brickwork, again using bricks like *bipedales* throughout the thickness, but not merely as bonding courses. The wall constructed entirely of brick had, of course, long been known in Egypt and elsewhere in the East. But the use of much larger well-fired bricks to give greater strength and durability must have been introduced from Rome. The finest early example is now to be seen in the remains of the basilica of the Serapeum in Pergamon. Right at the beginning of Justinian's reign similar mortared brickwork had been used for all the substructures of St Polyeuctos.

The adoption of this last form and the continued use of solid ashlar must have stemmed from experience of the possible shortcomings of mortared rubble, which would have been more prone to cracking even when reinforced by some bonding courses of brick. But there must also have been evidence that well-built ashlar walls and piers were not necessarily immune from similar cracking if the bearing of block on block was uneven, or if there was excessive side-load from any cause. Even if blocks did not split, it was possible for some to lift and rotate slightly under the combined action of upward and horizontal loads during an earthquake. And it would certainly have been known that the use of thick mortar-joints in brickwork entailed a fairly long wait for the full hardening of the mortar, and a likelihood of considerable settlement if construction proceeded too rapidly.

202 Detail of the walls of the basilica of the Serapeum, Pergamon

203 (*Below*) Fractured and displaced masonry of the extra-mural baths, Heirapolis. The lower projection from the pier at the right is an addition, made when the structure was converted to a church

204 The outward inclination of a column in the gallery of Sts Sergius and Bacchus demonstrated by a plumb-line held against it

The complete structural system

It is less easy to say what could have been learnt from existing complete structures about the ways in which the safety of high arches and vaults could best be ensured. Too few earlier structures have survived as well and as little altered as Justinian's Hagia Sophia itself. And there are uncertainties not only about the date, but also about some of the most important details of the construction of what may have been the most immediate prototype – the Church of Sts Sergius and Bacchus.

It is clear, at least, that the uses by Anthemius and Isidorus of cut stone and mortared brick for the walls and piers, and of mortared brick for the vaults, was not new. Nor was the way in which each was selected according to the differing requirements in different parts of the structure. A very similar selection can be still be seen, for instance, in what remains of the late-Roman theatre and 193 harbour baths in Ephesus.

There would also certainly have been evidence of the need to make ample provision to buttress the arches spanning between the main piers, and to make provision, also, to buttress the thrusts from all the semidomes. Some precedents for meeting these needs would have been provided by existing vaulted structures – in particular, for doing so by means partly of outer buttress-piers linked to the main piers by arches spanning across aisles or ambulatories. On a scale approaching that of the new Hagia Sophia, the Basilica Nova in Rome would probably 175, have been the best available guide. If completed, the 208 Church of Sts Sergius and Bacchus would probably have served chiefly to emphasize the need for buttressing. Even a casual inspection today shows that its piers lean outwards 179, considerably under the thrusts of the central dome. 204

There is, on the other hand, very little evidence now of possible precedents for the use of ties to contain some of the thrusts. Such evidence as there is relates only to timber ties across the minor arches of continuous arcades, and to the use of iron cramps to link together the blocks of a stone string course or cornice.[22]

Even the use of short-span timber ties in arcades cannot be attested with complete certainty before the time of Justinian, because of doubts about the precise dates of certain structures that may be relevant, such as the earliest covered cisterns in Constantinople. There was, on the other hand, a long tradition of placing arches ('relieving arches') over lintels, and the encasing of the tie beams in Hagia Sophia in decorated boxes to resemble architraves might indicate a direct derivation from the lintel.

The earlier use of iron cramps in string courses is much better attested.[23] It undoubtedly arises from the general practice, already noted, of cramping the blocks together in some pure ashlar construction. Particular attention was naturally given there to courses that might serve to strengthen the whole structure. The practice was simply carried over, when courses of stone were incorporated only in critical positions such as at the springing levels of vaults. It is nevertheless virtually impossible that anything better than rule of thumb could have guided the choice of size of the cramps.

The first definitive design

The design finally approved to allow construction to begin must have been the outcome of a good deal of give-and-take whose history is lost for ever. No design – and certainly not one that brings together ideas from different sources – springs entire into the designer's mind; it has to be built up gradually. Conflicts have to be reconciled, and order and unity achieved. A common problem is that of coping with the necessary thicknesses of walls, columns and similar elements, and reconciling desirable external, internal, and centre-line dimensions. Here, once the large hemicycles and their exedrae had been decided upon, there would have been the further need to reconcile their circular geometry with the rectilinear geometry of the forms within which they were set.

To see more of the process and gain some further insight into the basic intentions and concepts, and the relative importance attached to them, we must first establish what the design was. And we must do this in terms of the measure which was used at the time.

The ground plan
The only record we have is that preserved at ground level, in the outlines of the piers and walls, and in the setting-marks for the columns and the outlines of their bases. To reconstruct the design from this evidence calls for more than a precise survey, followed by the removal of those elements that were later additions (notably, as we shall see in the next chapter, the projections from the main and buttress piers into the aisles that are marked aaaa in the isometric drawing in Chapter 3). This is because, in building, achievement always falls short of intention. Absolute accuracy is unattainable, and deliberate adjustments may be necessary to accommodate the unforeseen. The significant outlines of the piers and walls are likely, moreover, to be those of the working masonry and not those of the subsequently applied facings. Allowance must be made for the inaccuracies and adjustments, and for the thicknesses of the facings. Great care is needed here: it is all too easy to round off measurements in such a way as to find whatever one looks for.

Fortunately the difficulties and hazards are much reduced by an unusually high degree of accuracy in some of the setting-out, and by the unambiguous nature of the evidence furnished by the scribed setting-marks for the columns. The four corners of the square from which, at a higher level, the pendentives that carry the dome were to spring, were so carefully located that the distances between them, measured to the facings, differ by a maximum of about 6 cm. This deviation, in about 31 m, is well within the range to be expected today when setting-out with a steel tape without any special control of the tension.[24]

Elsewhere the accuracy is not as high. At the worst, the 10.5 m north-south spacings of the columns in the corner bays of the aisles vary by about ±15 cm. But, since there are eight pairs of columns in all in these bays, and four similar pairs in the central bays, it is possible to come considerably closer to what was intended by using the average spacings.

This partial elimination of error by averaging is a starting point. The next stage is to establish the unit of measure, in the expectation that the primary measurements would have been set out in simple multiples of it.

Evagrius gives a clue.[25] He later recorded some dimensions in Byzantine feet, and his figures imply that this foot was equal to about 0.31 metre – a fairly normal value at the time but greater than the present value of 0.3048 metre. The closeness of the length of the sides of the central square beneath the dome to 100 of these feet suggests that the sides were intended to be precisely this. If so, we obtain a more precise unit of between 0.312 m and 0.3125 m, depending on the allowance made for the depths of the working masonry behind the facings.

This foot unit may be checked against the measured spacings between the setting-marks for the columns. The check confirms the validity of the approach, but the variations between the spacings of corresponding pairs of columns are too large to permit a closer determination. For each typical spacing, a dimension within the range of measurements and close to the mean converts to a whole number of feet, whether of 0.312 m or 0.3125 m.

Taking into account, also, several other measurements that will be referred to later, a foot equal to 0.312 m was finally assumed.[26] All subsequent references to feet will be to this Byzantine foot, modern equivalents and other dimensions being given, as before, in metres.

With this unit, all measurements that it was possible and reasonable to set out on a square rectilinear grid prove to have been whole number of feet, those determining the sizes and positions of the piers being always to the working masonry, rather than to the facings. Only around great eastern and western hemicycles and the exedrae does a different, geometric, procedure of setting-out appear to have been followed, leading to dimensions that are not whole numbers of feet.

Basilican origins, and the intention to retain a basilican character
The derivation of the design from the earlier basilican form and the desire to retain this character, despite the new emphasis on the centre, are betrayed in a number of ways.

If the proposed reconstruction of the Theodosian church is correct, it appears that (apart from a probable slight rotation of the alignments) the secondary piers were centred almost, if not quite, on the axes of its nave colonnades and that the nave colonnades of the new church were centred almost on the axes of the earlier intermediate aisle colonnades. The apse of the new church would also have corresponded very closely to the previous apse.

The desire to retain a basilican character is shown chiefly by the elongation of the central space under the dome. But it is also evident from the precise alignment of the backs of the most easterly and most westerly of the exedrae columns with the backs of the rows of four at each side of the central square – whereby this outer boundary of the nave is extended in a straight line into and even beyond the exedrae. This alignment confirms that the nave was envisaged as including, not only the large hemicycles, but also, with undiminished width, most of the exedrae.

Further confirmation of the importance attached to these colonnades is to be found in their positions in relation to the outer walls, and in the selection of leading measurements given by Evagrius:

> In order to make clearer the wonderful qualities of this building I have decided to set down in feet its length, width and height, as well as the span and height of the arches, which are as follows: the length from the door facing the sanctuary . . . to the sanctuary is 190 feet; the

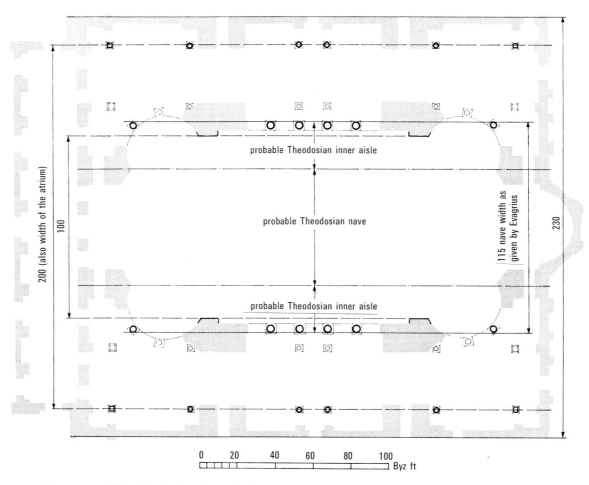

200 (also width of the atrium)

100

probable Theodosian inner aisle

probable Theodosian nave

probable Theodosian inner aisle

115 nave width as given by Evagrius

230

| 0 | 20 | 40 | 60 | 80 | 100 |

Byz ft

205 Setting-out alignments of Justinian's church probably based on some of those of the Theodosian church, together with others preserving a basilican character. A possible slight rotation of the alignments is ignored for simplicity. (Dimensions in Byzantine feet; scale 1 mm: 2 Byzantine ft)

width from north to south is 115 feet; the height of the crown of the dome above the ground is 180 feet; the width of each arch is? [lacuna] feet; the length from east to west is 260 feet; the span is 75 feet.[27]

Here the 'width from north to south' of 115 ft is neither the overall width from wall to wall nor the clear width between the foremost faces of the main piers (one or other of which might have been expected), but that between the two extended alignments of the backs of the colonnades. And this width is exactly half the overall width of 230 ft between the outsides of the outer walls – outside compared with outside, though the relationship was probably thought of initially at the time of design in terms of the spacings between axes of the colonnades and insides of the walls.

There is, moreover, an apparently deliberate correspondence between the relative positions of these outer bounding lines of nave and aisles and the relative positions of what must have been regarded as their secondary boundaries – for the nave, lines tangential to the foremost faces of the piers, and for the aisles, the axes of the outer

columns which are continued westwards as axes of the walls that bound the narthexes and atrium at north and south. Here, also, the spacing of the inner boundaries (100 ft) is exactly half the spacing of the outer boundaries (200 ft).

The one departure from basilican precedents that will be noted here is that, with a much wider nave, single aisles each half its width have taken the place of double aisles each about 40 per cent of its width.

Vaulting intentions and provisions
The more immediately obvious features of the plan are, however, those associated with the intentions for vaulting the nave. The proportioning and placing of the secondary piers and exedrae colonnades at the east and west in relation to the main piers confirm the intention to vault both ends of the nave by means of large semidomes covering most of the space, with smaller semidomes over the exedrae and barrel vaults at the far ends. The intention to have a central dome is similarly confirmed by the proportioning of the main piers to carry broad arches spanning from east to west at each side. Such arches would

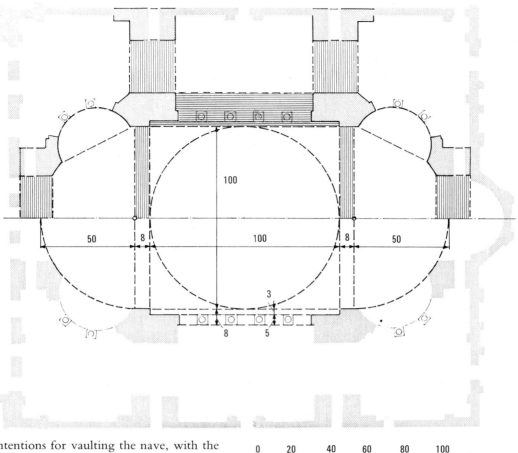

206 Indications of intentions for vaulting the nave, with the principal arches shaded. (Dimensions in Byzantine feet; scale 1 mm: 2 Byzantine ft)

have been unnecessary had a groined vault been intended because its thrusts would have come down directly to the four corners. But there is no means of knowing how, at this stage, it was intended to bridge the corners of the central 100-ft square between the arches.

The primary generator must have been this central square. It will be seen that the two large hemicycles do not directly abut it, but are each separated from it by 8 ft. These separations may have been introduced initially either to allow for the construction of a substantial arch at the forward edge of each large semidome, or to facilitate the placing of the main piers in relation to the corners of the square and the colonnades to each side. But it is characteristic of the design that it is permeated by multiple interrelationships, and this is no exception. For the central square is similarly bounded at north and south by 8-ft strips, now made up of 3-ft recessions in the main piers and the 5-ft widths of the side colonnades.

In relation to the centres of the 8-ft separations at east and west, the main piers extend 6 ft outwards and 18 ft inwards in the east-west direction, leaving an opening 72 ft wide at each side of the nave. The simple 1:3:12

relationship between these dimensions (or 1:3 between overall width and opening) indicates the importance attached to them.

If a basilican character was to be retained, the choice of the north-south dimensions of these piers would, however, have been less free. The aisles had to be left as open as possible from end to end. The one feasible way of leaving them reasonably open while providing adequate depth to resist the anticipated thrust to north and south was to separate the piers into paired main and buttress piers – perhaps taking as a model the piers of the Basilica Nova in Old Rome – and this is what was done. The dimensions chosen must also have taken into account the alignment of the outer columns within the aisles.

The actual dimensions appear to have been based on a module of 15 ft and a 1:2:1 relationship between pier-depths and the opening between them, with a slight adjustment of the depth of the buttress piers to accord with an apparently prior choice of the overall width of the church.

This module of 15 ft is seen also in the north-south width of the secondary piers, and seems to have been an

208

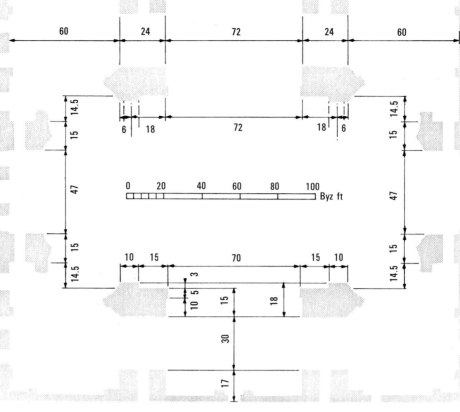

207 Setting-out of the piers. (Dimensions in Byzantine feet; scale 1 mm: 2 Byzantine ft)

208 **a** Half-plan of the Basilica Nova, Rome, compared with the ground plan of Hagia Sophia. **b** The central piers of the Basilica Nova scaled up to equate the main spans, as nearly as possible for a non-square bay, with those of Hagia Sophia. (Scale 1 mm: 2 Byzantine ft)

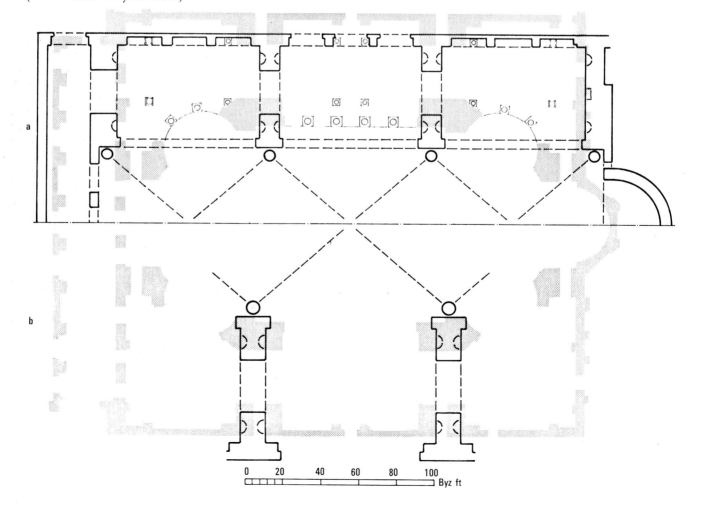

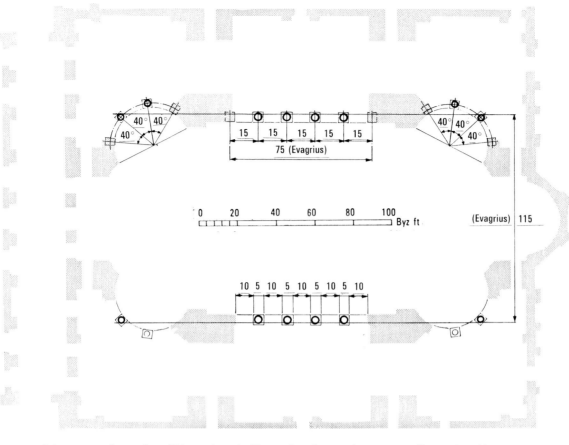

209 Setting-out of the nave colonnades. (Dimensions in Byzantine feet; scale 1 mm: 2 Byzantine ft)

The exedrae and the nave colonnades

The problems of marrying the circular geometry of hemicycles and exedrae with the rectilinear geometry stemming from the basilican origins were accentuated by the decision to open the exedrae to the aisles through colonnades similar to those between the main piers. Since the porphyry columns in the exedrae were almost certainly re-used from elsewhere – whether or not from Old Rome as stated in the *Narratio*[28] – it is even possible that their placing was one of the starting-points of the design.

For the similar *verde antico* columns obtained to complement them in the central colonnades, the module of 15 ft used elsewhere was a suitable spacing measured between centres, both in relation to the size of the columns and in relation to the clear space between the main piers of 72 ft. Five modules of 15 ft gave an overall length of 75 ft, including half of each notional end column absorbed into the pier – and, incidentally, the measure of the span of the main arches between the piers as given by Evagrius. The bases, 5 ft square, were spaced 10 ft apart, with 1 ft

projections from the piers to terminate the colonnades and make up part of the notional end columns.

The intention, then, seems to have been to space the columns in the exedrae as nearly as possible in the same way, the most significant measure of the spacing now being the clear spacing as seen from the nave. This is very close to 10 ft again. The necessary spacing on centres, measured around the curve, was no longer 15 ft, however, on account both of the curve and the slightly smaller widths of these columns and their bases. And there were other important requirements to be met if the basilican character of the whole nave was to be retained in all the ways suggested above – such as aligning the easternmost and westernmost columns with the central colonnades – at the same time as setting the openings in the centres of the exedrae.

The crucial choice was, of course, the size and placing of the exedrae themselves. As far as can be seen from what was finally done, they were planned primarily in terms of the curve running through the centres of the columns. This curve starts from the same point as the curve of the hemicycle, and terminates slightly more than 40 ft eastward or westward, which is half the distance at the east to the end of the apse.

underlying module for all main north-south dimensions, though not one that was allowed to override all other desiderata when conflicts arose.

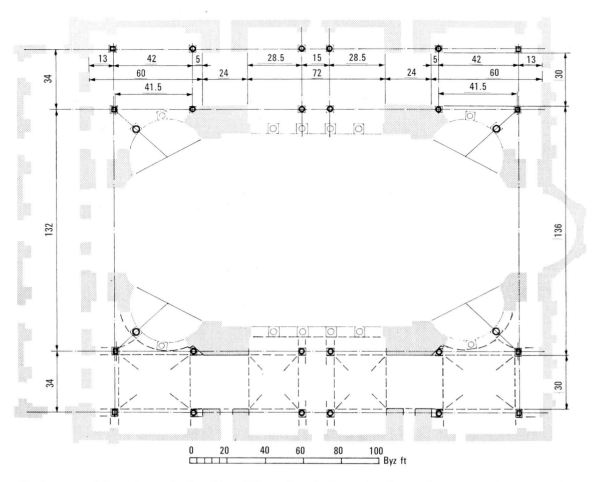

210 Setting-out of the columns in the aisles. (Dimensions in Byzantine feet; scale 1 mm: 2 Byzantine ft)

Around this curve, the columns are spaced 40 degrees apart measured to their centres and to the centres of notional end columns absorbed into the piers. Further evidence of the need for adjustments is the fact that these spacings are all rotated very slightly towards the east-west axis of the church to give the desired alignment of the end columns.

The aisles

The outlines of the aisles were determined by the placing of the outer walls, the piers and the main colonnades.

The provision of a group of four columns in each bay indicates an intention to cover the central parts of these bays by domical or groined vaults linked to the outer walls and piers in such a way as to carry over to these their outward thrusts. The columns are in two rows, so spaced as to maintain from end to end of each aisle the same unobstructed passage as that between the main and buttress piers.

The columns in each central bay are obviously aligned with the central columns of the main colonnades. Those in

210

the end bays have had to be placed in a manner largely dictated by the irregular boundaries of these bays. But, within these dictates, an attempt was probably made to reduce the east-west spacings to a minimum in order to reduce the necessary height of the vaults.

The precise placing of the end columns shows, however, interesting evidence of conflicting objectives. The columns nearest the exedrae are radially aligned with the outermost porphyry columns, which results in an east-west spacing in the end bays of about 41.5 ft. That was apparently considered undesirable where the choice was a little freer, in the outer corners. The spacing there was therefore rounded up to 42 ft, or seven times the basic 6 ft module for the other principal dimensions along the length of the aisles.

The elevation

The chief 'unknowns' of this first design are most details of the elevation. Galleries can reasonably be assumed on the basis both of previous practice and the lack of overall proportion that would result from their absence. But the only intended heights that are reasonably certain are those of the main nave colonnades and the principal arches and semidomes.

The acquisition of the columns for the colonnades must have been one of the critical first tasks, and construction is unlikely to have started until there was at least an assurance that those used would indeed be available – giving a height of 40 ft, as built, to the first cornice.

Then, it would be surprising if semicircular profiles had not already been decided upon for the arches and semidomes above the second cornice because of their obvious advantages in simplifying the geometry of the interpenetrating vault surfaces, and in helping to achieve overall visual unity. And, though the large semidomes need not have sprung from the same levels as the smaller ones, construction would have been easier and the final form more satisfying if they did so.

Finally, there are hints of what is likely to have been contemplated at gallery level, as we shall see in the next chapter.

211 The south-east main pier from the south east. Originally there were no projections from the pier into the aisle and the soffit of the upper arch over the aisle extended westwards uninterrupted by the pair of lower bracing arches carried on the projections

CHAPTER 8

Justinian's church: further development of the design, the construction and first partial reconstruction

CONSTRUCTION BEGAN, according to Cedrenus, on 23 February 532, and the new church was dedicated on 27 December 537, less than six years later.[1] No comparable building is known to have been completed in under thirty years: Chartres Cathedral was substantially completed in about thirty-two years, Salisbury took well over forty years, and Wren's St Paul's thirty-five years, after some five years of preliminary planning. A major reason for this was, of course, limitation of resources, which frequently led to total durations of between fifty and one hundred years. Justinian obviously ensured that his builders were never kept waiting, and it seems highly probable that he continually spurred them on towards the earliest possible completion.

The more usual slower progress had the considerable advantage of allowing time for new work to mature and settle before it was subjected to its full loading. Speed had its price. Difficulties were experienced even before the church was completed, some of them recorded by Procopius under the pretext of demonstrating that disaster was averted only by seeking Justinian's personal guidance.

A succession of earthquakes between 542 and 557 led to further problems, and then to the first partial collapse. Only with the rebuilding necessitated by this collapse and completed in 562 did the church receive its definitive form which survived unchanged for the following three centuries. The story will now be followed through to that point.

The sequence and progress of construction

How far Anthemius and Isidorus – or whoever planned and supervised the actual construction under their general direction – drew up in advance a programme of what had to be done, is unknown.

Today such planning would be considered essential to ensure, as far as possible, that labour and materials were available when called for, and that work on site proceeded smoothly within the total time allowed for completion. It would provide targets for individual operations, and allow progress to be checked and possible sources of delay to be identified. It might become clear that some operations or sequences of operations were critical for the successful completion of the whole. Special emphasis could then be placed on these.

In 532 it must at least have been clear that some tasks, like the acquisition of the columns for the main nave arcades and the construction of the piers, should initially

be given priority. But it would not have been easy to set realistic targets because of the novelty of many of the tasks.

As an indication of the actual progress of the work, it has been argued that the date which appears instead of the usual monogram on the nave face of the capital of one porphyry column of the south-west exedra should be read as the date 6042 AM, or AD 534, and that this must record the date when the capital was set in place.[2] If so, this would be the one known surviving record between 532 and 537. The date is not unlikely, but the authenticity of the inscription is open to doubt, and the reading is by no means obvious, or the only one possible.

In these circumstances we are left to reconstruct the sequence and progress on the basis of the recorded start and finish of construction, the other evidence afforded by the building itself, and a modern view of what would have been reasonable.

The bar chart indicates the likely progress with as much 212 accuracy as can be hoped for until fresh evidence – of brick stamps perhaps – comes to light. The relative timing of related operations can be established with more confidence than their starting and finishing dates. All terminal dates are therefore shown with a substantial margin of uncertainty – much as they might have been if such a chart had been prepared in advance to guide the work.

From ground level to the first cornice

After clearance of the site, the first tasks would have been to set out approximately the positions of piers, walls and columns, and to prepare their foundations. The limited exploration that has been undertaken below floor-level suggests that the preliminary excavation was taken down at least to the surface of the natural rock. There does not seem to have been complete consistency in the way in which the foundation was then brought up to floor-level. In the passageway through the north-west buttress pier, the tops of huge greenstone blocks can be seen extending beneath the masonry of the pier. Elsewhere, a concrete-like mat has been seen projecting. It is not, however, of the excessive size – 50 ft square and 20 ft deep – or of the unlikely composition described in the *Narratio*.[3]

Around these carefully prepared foundations, the area of the future floor would have been brought to the same level to allow the final precise setting-out to be done and construction of the piers to proceed. At this stage, those marble slabs of the floor which bear setting marks for the column bases must have been set in place, followed by the

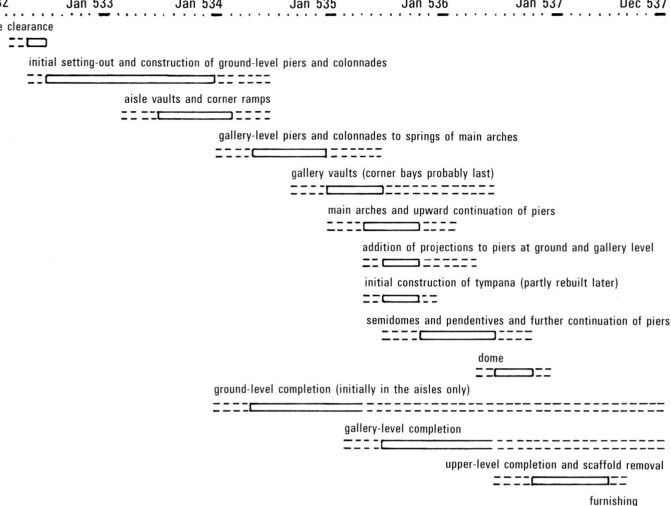

site clearance

initial setting-out and construction of ground-level piers and colonnades

aisle vaults and corner ramps

gallery-level piers and colonnades to springs of main arches

gallery vaults (corner bays probably last)

main arches and upward continuation of piers

addition of projections to piers at ground and gallery level

initial construction of tympana (partly rebuilt later)

semidomes and pendentives and further continuation of piers

dome

ground-level completion (initially in the aisles only)

gallery-level completion

upper-level completion and scaffold removal

furnishing

212 Bar chart of the probable progress of construction, assuming that it was complete by the date of the dedication

bases themselves. Elsewhere the floor was probably given a temporary surface only. Some brick-vaulted channels, possibly intended for drainage, were incorporated in the fill under the narthexes and the western part of the nave.[4] The later legends of cisterns beneath the floor have no factual basis and must have had their origin in the proximity of the Basilica Cistern (Yerebatan Sarayi) which was built at about the same time.

Most accounts stress the solidity of construction of the piers. Procopius described it as follows:

The courses of stone were laid down so as to form a four-cornered shape, the stones being rough by nature but worked smooth; and they were cut to the angles when they were destined to form the projecting corners of the sides of the pier, but when they chanced to be assigned to a position between the angles, they were cut in rectangular form. They were held together neither by lime . . . nor by asphalt . . . nor by any other such thing, but by lead poured into the interstices, which flowed everywhere in the spaces between the stones and hardened in the joints, binding them to each other.[5]

The early part of the description is confirmed by what can be seen of the bare masonry on the faces of the passages through the buttress piers and on the outside of the south-west buttress pier, and by what has been seen of it on other faces when limited areas have been exposed. Procopius is wrong, though, in stating that all joints were filled with lead. Sheets of lead have been found at the springings of arches and vaults, where its ability to creep, over long periods when relative movement took place, would have been valuable in equalizing pressures and 'gently compressing' the stone, as Silentarius put it.[6] But elsewhere only thin mortar joints are visible on the surface.

How closely the blocks were fitted together behind the surface cannot now be checked. The commonest procedure, even when they were cut to fit closely on exposed faces, was to leave them much rougher where they would not be seen, and then to fill the irregular interior voids (including the bed joints behind the faces) with larger quantities of mortar and rubble. Unless the mortar was of very high quality, this could result in highly uneven distributions of pressure, with most of the load falling on the faces.

84

Silentarius hints that subtantial quantities of mortar may have been used in the interior: 'In their midst the workman has mixed and poured the dust of fireburnt stone, binding them together with the builder's art.'[7] However, the unusual care displayed in the incorporation of lead in critical joints, and the manner of construction of the piers of the slightly later church of St John at Ephesus,[8] would suggest that the sounder practice was followed of cutting the blocks to fit closely throughout the mass, even if not quite as closely inside as on the surface.

This early stage of the work should have presented no problems, since the loading on the piers would have been purely vertical.

The main and secondary piers must have been completed up to the level of the capitals of the nave colonnades before any of the columns were erected, so that the columns could be stabilized immediately after erection by the iron ties which run between them just above the capitals. Construction of the buttress piers probably followed close behind, up to at least the level at which stone gives way to brick. The fitting of the marble facings would, of course, have come much later. One indication of this is the manner in which the facing slabs have been fitted around the capitals of the columns that stand close

214

213

213 Detail of the head of the aisle column set against the south-west pier

214 Remains of the church of St John, Ephesus, from the east

216 Looking up to the vaults of the central bay of the south aisle, with the soffits of the arches over the nave colonnade at the bottom

◁ 215 The central bay of the south aisle from the east

against the main piers in the corner bays of the aisles: they fit rather loosely, because it otherwise would have been too difficult to manoeuvre them into place. And, through gaps around the edges, brickwork fillings can be seen in faces of the piers, showing that shallow voids were left in the pier masonry to accommodate the capitals with greater ease.

The eight porphyry shafts probably came originally from more than one structure because they vary considerably in both height and cross-section, the tallest having a height of about 25 ft and the shortest less than 24 ft. They were given some extra overall height and their lack of uniformity was compensated for by the addition of pedestals to their bases.

The *verde antico* columns, as befitted their central position, were made somewhat taller without any pedestals. To give them an overall height, including capitals and bases, of about 34 ft (10.5 m), the shafts were made about 28 ft (8.75 m) tall. Shafts of this size were not particularly notable by earlier Roman standards, the monolithic shafts inside the Pantheon being slightly taller, those of its porch being almost 12 m high, and those originally inside the Basilica Nova being almost 16 m high. But they were large for a time when much less marble was being quarried, and this may be one reason why they also show an appreciable variation in size and irregularity of cross-section, even though they must have been newly cut.[9]

It would have been imperative now, if this had not already been done, to decide how to connect the main and buttress piers across the aisles, and how to relate the vaulting of the aisles to the arches over the main colonnades. The gap between the piers was 30 ft and the longitudinal spacing of the columns between which the aisle vaults had to span was up to 42 ft, measured between their centres. Whatever the types of vault- and arch-profile, these spans called for appreciable rises. Yet it was necessary to keep all the crowns below the gallery floors, and to keep the latter not much above the top surface of the first cornice.

, 211

, 215

217 Vaults of the
western bay of the
south aisle from
the east

The adoption of a semicircular profile for the arches connecting the main and buttress piers called for a rise of 15 ft, and all precedent would have shown the desirability of a considerable depth at the crown to withstand the action of large side-thrusts on the piers, with their tendency to cause the arches to fail in shear, as sketched in the illustration in Chapter 7. This in itself would not have presented any difficulty. But these arches, which continued through in the corner bays of the aisles to the columns adjacent to the piers, were also transverse boundary arches for the aisle vaults – more obviously so originally than after the addition of the underpinning arches between the later projections from the piers. And the aisle vaults had to be related, in turn, to the backs of the narrow arches over high nave colonnades.

The vaults of the corner bays of the aisles must have been the more troublesome because of their greater longitudinal spans. In the sixteenth and seventeenth centuries in the West, the arches over these spans would probably have been made elliptical in profile. But such was the preference here for the semicircular profile that they, too, were made semicircular, as were the longitudinal arches of the pairs of more nearly square vaults in the centre bays. The highest possible springing levels had then to be adopted to allow the longitudinal arches on the nave sides to be carried through to the backs of the arches over the nave colonnades without obtruding below them. To link together the two main vaults of the central bay on each side, the central arches over the colonnades were then simply extended backwards to meet transverse arches spanning between the free-standing columns.

The choice of springing levels also determined the height of the crowns of the arches connecting the piers and, in spite of the raising of the gallery floor more than a foot above the top of the cornice, severely limited the depth here. If the arches are similar to those at gallery level, they were finally made only one-and-a-half bricks thick. At most, they cannot have been more than about two bricks thick, though the connections were subsequently stiffened in the haunch regions by fills placed over them, up to the level of the gallery floor.

To leave room for the minimum depth of one brick at the crowns of the vaults, very little further rise was possible above the crowns of the arches. Each vault thus became, as we have seen, a slightly domical groined vault in which the groins died out in the central region, probably constructed without centering, like the slightly later vault illustrated in Chapter 3. This manner of construction had the further merit of not calling for a precise geometric definition of the form, which could have proved difficult.

Not all these arches and vaults would have been constructed at the same time, however. The main priority would have been the arches that connect the main and buttress piers.

The construction of the outer walls and the ramps that were built against them – necessary to give lateral support to the outermost columns in the aisles – would probably have been held back for a time to give less restricted access to the central area. Similarly, the construction of the narthexes and atrium would have been a matter of less urgency, and would have been held back by the need for extensive substructures in the atrium area to create a new ground-level well above the natural surface.

In the narthex, part of the problem encountered with the aisle vaults would have arisen once more. Direct lighting of the inner narthex was possible only through windows in the west wall above the roof of the outer narthex, and the overall height of the vault was again limited by the desire to have a gallery above. This ruled out a simple barrel vault from end to end, as was used over the gallery. It called for a succession of cross vaults, again with different spans in the two directions if the bays were to correspond to the bays of the outer narthex. Here the semicircular profile was adopted for the window heads and the arches running from north to south. But, for the only time, a segmental profile of the same rise was adopted 31 for the transverse arches.

From gallery level to the second cornice

At gallery level we encounter the most surprising feature of the whole design. All known precedents would lead one to expect that the plan at ground level would have been repeated here virtually unchanged – as it was, for instance, 218 at Sts Sergius and Bacchus. At most, the overall height of this storey might have been reduced slightly, with slightly shorter columns of slightly reduced diameter. Normal prudence would demand that column should stand above column, and that the cross-sections of the piers should be maintained, since the critical loading on them was likely to be the side-thrust of the high arches and vaults. which would act equally at both levels.

Yet the main and secondary piers were substantially reduced in cross-section, and the columns of the 219 colonnades around the nave do not correspond at all. As Silentarius wrote, referring to those of the exedrae:

> These are adorned not with two columns but with six Thessalian ones [so that] one may wonder at the resolve of the man who upon two columns has bravely set thrice two and has not shrunk from fixing their bases over empty air.[10]

When, and why, was it decided to depart so radically from classical precedent?

It appears that, at least in part, the decision was made only after the construction of the main piers had already advanced some way above the gallery floor. The evidence for this is the otherwise inexplicable form of the pilaster-like projections from the faces of these piers that serve as 20–1 terminations of the side colonnades (shown stippled on the 222 isometric drawing).

218 The south-west exedra of Sts Sergius and Bacchus

219 The south-west exedra of Hagia Sophia

220 The north–west
pier at gallery level
seen from across the
nave

221 The east face of the north-west pier seen from the central bay of the north gallery. The pilaster-like projection from the pier in line with the nave colonnade terminates abruptly alongside the top of the mosaic figure of the Emperor Alexander, and immediately below the white patch from which the painted wall-plaster has been removed

48 At ground level the projections have, as would be expected, the same widths as the colonnades themselves. Above the gallery floor they were given exactly this width again, up to a level at which they largely disappear from sight behind the arches over the colonnades. Only then were they abruptly cut back to the reduced actual width of the colonnades. This, surely, can only mean that it was first intended that the colonnades should have the same width at both levels.

It does not necessarily follow that it was first intended that the piers and colonnades at gallery level should correspond in all respects to those below. It is unlikely that there was any substantial demolition of masonry to create the arched openings through the main piers from nave to aisles. Also, the extent of the reduction of the projections of the main and secondary piers towards one another around the curves of the exedrae (as compared with the projections of the same piers below, seen in the drawing in

132 Chapter 4) corresponds so exactly to one inter-
columniation of the colonnades as finally erected here that
the decision to have very differently spaced colonnades
must already have been taken by the time these projecting
parts of the piers were built.

It nevertheless seems likely that it was originally
intended that the piers and colonnades at gallery level
should correspond much more closely to those at ground

222a level. Not only would this follow previous practice, but it
would be in line with the correspondence between the two
levels that was clearly sought and achieved at the east and

223–4 west ends of the nave. If so, the change in plan must have
222b been made soon after the gallery level was reached.

The most likely chief reason for it is either a realization
that the initial design had been too ambitious, or a desire to
speed completion. There may, indeed, be some factual
basis for the reference in the *Narratio* to the Emperor's lack
of gold at about this time, if not for the subsequent
miraculous discovery of a huge store of coins.[11]

A more specific reason may have been that difficulties
were experienced in obtaining suitable counterparts to the
large porphyry and *verde antico* columns of the ground-
level colonnades. These difficulties could have been
circumvented by making do with smaller columns for the
gallery colonnades, at the price of the reduced
intercolumniations. Though this would not have necessitated changes in the piers also, it might have been felt to
make changes desirable in order to give a consistently
greater openness and lightness to the gallery. It is also just
possible that an increased confidence in the effectiveness of
the tying together of the large marble blocks of the
cornices led to a hope that this tying would sufficiently
contain the outward thrusts soon to be experienced from
above as to justify reduced cross-sections.

As a sidelight on the change in plan for the side
colonnades, two different sets of setting-marks remain to
indicate the spacing along their lengths of the centres of

85, 118 the column bases (*Survey*, plates 18, 44). The first sets of
marks – obviously made after the major change – are on the
cornice just below the colonnades and are spaced
uniformly 10.7 ft apart. In other words, the 75 ft total
length (again including half of each notional end column)
was simply divided into seven equal parts. But, after the
stylobates for the colonnades had been set in place over
the cornice, further sets of marks were scribed on these
directly alongside the intended positions of the bases, and
it was then apparently considered preferable to round off
all but the end spacings to 10.5 ft. This left spaces of 9 ft at
each end, as measured to the faces of the projections from
the piers.

In the exedrae, similar marks exist only on the
stylobates, and appear to have been set out by dividing the
total angle of 120 degrees that was subtended by the
ground-level colonnades into five equal parts of 24
degrees, with similar spaces between the last columns and
notional end columns in the piers.

222 The gallery as probably originally planned and as built.
The stippled pilaster-like projections from the eastern main
piers, together with corresponding projections at the west,
are the principal evidence for the change in plan

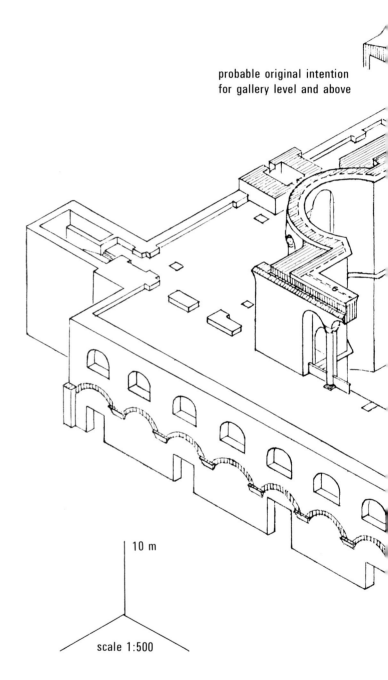

probable original intention
for gallery level and above

10 m

scale 1:500

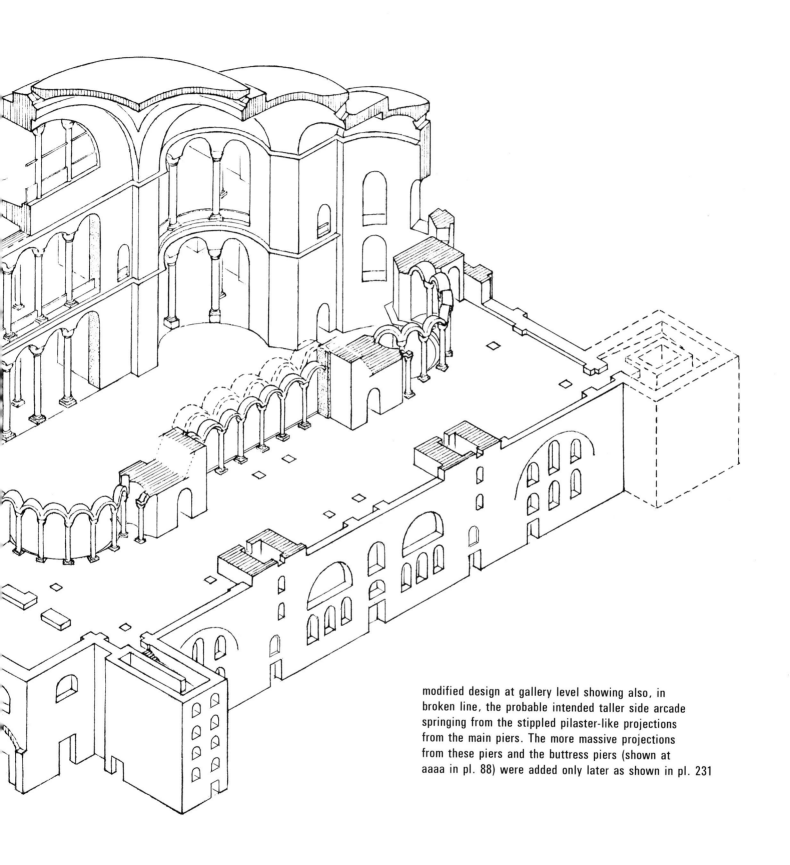

modified design at gallery level showing also, in
broken line, the probable intended taller side arcade
springing from the stippled pilaster-like projections
from the main piers. The more massive projections
from these piers and the buttress piers (shown at
aaaa in pl. 88) were added only later as shown in pl. 231

Justinian's church: design, construction and partial reconstruction   195

223 (*Left*) The east end of the nave   224 (*Above*) The west end of the nave

The columns of all the colonnades were here cut from the green Thessalian marble that was used below only for the side colonnades. The heights of their shafts are about 16 ft at the sides and 15 ft in the exedrae. They gave an overall height for this storey, measured to the underside of the second cornice, of 30 ft.

Behind the colonnades, the free-standing columns to carry the gallery vaults were set above the corresponding columns at ground level with only one minor variation. This was a slight setting-forward of the two columns that stand behind the central pair of columns of each side colonnade, matching a similar setting-forward of the axes of the colonnades themselves on account of their reduced widths.

These free-standing columns were again made lower than the columns of the main colonnades in order to drop 225 the springing levels of the arches carrying the vaults. But the fact that there was to be no second floor above the gallery meant that there was less constraint here on the rise of the vaults. The more dome-like form given to them 226 would have made their construction without centering easier. And the springing levels and heights of the columns could be the same in all bays (instead of a little lower in the corner bays, as they were below).

One other change was that, immediately behind and parallel with the side colonnades, tall barrel vaults were substituted for the simple extensions of the boundary arches of the main vaults that served the same purpose at 221, ground level. This may have been considered desirable on 225 account of the lower relative level of the upper cornice and the changed design of the side colonnade. Or it may have been thought that, if no change had been made, the clash of arch-profiles would inevitably have been more obtrusive when seen from below, from the nave floor. Though it has been pointed out already that this region was reconstructed subsequently, there is no reason to suppose that any significant change was introduced here.

Construction at this level would have proceeded much as below, benefitting no doubt from increased skill and confidence of the workforce. The only retarding factor would have been the need to raise everything to a new working level 12 m or more above ground. For this purpose, the four corner-ramps would have been of considerable value. Most of the lighter loads could have been manhandled up them. Heavier and bulkier loads would have had to be lifted vertically, probably using fairly simple guyed mast cranes similar to the one seen in 227 the illustration.

225 The centre bay of the south gallery

226 Vaults of the western bay of the north gallery from the east (compare with plate 217)

227 Roman guyed-mast crane operated by a treadmill. (From a relief now in the Vatican Museum)

There would, however, have been no need to complete everything up to the level of the gallery roof before proceeding higher. The chief emphasis would certainly have been on the piers, and there are clear indications that the corner bays were not vaulted until after substantial tilting of the piers had occurred – that is, not until after construction of the high arches and vaults over the nave was well advanced. There would not otherwise be marked differences in inclination of the main piers and the adjacent columns that support these vaults. The columns (now partly embedded in the Fossati fillings of the piers) incline much less, and do not appear ever to have been moved. It seems likely, therefore, that these corner bays, conveniently served by the ramp-heads, were kept open as working areas for as long as the higher scaffolds could easily be reached from them.

Close study of the brickwork of the stairwells in the buttress piers suggests increasingly rapid construction here above the gallery floor.[12]

228 The southern buttress piers, now rising almost to the foot of the dome

Construction of the main arches and strengthening of the piers

Some three years must now have passed since construction began, and the critical stage was fast approaching when the main arches and other high arches and vaults would have to be built, and the adequacy of the piers to support them would be tested.

The spans of the arches were all determined. So – given a likely decision early on to use semicircular profiles – were the rises of the soffits from springings to crowns. The only details that may not already have been finally settled were the heights of the springing levels above the upper cornice, the depths of the arch rings, and the amount of further buttressing to be provided.

The springing levels (as defined by the centres of curvature of the original profiles) were made about 1 ft above the cornice for all the shorter spans, about 3 ft above for the main east and west arches and the upper north and south arches, and about 10 ft above for the lower north and south arches.

The principal arches were, as we have seen, constructed with double rings of the extra-large bricks up to 0.7 m square that seem to have been specially imported for them. This gave the east and west arches a total depth close to 1/20th of their spans, and the lower north and south arches a total depth of about 3/40th of their shorter spans. Except for the upper ones at north and south, which received support from below, the other arches seem to have been given proportionately similar or greater depths. Provided that the supports remained firm and there was some firm backing to the haunches by the time the arches were completed, these depths were ample.

Trouble did soon ensue, nevertheless. Indeed it is for this stage alone that we have an almost-contemporary record of two major problems. But Procopius' account of them is far from complete and unambiguous, so that questions remain. How much further did the construction of the piers proceed before that of the arches and vaults began? How were these built? What precisely were the problems and when did they arise? And how, more precisely, were they overcome?

Initial heightening of the piers

In the structure as we see it today, the secondary piers rise to the haunches of the barrel vaults at the east and west ends and then terminate. The main piers rise into the large masses behind the pendentives at the corners of the square dome-base. And the buttress piers (excluding the aedicules at the heads of the stairs) rise in two stages of diminishing wall-thickness, as described in Chapters 2 and 3, to about the full height of the soffits of the principal north and south arches, each upper stage being connected by walls to the backs of the main piers.

It is reasonable to assume that, after completion of the cornice (composed, it will be remembered, of huge blocks of marble extending back over the full widths of the

229 Looking to the back of the main north-east pier between the upper walls connecting it with the north-east buttress pier above the gallery roof. At the top centre may be seen the filling of an arched opening which originally penetrated for an undetermined distance towards the back of the pendentive

230 Looking to the back of the main south-east pier between the lower walls connecting it with the south-east buttress pier above the gallery roof

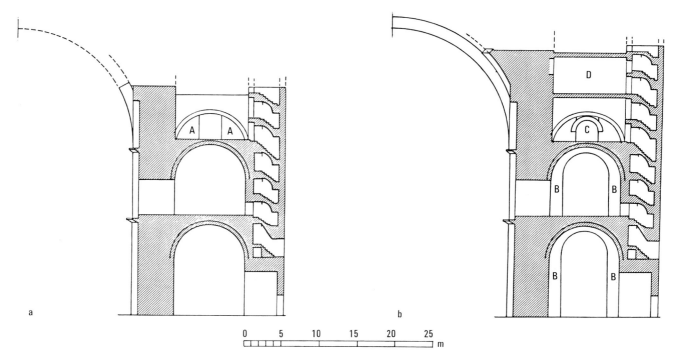

231 Part-sectional elevations of a typical main and buttress pier: **a** as already constructed prior to the start of construction of the main east and west arches; **b** as strengthened after the problems described by Procopius with the eastern arch. The letters A, B, C and D refer to the sequence of construction, as described in the text. (Scale 1:500)

arcades surmounting the colonnades and for indeterminate distances into the masses of the piers), construction above it would initially have proceeded without pause. It would now have been in brickwork throughout, and would have included the upward extensions of the secondary piers and the first part of the extensions of the main piers.

But how far would the main piers have been taken above the springing levels of the arches? And how much backing would they initially have received from the buttress piers? To answer these questions we must look at the exposed brickwork of the inner faces of the walls and arches that run from the buttress piers to the backs of the main piers.

The arches, now badly deformed at their crowns, were constructed at each side on the triangular sections of wall beneath them (AA in the drawings). The walls they carry must have been built up subsequently against the main piers, since they are not bonded to these in either stage. The sequence of construction, at least, is therefore clear.

Analysis of the deformations shows that the whole of the original lower stages must have been built before any major side-thrusts were exerted by the east and west arches to cause the piers to tilt outwards – in other words, before the construction of these arches had proceeded very far. The very marked shearing deformations of both the arches and the courses of brick immediately above them are wholly consistent with the total inclinations of the piers at gallery level.

The corresponding deformations of the upper stages of the walls are, however, significantly smaller, showing not only that these stages were added later (as is also suggested by the diminutions in wall-thicknesses), but also that they were added only when significant tilting of the piers had already occurred.

Thus it can be concluded that the lower stages only of the buttress piers and the walls, together with the arches that carry the walls, were part of the original design and were constructed at the outset. Before they were completed, though probably only a short time before, the main piers must have been built up at least to the tops of the walls – some 6 m above the upper cornice. They may have been built a little higher, to the tops of the barrel vaults that originally spanned between the walls. But only traces of these vaults now remain (the present vaults being later replacements), so it is impossible to confirm this.

Centering and construction of the arches

While this work was proceeding, the necessary centering would have been erected for the arches. In the absence of any record, we can only surmise what types were used on the basis of what would have been feasible at the time, and of such evidence as there is of provisions for supporting it.

We saw in the previous chapter that the more economical flying center was certainly used in earlier Roman construction. Its use in Constantinople is best attested in the eighth century by rows of arched holes at the feet of the rebuilt barrel vaults over the galleries at

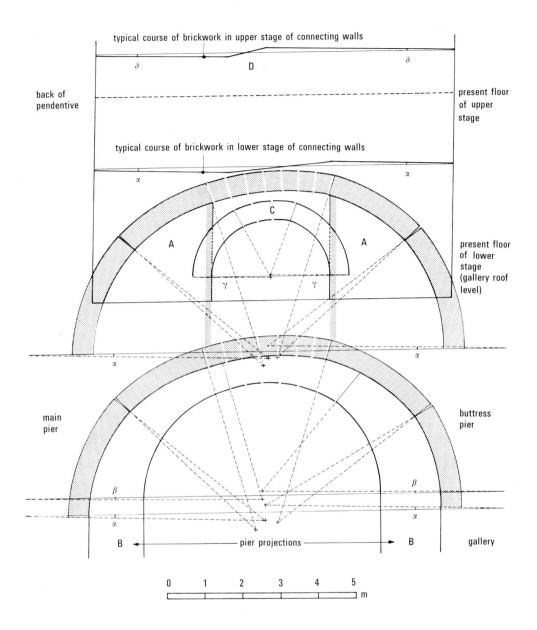

typical course of brickwork in upper stage of connecting walls

δ

D

δ

back of
pendentive

present floor
of upper
stage

typical course of brickwork in lower stage of connecting walls

α

α

C

A

A

present floor
of lower
stage
(gallery roof
level)

γ

γ

α

α

main
pier

buttress
pier

β

β

α

B ◄──── pier projections ────► B

gallery

0   1   2   3   4   5
                        m

232 Analysis of the present mean deformations of the arches connecting the main and buttress piers above and immediately below the gallery roof, and of the walls above the arches at the northeast. The letters A, B, C and D again refer to the sequence of construction. As in plate 104, crosses mark the present positions of the centres of curvature of individual sections of the arches, the lower sections having rotated with the tilting of the piers and the upper sections having rotated in relation to the lower ones. The rotations due to tilting of the piers are further shown by the light horizontal lines passing through the effective centres of rotation within the pier masses. Thus the different angles α, β, γ and δ denote different amounts of tilting since the construction of the arch or wall to which they relate. For simplicity, the centres for setting-out the original complete semicircular profiles of the arches are not shown here, since all the springings have also been displaced horizontally to the right. In the crown regions of the arches – shown in broken outline, and with interrupted shading – there are relative slips as well as joints that are splayed open at top or bottom. The pattern of these is not shown in detail, since it varies from arch to arch. (Scale 1:100)

233 Interior of Hagia Irene showing, immediately above the cornices from which the main arches spring, arched holes for projecting timbers to support flying centers

233 Hagia Irene. But similar holes exposed by the removal of external stucco from the original sixth-century brickwork of the lower parts of the eastern semidomes of Hagia Sophia have shown that it was used there also.

It seems likely, therefore, that the shorter-spanning arches at the forward edges of the exedrae and apse, and the barrel vaults at the east and west ends, were constructed on centers of this kind. They should not have presented much trouble, and there is no indication that they did.

Today we should probably also construct the main arches on flying centers. But this has never been the universal practice. We have seen that, in the sixteenth century, flying centers were used at St Peter's. Yet in the nineteenth century, centers supported partly from below were often preferred for large-span arches of masonry bridges, and it would have been difficult in the sixth century to dispense with this support over spans of more than 30 m. Over the lesser spans of the lower arches at the north and south it would also have been difficult to resist

taking advantage of the support offered by the colonnades below, in spite of the risk of loading these prematurely. Indeed, we have seen that the lower parts of these arches were built in horizontal courses which were presumably continuous with those of the original tympana up to a level well above the gallery roofs, though this does not necessarily mean that the tympana were then immediately carried up beyond that level to serve as permanent centering.

In any case it seems unlikely that all the conditions for minimal thrust on the piers while the centering remained in place would have been met: progressive developments of thrust seem almost certain. On each main pier and its associated buttress pier the final thrusts to north and south, after completion of the east and west arches and the pendentives, would have been about 3 MN acting some 8 or 9 m above the upper cornice. To east and west, after completion of the lower and upper north and south arches and the pendentives, they would have been similar in magnitude but would probably have acted a little lower.

East and west arches, and the strengthening of the piers

Procopius refers first to difficulties experienced with the main east arch:

One of the arches that I have just mentioned (called *loroi* by the *mechanopoioi*), namely that towards the east, had already been built up on either side but had not yet been completed in the middle and was still waiting. And the piers [*pessoi*] on top of which the structure was being built, unable to bear the mass that was pressing down on them, suddenly began to part asunder and seemed to be about to collapse. So Anthemius and Isidorus, terrified at what had happened and losing confidence in their ability, referred the matter to the Emperor. And immediately the Emperor, impelled by I know not what, but I suppose by God since he is not himself a *mechanicos*, commanded them to complete the curve of the arch. 'For when it presses against itself', he said, 'it will no longer need the piers [*pessoi*] beneath it.' If there were no witnesses to this story I know that it would seem to be a piece of flattery and altogether incredible, but since there are many witnesses of what happened at that time we need not hesitate to finish it. So the builders did as he ordered and the entire arch then hung secure, thus demonstrating the validity of his idea. In this way it was completed.[13]

Procopius would not have told the story without some factual basis. Yet it is simply untrue that the arch would no longer need the piers beneath it once it was completed. Completion would add to the load on them, and subsequent removal of the centering might add to it further. Only through some serious misconception of arching action could it have been thought otherwise.

It has been suggested that the word *pessoi* should be translated 'props' – probably the vertical props of a ground-supported center, though they could also have been the raking props of a flying center.[14] The story would then make rather more sense, particularly if the first ring of the arch were already complete, and it remained only to complete its second ring using the same special large bricks. This completion would not have immediately rendered the centering superfluous because the mortar needed time to harden. Also, it could have been hazardous because initially it would merely have added to the weight on the props. But, by doubling the overall depth of the arch, it would have reduced the risk of a complete collapse if the props then continued to yield.

This suggested translation does, however, run counter to Procopius' own earlier statement that the name *pessoi* was given to the piers themselves:

In the middle of the church stand four man-made eminences which they call *pessoi*, two on the north side and two on the south, opposite and equal to one another, each pair having between them just four columns.[15]

There is also no doubt that, as the arches were built, the main and buttress piers did start to shear apart at their weak interconnections, to an extent that must have made it seem that they might soon collapse.

It must be remembered that Procopius was writing twenty years or more after the event, most likely on the basis of half-understood hearsay, and that he goes out of his way to profess ignorance of technical matters. What he must have done was to conflate accounts of two separate problems, one that of the inadequacy of the centering of the east arch, and the other that posed by the alarming behaviour of the piers. He first refers to the second problem, and then indicates the response to the first, though perhaps with some hint also of the response to the second.

The response to the yielding of the piers was, as might be expected, to stiffen them – the second major change in design during construction.

The stiffening was accomplished primarily by adding the projections from the main and buttress piers, at both ground and gallery levels, that narrow the original 30-foot aisles and side galleries to 20 ft between their central and end bays, and carry bracing arches beneath the original shallow brick interconnecting arches (BB in the drawings). The shallowness of these original arches was part of the cause of the problem; the plentiful use in them – and in the walls built above the uppermost arches above the gallery roofs – of a slow-hardening mortar was another. To allow the additions to take load immediately the existing main piers leant on them, they were constructed throughout of closely fitted blocks of stone set tight against these piers and the existing interconnecting arches.

231b, 232 234–5

92

The present tilts of the free faces of the projections and deformations of the soffits of the arches are between 75 per cent and 80 per cent of those of the piers and their original interconnecting arches. This shows that the piers had already inclined by 20 to 25 per cent of their present inclinations when the additions were made.

232

The earlier analysis of tilts and other deformations described in Chapter 4 showed that, by the time the first dome was completed, the inclinations of the piers were between 40 and 45 per cent of their present inclinations – or twice those at the time when the additions were made. With the construction of the dome, the thrusts responsible for the inclinations would also roughly have doubled (the precise increase being dependent on both the design of the first dome and the efficacy of any circumferential tying at its foot), and they would, in part, have acted at a higher level. Allowing for the compensating factor of the stiffening of the piers by the additions, it must be concluded that the additions were made before construction of the dome commenced.

It was probably at the same time that additional short arches were constructed beneath the arches over the gallery roofs (C in the drawings).

231b, 232

Did the first signs of serious movement of the piers lead to a pause in constructing the main arches while the

234 The south-east pier at ground level looking north west, showing the pair of projections carrying bracing arches which stiffen its connection with the buttress pier

235 The same pier at gallery level looking north east, showing the similar projections and bracing arches there. The small holes in the plaster facings of the pier disclose some of the fractures of its stone masonry, and, in one case, the edge of the filling of the former opening through the pier to the nave. A detail of the masonry of the arch carried by the nearer projection may be seen in plate 92

additions were made, this pause then being part of the cause of the problem with the eastern arch itself? Or was the completion of the arch rushed forward while the piers were temporarily shored, and before more permanent measures were taken to halt the movement?

All we can now say is that the movements of the piers would have been a major contributory cause of the problem with the arch in any circumstances but the most unlikely one of the use of a type of centering that relieved the piers of nearly all thrust while it remained in place. This makes it even less surprising that Procopius confused the two problems.

Lower and upper north and south arches, and the great tympana
Procopius' reference to these is less confused:

> In the case of the other arches, namely those towards the north and south, the following chanced to happen. The so-called *loroi* had been raised up and some of the adjacent construction [presumably the lower parts of the pendentives and the masonry above the haunches of the lower arches], but everything beneath was labouring under their weight, and the columns that stood there were shedding little flakes as if they had been planed. So the *mechanicoi* . . . reported the problem to the Emperor. And once again the Emperor suggested a remedy. He ordered that the parts that had suffered, namely those in contact with the arches, should be removed and replaced only much later when the masonry had sufficiently dried out.[16]

The problem here was that the arches were weighing down on the columns directly beneath them, overloading these, and causing the marble to split and parts of it to spall off at the top or bottom. The outward tilting movements of the whole bearing structure would have made matters worse by accentuating any initial unevenness of the bearing pressures.

If the report is accurate, not only had the arches been completed, but also whatever originally filled the spaces beneath them where the great tympana now stand. If, also, the filling was of the character that has been suggested in Chapter 4, it would have been sufficient, in order to relieve the load, to remove the columns separating the lights of the single large window at the top. The damage may, however, have extended to some of the columns at gallery or even ground level, and it may have been only at this time that some of the bronze collars were added to these, to limit further similar damage.

But was this the whole story?

We have already seen that, at the relevant time, the arches would have been exerting thrusts to east and west similar in magnitude to those exerted to north and south by the main east and west arches. The more effective absorption of these thrusts, and of those due to the dome, by the main and secondary piers (assisted to an indeterminate extent by ties at four levels) has meant that present inclinations of the piers to east and west are only about half those to north and south at ground level, and less than a third of them at gallery level and above. But it certainly did not eliminate such inclinations. Indeed the outward movements of the springings of the arches resulting from the initial inclination would have been partly responsible for the settlements of their crowns 104 which led to the problem described by Procopius.

There is less basis for estimating the magnitudes of these inclinations at the time of completion of the arches than there was for estimating the inclinations to north and south. Assuming (as is not unreasonable, taking into account all the relevant factors) that they were a similar proportion of the present inclinations, they would still have been large enough to initiate some of the failures that can be seen today. The most important are the shear failures which run through the exedrae close to the terminations of the main piers. These are especially noticeable in the two western exedrae on account of the 100 weaker terminal buttressing at the west end of the church before the flying buttresses were added.

This raises the question whether any other, and unrecorded, steps were taken at this time, comparable with those to stiffen the resistance to the side-thrusts to north and south.

The chief possibility is that the long tie bars which run round the western exedrae in chases cut into the upper cornice were added then. The extent to which the east end 77 of the easternmost bar in the south-west exedrae is now separated from the hole in which it was originally set shows that the addition was certainly an early one. But it may not have been made until the time of the first reconstruction of the dome.

Semidomes and pendentives

As the main and secondary piers were raised to permit construction of the arches, the almost-horizontal bottom courses of the brickwork of the exedrae semidomes would have been laid between them. But, from about the height of the sills of their window openings, the inclination of the brickwork would increase, and further progress would call for the end abutments for the incomplete rings that were provided by the arches at the forward edges. Only when construction of these arches was complete was work on the semidomes likely to have been resumed. Construction of the pendentives could have proceeded in step with that of the main piers to a somewhat greater height, before it similarly would have had to be halted.

With the arches completed, construction could have been continued with no more need for centering than there is when building a complete dome. The only requirements for temporary support would have been those introduced by the interruptions of the horizontal rings by window openings, and by the need to construct successive rings brick by brick.

Any problems that might have arisen on account of the interruptions of the rings by the windows were probably avoided partly by placing temporary strutting across the openings, and partly by building-in the permanent timbers across the window heads. Whatever the primary intended purpose of these permanent timbers, they would initially have been acting as struts, and only much later, after cracking developed around the bases of the semidomes, would they have been put into tension.

Among the techniques used to assist the setting in place of individual bricks as the inward slope of the surface of a vault increased have been the use of fast-setting gypsum mortars which virtually glued the bricks in place as they set, the use of interlocking earthenware tubes instead of normal bricks (notably in Ravenna), and the setting of the bricks at a flatter inclination than that indicated by a radial line to the centre of curvature. Where a greater overall thickness was desired than that of a single brick or other unit, it has also helped if the additional thickness was built up later, on the back of the first layer.

The semidomes and pendentives in Hagia Sophia were built of normal bricks set in a normal slow-setting mortar. The large face-dimensions of the bricks in relation to their thickness were, however, an advantage; and the available evidence seems to confirm Choisy's suggestion[17] that the bed joints were made flatter than the radial inclination. Thus no temporary local support should have been necessary in the pendentives, or up to the heights of the window heads in the semidomes.

Where the semidomes became flatter towards the top, the least possible inclination would still have allowed bricks to slide off if unsupported. The procedure here was probably to use relatively light local supports or flying centers. These could have been attached to short timbers built into the brickwork below, similar to those that would have been necessary at regular intervals lower down to support working platforms. Any surviving evidence of such holes is hidden behind the internal plaster 97 rendering. But such evidence can readily be seen in Hagia Irene.

As the work proceeded, there would have been further increases in the outward thrusts on the piers, and further outward tilting.

In a final attempt to stem the tilting to north and south, the top stages of the buttress piers and the walls running from them to the backs of the main piers were now added 232 (D in the drawings). These additions gave the main buttressing-arms essentially their present form, lacking only the squinch arches that connect the inner walls to the masonry above the lower north and south arches.

The tilting of the piers to east and west would still have been only about a third as large, however, and there would have been inward movements of the crowns of the main east and west arches after completion of the semidomes, on account of the inward pressures exerted on them by the semidomes. These would have been greater than the present movements in the absence of any counter-192b thrust from the dome.

Thus the central square, measuring precisely 100 ft across in each direction, with which Anthemius and

Isidorus so carefully started at ground level, would no longer have been square, and the curve formed by the tops of the pendentives would not have been a true circle. Measured between the faces of the main arches at their crowns, the north-south diameter would have been increased to about 102 ft by the tilts of the piers, whereas the east-west diameter would have increased initially to no more than 101 ft in this way. The subsequent collapse of both the east and west arches leaves no firm basis for estimating the final change in the east-west diameter, taking into account also the forward bends of the arches. But if the forward bends of the present arches and that of 103, 114 the arch of the apse semidome are taken as a guide, there 236 would have been a net reduction of almost 1 ft in this span, giving a difference in diameters of almost 3 ft.

All the subsequent changes have left so little of the original pendentives that it is more difficult to establish their intended form. What can now be seen suggests that the centre of curvature was some 2 ft above the centres of curvature of the bounding arches, with an intended radius equal to half the diagonal of the 100 ft by 106 ft rectangle 237b of the clear central space. If, however, the original centre was at the same level as that of the arches, which would seem more likely, the intended radius was probably 75 ft – half the diagonal of a 106 ft square. 237a

Dome

Once the pendentives were completed, the next task would have been to set in place the topmost cornice. But before this was done, some decision would have been necessary on how to deal with the non-circularity of the base that had been provided. The initial choice would have been between making the cornice follow the curve formed by the lips of the pendentives, and making it circular by giving it a greater projection in front of the lip at the north and south to compensate for the greater span on this axis.

The subsequent collapse and complete reconstruction have destroyed all direct evidence of what was done. It is probable, however, that the cornice-blocks under the surviving sixth-century sections of the dome at the north and south are the original blocks, reset after the modifications to the arches below. If so, the front edge of the original cornice would have projected uniformly all round, and the first dome, like the second, would have been non-circular in plan from the outset, with a north-south diameter about 3 ft greater than the east-west diameter. The critical cross-section would then have been the north-south one.

Form

The most likely profile, suggested in Chapter 4, was a simple part-circular one, lifted somewhat above the cornice by a low drum-like section at the foot to afford reasonable passage around it. The only clues to its possible precise form are what we are told about the height of the crown in relation to that of the reconstructed dome,[18] and

236 Looking vertically up to the apse semidome, showing the inward movement of its forward edge

what we can deduce about the precise forms of the pendentives and cornice.

In following up these clues, it soon becomes apparent that the radius of curvature of the main curved surface cannot have differed much from that of the pendentives themselves, which makes it highly probable that the same radius was adopted for both. In effect, construction of the notional continuous hemispherical dome – of which the pendentives were the only parts that had so far been built – would simply have been resumed a little higher up, after being cut off by the cornice.

Perfectly possible profiles for a dome of this kind can be suggested for either of the likely radii of curvature of the pendentives. If the slope of the exposed upper surface of the cornice was the same as now, a radius of 75 ft would call for notional springings set back about 5 ft behind the faces of the arches below – these notional springings being the intersections of the curved profile with the top of the cornice, ignoring the likely drum-like filling of the re-entrants up to the splayed sills of the windows. A radius of

237a

72.85 ft – half the diagonal of the 100 ft by 106 ft rectangle – would call for notional springings similarly set back 3 or 4 ft. The first radius would give a crown height slightly more than 20 ft below the present crown, and the second would give crown heights 22 or 20 ft below the present crown, according to the actual setback. The north-south diameter measured between the inside faces of the low 'drum' might then have been 108 ft and the east-west diameter some 3 ft less. This difference in diameters would have called for a setting-out of the 'drum' as shown in the drawing.

Since a design on these lines would have conformed closely to the principles followed in the other main vaults, it is probable that similar principles were followed also in the choices of thickness and of the form of the windows. This would have meant the adoption of a uniform thickness of about 5 per cent of the radius of curvature, or about 1.1 m, which would have called for one and a half of the special large bricks, if they were set truly or almost radially.

237

237

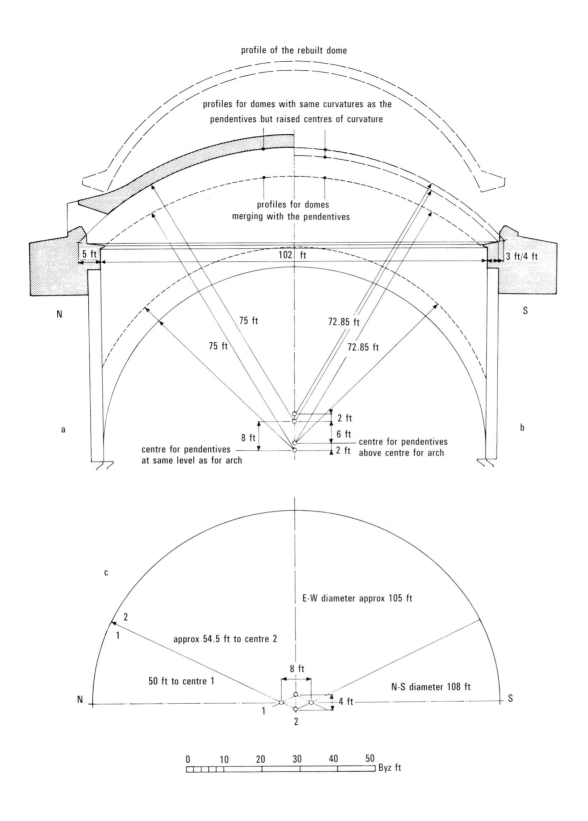

profile of the rebuilt dome

profiles for domes with same curvatures as the
pendentives but raised centres of curvature

profiles for domes
merging with the pendentives

5 ft

102 ft

3 ft/4 ft

N

S

75 ft

72.85 ft

75 ft

72.85 ft

a

b

2 ft

6 ft

8 ft

centre for pendentives
above centre for arch

2 ft

centre for pendentives
at same level as for arch

c

E-W diameter approx 105 ft

2

1

approx 54.5 ft to centre 2

8 ft

50 ft to centre 1

N-S diameter 108 ft

N

S

4 ft

1

2

0   10   20   30   40   50
Byz ft

237 Possible setting out of the original pendentives and dome: **a** and **b** in section;
c in plan at cornice level. (Scale 1 mm: 1 Byzantine ft)

The windows would presumably have been similar to those in the semidomes, the lower part of the dome up to their rounded heads being seen externally as a taller, but still relatively low, vertical-sided drum. The much closer spacing of the windows and the narrowness of the sections of the dome between them, may, however, have suggested the desirability of one departure from previous practice – the extension of these narrow sections into the continuous shell above as protruding ribs.

Construction

Once the profile and springing line and other details of the construction had been decided, the chief outstanding choice would have been between different possible construction procedures.

The flatness of the profile meant that some temporary support would have been essential for setting the bricks, as soon as the surface closed in above the windows. Working platforms, too, would have been necessary before this, for setting out the springing line and afterwards for the final plastering of the soffit and setting of the mosaic. Finally, some control of the profile was necessary.

Centering would have served the last as well as the first purpose. Without it, there would have been a choice between using templates and swinging a cord attached at the centre of curvature. The latter would have been far from easy, however, on account of the location of this centre well below the cornice. It would have called both for a second working platform at this lower level, or some other firm means of attachment there, and for a sufficiently unobstructed space above it for swinging the cord.

Bearing in mind also that the strength and stiffness requirements for templates spanning 100 ft would have been far from negligible, and that those for centers would have been considerably less than they were for the centers for the main east and west arches, it seems most likely that centers were used above the level of the window heads. It would have been feasible to support them largely by means of heavy timbers projecting back through the window openings, and to link the radial frames together circumferentially for added strength and stiffness. If the dome was ribbed like the present one, there would have been one frame for each rib. But it would still have been desirable to construct the ribs and the intermediate webs together, to gain the dual benefits of unbroken bond and complete self-supporting horizontal rings as construction proceeded.

Further thrusts and their effects

Whether truly circular or not, the dome would have developed its own outward thrusts as it began to close in over the central void. Without knowing for certain the precise form, it is impossible to estimate the thrusts other than very approximately. But they would probably have exceeded those of the present dome by 50 per cent or more, and would certainly have broken any tie likely to

have been formed at the base by cramping together of the marble blocks of the cornice. Thus they would have passed over to the piers through the pendentives, the north and south arches, and the semidomes.

It is at this stage that the most marked difference between the ways in which the loads exerted by the high vaults were transmitted in different directions would have come into play.

The diagonally aligned thrusts would have passed directly through the pendentives to the main piers. The thrusts acting more to east and west would have passed largely through the semidomes, to act finally, at a less damaging lower level, on the secondary piers and the walls of the apse. But those acting more to north and south would have reached the main piers much less directly, after passing, both downwards and outwards, through the main north and south arches. In so doing, they would finally have caused thrusts not only to north and south, but also to east and west, as well as causing the arches to bow outwards.

The net effects on the piers would have been additional thrusts of about 1.5 MN to north and south on the main and buttress piers, additional thrusts of about 2 MN to east and west on the main piers, and additional thrusts of about 1.5 MN to east and west on the pairs of secondary piers, together with the walls of the apse at the east.

Independently of these additional thrusts, the added weight of the dome would alone have increased considerably the thrusts of the main arches on the piers. How much depends, of course, on the weight of the dome, which is unknown. If it is assumed that the most significant change made in the first rebuilding was the change of profile, these additional thrusts would have been about 2 MN to east and west (of which part would have been passed on to the secondary piers) and 3.5 MN to north and south.

Some further tilting-apart of the piers would have been inevitable, though not quite proportionate to the increases in the thrusts because the piers had been strengthened substantially. According to the estimate referred to earlier, the tilts would have reached 40 to 45 per cent of their present values. This, together with the outward bowing of the north and south arches would have meant a further increase in the north-south diameter of about 0.4 m (or almost 1.5 ft). There would have been a much smaller increase in the east-west diameter, resulting in an increased difference between the two. These increases in diameters would have entailed noticeable cracking of the dome above the window heads, especially in the regions over the crowns of the main east and west arches.

The final stages before the first dedication

Whatever relief was felt on completion of the dome must have been tempered by the continuing signs that all was not well with the structure. And much remained to be done before all scaffolding could be cleared and the church handed over to the clergy.

During the final year, it is likely that work of many kinds proceeded simultaneously, under continuous pressure to meet the desirable Christmas deadline for the formal dedication – Christmas being the patronal feast.

The principal remaining tasks would have been the rendering and other facing and weatherproofing of the exterior, the replacing of those columns of the tympanum windows that had been removed temporarily, the glazing of the windows, the facing of the interior with marble and mosaic, and the installation of the liturgical furniture. It is possible, also, that some of the corner bays of the side galleries still remained to be vaulted.

In general, this work would now proceed from the top downwards, to simplify the progressive removal of scaffolds and reduce the risk of damage to finished surfaces. It would, however, have been possible to work in the aisles and galleries largely independently of what remained to be done in the nave.

One needs only to look closely at the surviving original finishes to see that there was no striving for meticulous accuracy and uniformity. Everything possible seems to have been done to speed the work, and perhaps also to hide the cracks in the masonry, which would have been very noticeable by this time.

This emphasis on speed is particularly evident in the marble revetments – in the simple butting-together of the larger slabs, in the simple cutting-to-length of the narrow bands that frame them without any attempt at mitred joints, in the cutting and fitting of the slabs that cover the tapered soffits of the arches over the porphyry columns in the exedrae, and lastly, in the character of the carving. As might be expected, the wall revetments were set in place before the paving, which was then butted up against them.

The desire to complete the work as quickly as possible may also have been one reason for the apparent absence of figural mosaics, although it is unlikely to have been the only reason. The vast interior did not lend itself as readily to figural decoration as did, for instance, that of San Vitale in Ravenna. Nor was there the same need for it: space, form and light spoke for themselves. It has further been suggested that the absence could have been a deliberate choice by Justinian in deference to his monophysite subjects, whom he was still, at the time, trying to win over by persuasion.[19]

The installation of the altar, chancel screen, ambo and other furniture would have come last. To a great extent, these could have been made ready elsewhere while construction proceeded, needing only to be assembled when brought at the last minute to their final positions.

From the first dedication to the first collapse

Whether or not everything had been completed, the new church was solemnly dedicated on 27 December 537. According to Theophanes, the procession started from the church of Hagia Anastasia.[20] The patriarch Menas rode in the imperial chariot while Justinian walked with the people. The late *Narratio* tells a more colourful story,

weaving around the bare facts new details of Justinian's largesse, and of his first entry and oft-quoted exclamation exulting in having outdone Solomon.[21]

Twenty years later, on 14 December 557, the structure was shaken by an earthquake,[22] and on 7 May 558 parts of the eastern arch and semidome and dome fell. The collapse is referred to in very similar terms by Malalas, Theophanes, and Cedrenus, in passages immediately preceeding their descriptions of the subsequent restoration that were quoted in Chapter 4:

> On Tuesday 7 May of this year at the 5th hour, while the dome of the great church was being repaired – for it had been cracked in conspicuous places by the earthquakes that had occurred – and while the Isaurians were at work, the eastern part of the vault over the sanctuary fell down and crushed the ciborium, the altar table and the ambo.[23]

The chronicles also report unusual earlier seismic activity in Constantinople over the years 542 to 557. No less than five earthquakes were said to have been felt in the city, and two of them – those in 542 and 557 – were said to have been severe. Damage to the city walls is specifically mentioned in 557.[24]

It is difficult, however, to decide how much weight should be placed on the reports. The extensive data acquired in recent years show quite clearly that the city lies somewhat to the north of the main earthquake-belts that run across modern Turkey.[25] The frequency with which the chronicles mention it when reporting earthquake disasters must stem partly, and perhaps primarily, from the fact that it was the capital, the site of the largest number of important buildings, and the place where events of note were most likely to be observed and recorded.

From observations of the effects of recent earthquakes in several parts of the world, it seems probable that the partial collapse, when it occurred, could be blamed only partly on the earthquakes.[26] Even without them, the progressive tilting of the piers and associated deformation of the arches and vaults would have continued, though at a diminishing rate, after the completion of construction. The effect of the earthquakes would have been further movements, some of them irreversible, caused in the manner described in Chapter 7. The movements to north and south would have been largest on account of the weaker buttressing of the thrusts in those directions.

During the 558 shock, the movements of the north-east and south-east piers must have been sufficient to allow some highly dangerous slips of the crowns of the main eastern arch and semidome – which must, ever since completion, have been more deformed than their counterparts at the west on account of the difficulties experienced during construction. Thus the situation which the Isaurian masons were trying to remedy probably resembled that seen (in a much smaller structure) in the illustration. Even today it would be hazardous to 238

238 Damage to a small dome in the 1979 Montenegro earthquake

tackle this directly, and great care would be necessary to avoid precipitating the threatened collapse. Temporary centering or similar support would be desirable, and there may have been an unwise attempt to manage without it, to avoid interference with the normal use of the church. This, however, is pure speculation. It is equally possible, as we shall soon see, that the Isaurians were engaged in attempting to improve the resistance to the damaging thrusts.

The extent of the collapse can be roughly determined from the reference to the damage done to the ciborium, altar and ambo. As we shall see in the next chapter, the altar was probably situated slightly in front of the two eastern secondary piers, and the ambo between the western ends of the two eastern main piers. This implies that the whole upper part of the eastern semidome and eastern arch collapsed. The adjacent part of the dome would thus have lost its support and must also have fallen.

That conclusion is supported by the further account given by Silentarius:

> Now the wondrous curve of the semidome, although standing on firm foundations, fell . . . The whole broad-breasted church did not sink to the ground . . . but the upper part of the eastern arch slipped off and part of the dome was mingled with dust. Part of it lay on the floor, and part – a wonder to behold – hung in mid-air as if unsupported.[27]

Further indications are given by the present profile of the eastern arch and by the likely condition of the dome immediately before the collapse.

Up to the height of the sills of the semidome windows, the profile of the arch is still close to the original semicircle. This suggests that below this level the arch has remained in place, undamaged by either this or the later collapse. The actual breaks might have been a little higher. Above the arch, they probably continued almost vertically through the pendentives. Behind it, most of the semidome above the windows is likely to have fallen.

Since the dome would already have been cracked radially on the line of each of its windows to within, say, 5 m of its crown, two of these cracks would have constituted the side-boundaries of its collapse. The uncracked crown-region itself would have been supported by the rest of the dome to north and south, and should not have fallen.

239

104

239 Shoring of an arch damaged in the 1976 Guatemala earthquake prior to repair

First reconstruction

We have already seen something of the reconstruction in Chapter 4. One of the most notable facts about it is that, according to the records, it took almost as long to complete as the original construction of the entire church. It was preceded by the complete demolition of all of the dome that remained aloft, and it was clearly undertaken with much greater caution.

Modification of the upper north and south arches and pendentives
We saw that reconstruction began with a widening of the upper parts of the upper north and south arches in order, it may be assumed, to make their inside faces vertical again. Precisely how this widening was accomplished, we do not at present know. It must have involved some cutting-back of the original faces to bond-in the additions. Similarly, there must have been some cutting-back of the faces of the pendentives to bond-in new brickwork to these to conform to the new arch-faces. But nothing has been seen of any of the faces since Fossati partly exposed them in the mid-nineteenth century.

The widening of the arches and associated bringing forward of the adjacent parts of the pendentives did, in the words of Agathius, 'make the equilateral harmony more perfect'.[28] Before construction of the new dome began, the remodelled pendentives and the cornice above them would again have had much the same form as immediately before construction of the first dome. Nevertheless, the widening and remodelling would still not have achieved the equality of the north-south and east-west diameters that must originally have been intended.

To be more precise, the distance between the inside faces of the crowns of the upper arches at north and south would have been a little more than 104 ft at the time of the collapse and was reduced to a little less than 102 ft by the widening of the arch soffits. Since nothing now remains of the sixth-century crowns of the east and west arches, we cannot be as sure of the corresponding distance between their faces. Taking the present distance and the increases in pier tilts since 562 as a guide, the distance here was probably a little less than 100 ft at the time of the collapse, and is unlikely to have been changed much by the reconstruction of the semidomes.

115c

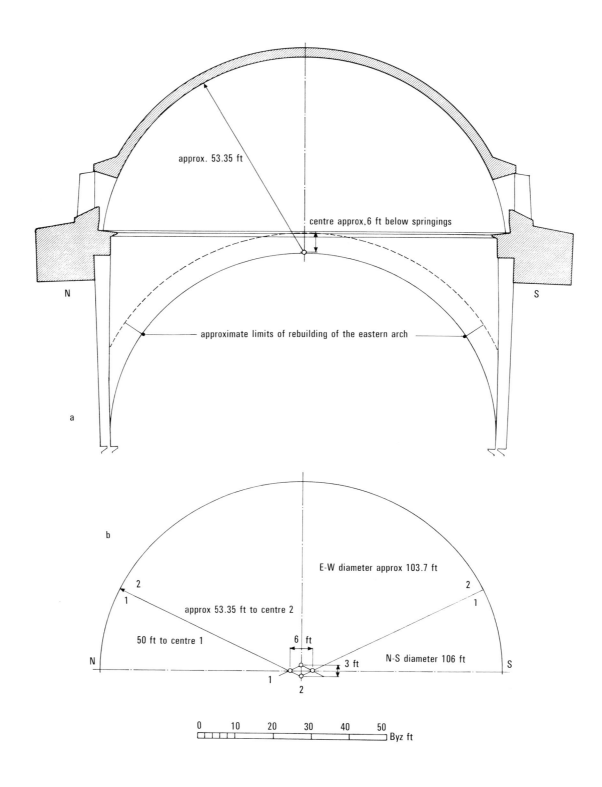

approx. 53.35 ft

centre approx.6 ft below springings

approximate limits of rebuilding of the eastern arch

N

S

a

b

E-W diameter approx 103.7 ft

2

1

approx 53.35 ft to centre 2

2

1

50 ft to centre 1

6 ft

N

3 ft

N-S diameter 106 ft

S

1

2

0   10   20   30   40   50
Byz ft

240 Possible setting-out for the reconstruction of the dome in 559–562: **a** in section; **b** in plan at cornice level. (Scale 1 mm: 1 Byzantine ft)

Reconstruction of the dome

We are on firmer ground in seeking to discover the way in which the new dome was set out than we were with the first dome because the setting-lines are still preserved on the cornice at north and south. These lines deviate only marginally from circular arcs of 50 ft radius, and the deviation can be wholly accounted for by the subsequent slight movements of the cornice. They are definitely not parts of a continuous ellipse with a wider north–south diameter to match the greater north–south distance between the faces of the arches.

At present the centres of the two arcs are 2.83 m or a little more than 9 ft apart. Originally (allowing for the separation due to subsequent movements of the piers) they must have been 6 ft apart. The east and west portions were therefore presumably set out as arcs of 53.35 ft radius with centres 3 ft apart, the centre of each of these arcs being on the far side of the transverse centreline.

As elsewhere in the church, the profile chosen was again a circular arc, at least transversely. But it was no longer of the same radius as the surfaces of the pendentives. It must have been realized that this resulted in too flat a surface and unnecessarily large outward thrusts. The new radius was very close to, if not identical with, the presumed 53.35 ft radius of the setting-lines at east and west, though still greater than the transverse semi-diameter of 53 ft. So the dome became, geometrically, a wholly independent element without yet being a complete hemisphere. Its centre of curvature was now about 6 ft below the springing level.

It is probable that the new dome like its predecessor was constructed on light centering. Indeed the *Narratio*, perhaps preserving some earlier tradition, tells us that the supports were left in place for a year.[29] The setting of the bricks was slightly flatter than radial near the foot, presumably to reduce the need for centering there.

Other works

In his garbled account of the restoration, Cedrenus referred to the erection, outside the church and from the ground up to the dome, of new spiral stair towers opposite the interior piers.[30] This reference was ignored previously because it is clear from the structure itself that the buttress piers – which Cedrenus must have had chiefly in mind when writing – were completed to their present heights well before the collapse.

The one addition that we have seen was made at about this time was that of the four corners of the dome base and the adjacent squinch arches. This addition could provide a partial justification for the reference to stair towers, because the corners do contain the now-blocked short flights of stairs that once furnished the final means of ascent to the dome.

There is, however, a puzzling feature here – though there is now little to be seen of it externally. The stairs are remarkably different in their slightly skew alignments and detailed design. This strongly suggests that these were left to the discretion of the four masters in charge of four different gangs of workmen. Was this because they were considered to be matters of no importance? Or was it because the addition was made hastily in the months immediately before the collapse, as part of the effort by the Isaurians to forestall it? Certainly the apparent lack of care contrasts strongly with the care evident in the work on the dome itself.

We cannot now tell for certain. But it seems most likely that the reconstruction recorded by Cedrenus embraced work already in progress before the collapse – some of it perhaps begun considerably before.

Some further strengthening cannot be excluded as part of that programme. It could, as we have just seen (p. 208), have included the setting of the long tie bars in the western exedrae. It is also possible that it included the first additions to the main piers alongside the exedrae at gallery level, to give them the form that lasted until the nineteenth century. But, until deeper exploratory tests can be made, even the fact that the masses in question are additions to the original form must remain in doubt.

241 A tenth-century representation of a sanctuary, showing
chancel screen, altar and ciborium, and, behind these, the
steps and seats of the synthronon. The ceremony portrayed
is the adoration of the chains of St Peter on 16 January.
(Menologion of Basil II, Vatican Cod. Gr. 1613, folio 324)

CHAPTER 9

Furnishing and use: architecture and liturgy

THE COMPLETION OF THE RECONSTRUCTION was celebrated by a second dedication on 24 December 562, and, probably, shortly afterwards, by a further ceremony in which the long verse-description or *ekphrasis* by Paulus Silentarius was read. For the dedication, we are told that Justinian rode to the church in a chariot with the patriarch Eutychius, Eutychius holding the Gospel in his hands. As they did so the people chanted verses from the 24th Psalm:

> Lift up your gates, O ye princes; and be ye lift up, ye everlasting doors; and the King of glory shall come in.[1]

As they re-entered the church after an absence of almost five years, the impression made upon them by its vast unobstructed interior, sheathed in insubstantial-seeming marble, roofed by gold mosaic, and flooded with light from innumerable windows, may not have been quite as startling as that on the first entry twenty-five years earlier. But in a world that knew no other building even remotely comparable, it must still have been overwhelming. As Silentarius expressed it:

> Whoever lifts his eyes to the beautiful firmament of the roof can scarcely keep them on its rounded expanse, sprinkled with dancing stars, but soon turns to the fresh green hills below, eager to see there the flower-bordered streams . . . and the green tendrils of the vine . . . Whoever puts foot inside the sacred temple would never wish to leave, but would lift up his head and, with his eyes drawn first this way and then that way, would gaze around.[2]

Looking back to the re-dedication itself, he described it thus:

> At last the holy morn had come, and, as dark night was driven away by the dawning light of day, the sounds of the opening of the everlasting door of the newly restored temple invited Emperor and people to enter. As they looked inside, dark sorrows were similarly driven away and all were filled with radiant joy.
>
> It fell to you, all-powerful Emperor . . . to lead the people and, after this holy day, to celebrate next day the birth of Christ. . . . As the rose-coloured light drove away the shadows from vaults, the whole people and all the princes came in together . . . bringing gifts of thanksgiving to Christ the King and singing songs of prayer with melodious voice. The Patriarch led the singing . . . And, as they came into the sacred precincts, he offered up the thanks of all, and it seemed to them as if the very vaults were set in heaven.[3]

Silentarius gives here a rare, brief glimpse of the church in use. Later he gives a few others, which will be referred to below. For the most part, we must piece together a picture of the use in Justinian's time from what we know of the building and its furnishings, and of those of other contemporary churches in the capital, and from the evidence of the form of the liturgy in slightly earlier and slightly later periods. For this purpose, his description is valuable, above all, for its very detailed accounts of the liturgical furnishings – the altar, ciborium, chancel screen, ambo and solea – as they were restored after the collapse.

Since the church was built not only as the patriarchal cathedral but also as a setting for ceremonies in which the Emperor participated, the manner of his participation is also of great interest, and will be discussed at the end.

Liturgical furnishing and imperial metatorion and throne

About a third of the *ekphrasis* is, in fact, devoted to the furnishing of the church to fit it for the liturgy. Silentarius refers first, in the course of his description of the apse, to the synthronon – the seats there for the patriarch and other clergy.[4] Having, some three hundred lines further on, completed his description of the structure and referred briefly to the emperor's metatorion, he returns to the liturgical furnishing and deals, in turn, with the chancel screen,[5] ciborium,[6] and altar.[7] Finally, he devotes a complete second section to the ambo[8] and solea.[9] The probable arrangement is shown in the drawing, and, more 252 schematically, in an illumination in a tenth-century manuscript. 241

Synthronon

The synthronon took the usual form of a ring of seats around the wall of the apse, approached by tiers of semicircular steps which raised the seats well above the floor. The basic structure must have been almost identical, except in size, to that seen today in Hagia Irene, and it 242 presumably had a similar curved passageway beneath the seats. The patriarch's throne would have been in the centre, probably raised higher than the other seats, as we see it today in the cathedrals of Porec and Torcello. The seats, we are told, were covered in silver.

242 The synthronon in the apse of the Hagia Irene

243 S. Maria in Cosmedin, Rome

244 The stylobate (incomplete at the right) of the chancel screen of St Euphemia with the remains of the synthronon behind and, beyond this, Hagia Sophia

Chancel screen

269 The chancel screen was very different from the solid barrier of the modern Greek or Russian iconostasis. It took the form of a low parapet set between taller, free-standing columns which carried an architrave at a higher level, larger and more splendid than seen in other illustrations in 243 the same manuscript and in Sta Maria in Cosmedin Rome, but closer to this in its open character.

There were twelve columns in all, and doors between them in three places for the clergy. Columns, parapets and architrave were also sheathed in silver, on which various designs were incised – discs bearing representations of Christ and the Virgin, angels, prophets and apostles, and the monograms of Justinian and Theodora. Above the architrave were some of the many lamps that have been noticed already, and a pathway for the lamplighter. Most of these lamps were in tree-like clusters. But those over the central door shone like 'bright nails' studded on a cross.

261 On the analogy of the usual later arrangement, it used to be thought that the screen must have extended in one straight line between the eastern secondary piers. It has since been shown conclusively that this was not so.[10] It must have been anchored to these piers at each end. Indeed there are unmistakable later patches in the facings of both piers (those on the north side just discernable in an illustration in Chapter 8, to the right of the sultan's box) 223 showing where the anchorages must have been. But at each side, it first projected forward from the pier in a westerly direction before it turned through 90 degrees to meet the opposite half at the central door-opening.

The precise projection westwards cannot, at present, be determined, though there may still be evidence of it below the much-repaired floor surface. It has been plausibly suggested that it corresponded to the east-west distance between the remains of the two most easterly bands of green marble that run transversely across the floor.[11] These bands are far from complete, the remains of one being confined to the vicinities of the piers, and those of the other to the centre of the nave. But between them are the remains of two bands set in an east-west direction and very close to what must have been the alignments of the outer sections of the screen. So it is possible that there was originally a single band which projected westwards in its 250 central part, keeping a constant distance from the screen.

Numerous remains of early chancel screens of this form have now come to light, indicating that it was a normal form at the time. The stylobate of one is still preserved *in situ* near-by in the sixth-century Church of St Euphemia.[12] 244

245 The ambo from Beyazit Basilica A, now restored and set in the garden of Hagia Sophia

And it has been shown that the stylobate in the Studios church must also have been of this form before its marble blocks were rearranged in the adaptation of the church to Moslem use.[13]

The presence of the three doors is further evidence for the rectangular plan-form. Three doors all facing westward would have been most unusual at the time, and later references to doors at the north and south – in the *Book of Ceremonies*, for instance[14] – are more intelligible if the doors also faced in those directions.

Altar and ciborium

The altar, set behind the screen but not hidden by it, was sheathed in jewel-studded gold, and covered by a cloth with rich silk and gold embroidery. It was also said to stand on gold foundations, meaning either that it was raised on a stepped platform also sheathed in gold, or, more likely, that the columns that supported the slab stood on gold bases. On the altar cloth, Christ was represented standing between Peter and Paul, and there were numerous smaller representations of divine miracles and deeds of the emperors.

Over the altar rose a silver ciborium. This was of the pattern seen in the tenth-century illumination and well known from surviving examples of somewhat later date in the West. Four columns were spanned by arches, and here these supported an eight-sided pyramidal roof. This was decorated with sprays of acanthus, and culminated in a silver orb surmounted by a cross.

There is no reason to believe that any veils hung between the arches to hide the altar, so that whatever took place there would have remained fully visible to anyone in the congregation whose view was not otherwise obstructed.

Ambo and solea

Much more prominently placed, however, was the ambo. Set near the centre of the nave but slightly to the east, it would have been the first feature to catch the eye of both Emperor and Patriarch as they stepped through the Imperial door from the narthex to perform the dedication. In this first strictly axial view it must, indeed, have largely hidden both ciborium and altar, as well as the patriarchal throne. And, though Silentarius left his description of it to the end, we have seen that he devoted the whole second part of his poem to it and to the solea.

245 Today, we know the form directly only from smaller and simpler examples, such as the one now reassembled from fragments in the garden, though better-preserved examples in the West are some help in visualizing the richness in detail on which Silentarius chiefly dwells.

It was essentially a raised platform approached by stairs at west and east, and more akin in its normal use to the lectern than to the pulpit in a modern English church. Here, in spite of its considerable size, the platform apparently still consisted of a single slab of stone, probably oval in outline. It was supported on eight columns, leaving the space beneath free for the choir of professional singers. Both the platform itself and the stairs were protected by parapets sheathed in silver.

A more unusual feature was that it stood on a wider raised plinth which was surrounded by a second open screen, apparently very similar to the chancel screen, except that each side was crescent-shaped in plan. On each side there were four columns with gilded capitals, carrying an architrave on which crosses and lamps were set. Between these columns there were again low marble parapets – high enough, though, to hide the singers within. Two doors were provided, one at the north west and one at the south east.

Whether the colonnades and parapets on the two sides met at the west is not clear. If they did so, the only access to the western stair of the ambo would have been through the off-centre north-west door in the parapet. It seems equally likely that they did not meet, and that this stair was accessible directly from the nave floor, presumably with its own gate at the foot.

At the east, the arrangement is clearer. Silentarius concluded his description of the ambo by likening it to an island rising from the sea of the nave and joined to the mainland sanctuary by an isthmus:

> And as an island rises from the waves of the sea . . . so in the midst of the vast temple rises the towering stone ambo, adorned with its marble meadows wrought by the craftsman's art. Yet it does not stand entirely cut off in the centre of the space like a sea-girt island; it is more like some wave-washed land, projected forward through the billows by an isthmus into the middle of the sea . . .[15]

In more prosaic language, the raised plinth was continued eastward as a raised walkway to the sanctuary, protected by its own parapet. Two more doors or openings at the east end allowed passage across it in front of the chancel screen. This walkway was the solea. It had no direct equivalent in the West, though it had something in common, on the one hand, with the *schola cantorum* of some early Roman basilicas, and, on the other, with the railed-off passageway that later linked the *coro* and the sanctuary in Spanish cathedrals. In the East it is otherwise known chiefly from excavations, though there is a small

246 Detail of the carving on the lower right-hand side of the screen in the south gallery

well-preserved example of the complete arrangement of ambo, solea and chancel screen in one of the Cappadocian rockcut churches near Avcilar.

Imperial metatorion and throne

It is less easy to be certain precisely what special provisions were made in Justinian's time for his and his court's participation in the liturgy, since most of the relevant documentary evidence relates to later centuries, and the evidence to be seen in the building itself is far from clear. In his single brief reference Silentarius mentions a screened area and throne in the south aisle, but gives none of the kind of detail that helps us to visualize the other furnishings:

247 Detail of the carving on the soffit of the transom of a window in the south gallery

248 The screen in the south gallery, looking eastwards

On the south side you will see a long aisle just like that at the north, but it has something more; for it has a space set apart by a wall for the Emperor of the Romans on solemn feast days. Here my King, seated on his customary throne, gives ear to the sacred books.[16]

Paradoxically, the only surviving screen that separates a part of the church from the remainder is that between the western and central bays of the south gallery, and neither Procopius nor Silentarius makes any mention of this. They write of the galleries as if each was completely open. The carving of this screen is, however, so similar to that of the other sixth-century work that it is almost certainly of sixth-century date. Could it originally have been set similarly between the south-east main and buttress piers to separate off the eastern bay of the south aisle?

This seems unlikely. There are no signs on the facings of the piers to indicate the possible earlier attachment of such a screen to them. Equally, there are no signs of disturbance of the facings and flooring at gallery level, where the screen is now set, to suggest that it is a subsequent insertion.

In fact, the central and eastern bays of the gallery beyond the screen seem later to have been set aside largely for a variety of uses by the clergy and the emperor, who both then had direct access to them – the clergy from the patriarchate and the emperor by a high-level walkway from the palace that led to the door seen at the bottom left of a view in Chapter 2. We can only conclude that there must have been similar occasional uses of this gallery from the beginning, calling for some demarcation that was not a complete barrier and thus did not preclude other uses.

Returning to the south aisle, we may note evidence in two places of points of attachment for screens or other items of furniture now gone. The first is on the line of the two free-standing columns nearest to the south wall of the eastern bay, where there must once have been a screen enclosing an area about 3.5 m wide beside the wall. The second is immediately to the north of the south-east main pier, in the corner of the central bay that is nearest to the ambo and sanctuary. Here there are several sets of filled sockets in both the stylobate of the colonnade and the slabs of the floor behind this.

Mathews suggested that the throne was in the second of these areas, with the metatorion elsewhere, possibly further east.[17] Against this, it has been argued that the spacing of the sockets is too irregular to have served as fixings for a throne, and that there is no documentary support for such a publicly exposed location, or for different sites for throne and metatorion.[18]

Of the two sites, that against the south wall of the eastern bay seems more likely. It would have had direct access from outside, and would have afforded an adequate view of ambo and sanctuary and easy access to them, while

249 Markings in the paving immediately to the west of the main south-east pier, seen from the nave

remaining withdrawn from public gaze. It is also more likely to have appealed to Justinian's architects because an enclosure here would have been far less visually obtrusive and disruptive than one at the site suggested by Mathews.

On occasions when thrones in a more conspicuous place were called for – as, in later years, at a coronation – these could have been temporarily set further forward. An area within the south-east exedra where the original paving has been lost is one possible setting; and the large square of cosmati-like paving later inserted towards the south east in the central part of the nave was probably the final setting in the last centuries of the Empire. Later descriptions of coronations suggest that, when the throne was in this last position, there was a secondary dais in the position beside the south-west pier, to which Mathews drew attention.

The liturgy of Constantinople in the sixth century

Apart from the special provisions made for the emperor, these furnishings differed from what we know of the corresponding furnishings of contemporary and slightly earlier churches in Constantinople only in their greater size and magnificence. Similarly, the large atrium preceding a double narthex with multiple entrances, the axial plan of the church itself with side aisles and galleries and no barriers between aisles and nave, and the separate

skeuophylakion, all reflected on a larger scale and with a new architectural splendour the layout of earlier churches such as the Studios and the presumed Theodosian Hagia Sophia.[19]

Thus there is no architectural or archaeological reason to believe that there was any essential difference between the liturgy celebrated in the new church and that which had been celebrated in the Theodosian church, and which continued to be celebrated in other churches in the city. Nor do we have any other evidence that points to any such difference.

The Eucharistic liturgy

The liturgy with which we are here concerned was the celebration of the Eucharist. It was this, above all, for which non-monastic churches were designed at the time. The singing of the Divine office may have occupied more priestly time, and may have been the chief justification for some of the provisions for lighting the interior during the hours of darkness. The existence of two baptisteries at Hagia Sophia testifies to the importance, also, of the baptismal rite. But the singing of the Divine office made fewer architectural demands than the celebration of the Eucharist, and the fact that separate structures were provided for baptism means that its needs can have had little influence on the design and use of the church proper.

250 Looking down on the nave floor from the dome. North is at the top. The probable original completion of the northern half of the easternmost band of green marble is shown in broken line. Also superimposed on the pattern of the paving are the suspended lighting-hoops dating from the Fossati restoration

This Eucharistic liturgy had already acquired its basic shape in the second century – at a time when it could still be celebrated only in relative privacy by small groups of converts, possibly in the home of one of their number.[20] We know from Justin Martyr that it began with readings and a sermon or sermons by the presiding bishop. These were followed by prayers, the exchange of the kiss of Peace, the transference to the altar of the gifts of the faithful, their consecration by the bishop, communion by all present, and dismissal.

There were two clearly distinguished parts, which were sometimes separated. The readings and sermon or sermons which made up the first part were probably closely modelled on the Jewish synagogue service. The emphasis was on the ministry of the Word, and those not yet admitted to full membership – the catechumens – could attend for instruction in the Faith. The Eucharist proper which constituted the second part was more specifically Christian. Only those already admitted to full membership were allowed to participate in the communal prayer and in what followed, so that any catechumens present had to be dismissed before it began.

With the official recognition of Christianity, a number of changes inevitably occurred.[21] Attendance could now be open instead of somewhat clandestine. The numbers attending increased – in the first place, particularly the numbers of catechumens seeking full admission and of penitent apostates seeking readmission. New and larger churches were built to accommodate them, and there was a need for a more formal ordering of the proceedings. To facilitate this, clergy and laity were segregated by means of the enclosed sanctuary around the altar, and catechumens, too, seem to have been segregated when the Eucharist was to follow immediately after the ministry of the Word.

The changes did not everywhere take the same form. Differences developed between the principal sees in matters such as the ordering of the initial entry into the church, the places allotted to different groups in the congregation, and the provisions made for receiving the gifts of the faithful – originally a small loaf and a small quantity of wine from each – and then selecting and transferring to the altar those gifts to be consecrated for the communion.

The sixth-century shape

In the absence of contemporary service books, it is necessary to reconstruct the shape as it had developed in sixth-century Constantinople primarily by looking backwards from later sources – in particular the commentaries of Maximus Confessor in the *Mystagogia* written about 630, and of Patriarch Germanus in the *Historia ecclesiastica* written about a century later.[22] The major changes in the century before 630 are recorded in the *Chronicon Paschale*, and the picture that emerges can be further checked against the architectural, archaeological and documentary evidence of planning and furnishing that has already been considered.

The liturgy would have begun with a formal entry into the church.[23] This would have been led by the principal celebrant – at an important service by the patriarch, who would have been already vested in the silk patriarchal stole or pallium. But he would have been preceded by a deacon carrying the Gospel, since this was seen as representing Christ, and the Byzantine rule, unlike the Western one, was that the highest led. The other clergy would have followed, also having vested beforehand.

This entry would have been preceded by a prayer before the central door of the narthex, and would have been accompanied by an introit psalm – much as was the entry for the rededication of Hagia Sophia.

On major feasts the whole congregation would have come in procession with the clergy from another church. They would then have entered with the clergy, probably flooding through all the side doors from the narthex as the clergy (and the emperor and his court if present) entered through the central door or doors. On other occasions, they seem usually to have awaited the clerical procession in the atrium and narthex, probably being marshalled there as necessary for a seemly entrance. Sometimes, however, they may have awaited the procession in the church, being led in their singing by a few of the clergy who had entered informally ahead of it.

The clergy procession would have passed down the centre of the nave and then, on reaching the ambo, would have entered the solea. They would have passed down this and entered the sanctuary. The Gospel would have been placed on the altar and the patriarch or other principal celebrant would have ascended to his throne on the synthronon with the other clergy beside him, and would have greeted the assembled congregation.

The readings would now have followed. Whether they would have been preceded by antiphonal chants at this time is not clear. These may not have been introduced until later. At all events there would have been three readings, all from the ambo, by appointed lectors and a deacon. First a reading from the Old Testament, then the Epistle, and then the Gospel. The first two would have been accompanied by no special ceremony, but for the third the Gospel would have been ceremonially carried down the solea from the altar by the deacon, and afterwards returned to it in the same way.

This entry of the Gospel and the Gospel-reading would normally have been the climax of the first part of the service. If there was a sermon next, it would have been expected to expound the readings. The tradition was that it should be delivered by the bishop or patriarch seated in his throne while the congregation, as usual, stood.

At the conclusion of the readings and sermon, the principal celebrant and other clergy would have descended from the synthronon and moved to the altar for the second part of the service – the Eucharist proper. Meanwhile a deacon, or perhaps a priest, would have dismissed the catechumens after a prayer on their behalf, and the doors would have been closed. In the words of

251 A tenth-century representation of St Flaviano, Archbishop of Constantinople, holding the Gospel in front of the chancel screen. (Menologion of Basil II, Vatican Cod. Gr. 1613, folio 410)

Maximus Confessor:

> After the reading of the Holy Gospel, the bishop comes down from his throne and the priests dismiss the catechumens and the rest who are unworthy of the sacred sight of the mysteries that are about to be shown. . . . And there takes place the closing of the doors of the church.[24]

The Eucharist would have begun with prayers at the altar while this was made ready to receive the gifts, and while some of the deacons, taking a thurible, left to fetch them. The deacons would have proceeded to the skeuophylakion – the equivalent of the prothesis chapel or sacristy, where a suitable selection of the gifts would previously have been made ready – and would have returned with them to the altar.

At least from shortly after Justinian's time, this procession had acquired enough solemnity to be greeted by the people with a special chant – the Cherubic Hymn – when it re-entered the church:

> We who mystically represent the Cherubim and sing the thrice holy hymn to the life-giving Trinity, let us lay aside all worldly care to receive the King of All, escorted unseen by the angelic hosts. Alleluia.[25]

This hymn seems, however, to have been originally an addition to the latter part of the 24th Psalm, which, we have seen, was sung also on the way to the church for the rededication. So, in the early sixth century, the Psalm by itself probably greeted the procession.

The celebrant now moved to a position just inside the sanctuary doors, where he asked for the prayers of the other clergy. He returned to the altar for the preparatory prayer known as the *proskomide*, and, after this, gave the greeting of the Peace. The kiss of Peace would then have been exchanged by all in the church.

The ensuing central rite of the consecration of the gifts involved only the almost silent prayers and accompanying action of the celebrant and any con-celebrating clergy in the sanctuary. After the fraction, celebrant and clergy would have taken Communion. Communion would then have been given to those others present who wished to partake.

The liturgy must have ended rather as it began. After a prayer of thanksgiving and a pronouncement of dismissal, all would have left in much the same order as they came in. The celebrant and other senior clergy would normally have processed back down the solea and out through the narthex, probably to the skeuophylakion. The people would then also have left, and the sacred vessels and any residue of the consecrated gifts would have been taken back by a more direct route to the skeuophylakion.

The patriarchal liturgy in Justinian's Hagia Sophia

The similarity between the liturgy of the new church and the typical liturgy of the capital at the time does not mean that there would have been no differences in the way in which it was performed. Still less does it mean that the impact on those present would have been unchanged.

If we exclude the fact that the emperor and patriarch would have participated more frequently, the most obvious differences would have been differences of scale. The new church was much larger, was served by more clergy and, on major feasts at least, would have accommodated much larger congregations. Some indication of the numbers that may sometimes have been involved is given by the fact that, during his reign, Justinian found it necessary to limit the establishment of the Great Church to not more than 60 presbyters or priests, 100 deacons, 40 deaconesses, 90 subdeacons, 110 lectors, 25 psalmists and no less than 100 *ostiarii* or doorkeepers.[26]

There would also have been greater distances to be covered in moving from one place to another, and greater distances over which it would be necessary to project the voice intelligibly.

These differences of scale would, if nothing else, have tended to lengthen the service, especially those parts of it that involved movements.

The impact of the new architectural setting probably reached further in its ultimate effect. This, after all, must have been part of Justinian's intention in choosing to rebuild in the way he did, though it is doubtful whether the profound changes in what was experienced by those present could have been fully foreseen.

To explore these effects and their ultimate influence on the shape of the liturgy itself, we can best start by looking at certain practical aspects of the necessary adaptation to a new building, such as the allocation of the available space to different groups of those present. We shall do this chiefly in terms of the normal patriarchal liturgy, leaving imperial participation for separate consideration later.

The places of the clergy, psalmists and congregation

The principal place of the clergy was within the chancel screen in the sanctuary. There, as we have seen, were the seats for the priests and the throne of the patriarch. The ambo and solea were also reserved spaces, used chiefly in the early parts of the service. And, beneath the ambo, the professional psalmists had their place.

The sources are less informative about the allocation of the remaining space in the nave. This relative silence, coupled with the existence elsewhere of barriers between aisles and nave, allowed a belief to gain ground that it too was a reserved space from which the laity were wholly excluded except, at certain points in the service, the emperor and his retinue. Had the laity been thus confined to the aisles and galleries, they would have had even less opportunity for real participation than in the Theodosian church. But the belief has now been shown to be unjustified.[27]

Even the presence of barriers around the solea and ambo implies some presence of laity in the nave. More conclusively, Silentarius twice refers to laity there. In the first passage he refers to singers (not the professional psalmists) in the two eastern exedrae, embraced by the curved arms of their colonnades. Then, in his description of the solea, he refers to the press of people about it as the Gospel was carried along it for the Gospel-reading:

> Here the priest who brings the Gospel passes on his return from the ambo, holding up the golden book, and as the crowd surges forward in honour of the immaculate God to touch the sacred book with their lips and hands, countless moving waves of people break around.[28]

Thus, though there must have been restricted entry to the south-east exedra when the emperor was taking part in the service, and it would have been necessary at times to keep a way clear elsewhere for the clergy, it does not appear that there was any part of the nave outside the chancel, solea and ambo barriers from which the congregation was wholly excluded.

Within the remaining space it is reasonable, however, to assume that there would have been some ordering of those admitted according to rank or status. Guidance for such ordering is one possible explanation of the bands of green marble in the floor. (The other possible explanation, suggested by Majeska, is that they were to indicate intermediate stopping-places of the processions on certain occasions.[29])

At all events, it is unlikely that women would have been admitted to the nave for major services. Their place would have been in the aisles or galleries.

There can be no doubt that the aisles and galleries were given over to the lay congregation, including the emperor and his court when they were present. There are, nevertheless, conflicts and ambiguities in the record here which strongly hint at a changing pattern of use.[30] Procopius, who never mentions the use of the nave, refers to the aisles and galleries in passages that can be translated in more than one way. Essentially they read:

> There are two colonnades [*stoai*], one on each side, and these are not structurally separated from the nave in any way, but rather add to its width and extend along its whole length, without rising to its full height. . . . One of these colonnades [*stoai*] is assigned to men worshippers, while the other is used by women for the same purpose. But there is no difference or distinction between them . . .
>
> But who could describe the galleries [*hyperoa*] of the women's part [*gynaikonitis*] . . . ?[31]

Apart from the possible further (but hazardous) inference that neither men nor women initially had any place in the nave, there are two possible interpretations of the first passage taken by itself. One is to take the word *stoai* to refer solely to the two aisles. The other is to take it to refer to the two aisles-plus-galleries. But neither of these interpretations is consistent with the subsequent use of *hyperoa* in the plural to refer to the women's part.

Evagrius is equally ambiguous, in his description of the rebuilt church, in referring first in the masculine to those who wish to look down on the service from the galleries, and then stating that the Empress, presumably with her court, sometimes attended the liturgy there.[32]

Only Silentarius is completely consistent. He refers no less than four times to the galleries as the women's place, implying that only men were at ground level.[33]

Unless the surviving texts of Procopius are corrupt, it can only be concluded that he is describing alternative ways of allotting the spaces bounding the nave. And Evagrius seems to be doing the same. This suggests either a continuing flexibility, with Silentarius recording what had become the more usual practice by 562, or an initial period of experimental adaptation to a new building, leading to this practice as the norm by 562. No one who has been concerned with taking over a new building and deciding how best to use it need be surprised at the latter. It would be all the more likely here on account of the different characters of the new and old churches.

Readings, sermon, and dismissal of catechumens
In the earlier part of the service, the readings could have been intoned or chanted for greater intelligibility in the larger space. Doubts arise, though, about the practicality of delivering a sermon from the patriarchal throne in the apse. Even if this were raised as high as the available space allowed – say to the height of the present mimbar, or just below the lower central window – the throne would not even have been visible from all points in the nave, and would have been invisible from most points in the aisles and galleries. And the great distances involved, coupled with a reverberation-time for the interior of the order of 10 seconds, would have made it next to impossible to project normal speech intelligibly to the whole area.

223
252

There is, in fact, no evidence to confirm that the practice of preaching in this way was still followed in Hagia Sophia in Justinian's time, and we saw earlier that John Chrysostom had already departed from it to the extent of having a pulpit set in the nave of the first church, so that he could be better heard. Perhaps the greater difficulties in the new church were met by restricting this part of the service to a very short homily whenever there was a large congregation.

Whether the dismissal of catechumens was a reality or merely a formal observance of an earlier rubric it is not possible to say with certainty. Mathews has tentatively suggested that the galleries were originally allocated to them, largely on the grounds that (much later when the catechumenate no longer existed in its original form) these were referred to as *catechumena*, and that it would have been relatively easy to segregate people there, and then to

dismiss them without disturbing others.[34] But this evidence is very slight when set against the repeated contrary statements of Silentarius about the use of these areas, and the complete silence of all the records of Justinian's time about even the continued existence of the catechumenate. This silence suggests that it had already fallen into abeyance, and that the dismissal had become a mere formality, at least in Hagia Sophia.[35]

Offertory procession, consecration and communion
The outward route of the deacons to the skeuophylakion to fetch the gifts would have been through the left-hand or north door in the chancel screen to the external door in the east bay of the north aisle. What route they took on their return in Justinian's time, we do not know. Since, in origin, this bringing in of the gifts was a mere practical necessity brought about by the physical separation of skeuophylakion and altar, the most direct route would again seem likely initially. But we do know that by the tenth century, at least when the emperor was present, a longer route was taken via the ambo and solea,[36] and this longer route might already have been adopted much earlier.

The size of this procession must have depended partly on the number of communicants, which would determine how much plate, as well as bread and wine, had to be brought in. Even before the developments referred to below, it could have been quite large.

The consecration would have followed the procedure already outlined, differing from what would be done elsewhere only in the larger number of priests participating, and in its greater physcial remoteness from most of the congregation.

For the communion, some sort of informal procession or processions must have formed, to distribution-points by the chancel door, and perhaps also along the solea and up in the western gallery.[37]

The impact of a new scale
We must now ask what part the congregation would have been able to play in this liturgy, and what the overall impact would have been.

Certainly the part would have fallen far short of that played by members of the small groups of faithful assembled with their bishop, perhaps in the home of some patrician convert, in the days of Justin Martyr. The congregation in Justinian's Hagia Sophia could have joined in much of the singing, and some, if not all, would have been able to receive communion. But, apart from this limited participation, its role would have been a largely passive one. It would have been restricted to listening to the readings and prayers, and observing as much as could be seen of the actions of clergy, and of the emperor and court when they were present.

Some would have been much better placed than others. Those close to the sanctuary and ambo would have seen and heard most. Those further away, even in the nave, would have seen less, and may have heard little of the spoken prayers and of any sermon. Of those in the aisles and galleries, only those fairly well forward and clear of the dead areas created by the massive piers would have seen anything. Real participation from the galleries would be possible only for those right at the front. Indeed, Silentarius wrote of the women there resting their elbows on the parapets, no doubt partly to see more.

The problem was partly one of the sheer size of the building. But, for those less fortunately placed in the aisles and galleries, it would have been made worse by the intrusions of the piers, and by the depth of the galleries and their height above the floor.

In the long run, two consequences might be expected to flow from these restrictions on real participation. One was a greater emphasis on actions in the centre of the nave than on those in the sanctuary – not because these latter actions were hidden by screens or veiled by curtains but just because they were more remote. The other was a greater emphasis on singing, in which all could participate. Linked with this, it might be expected that new chants would be added to fill the greater time taken by the entries, processions, and some other parts of the service.

Though the changes in the liturgy which did ensue cannot all be attributed to the special requirements of Hagia Sophia, they were of precisely these kinds. There was a progressive filling out of the liturgy with new chants.[38] And there was an increasing emphasis on the two processions into the midst of the congregation – the ceremonial carrying of the Gospel to and from the ambo, which came to be known as the Little Entrance, and the offertory procession which developed into what came to be known as the Great Entrance.[39]

An increased emphasis on the Gospel procession is already apparent in the reference by Silentarius to the press of people to touch the book as it was carried down the solea.

The corresponding emphasis on the offertory procession probably did not develop until somewhat later. But it becomes progressively apparent, through the introduction of the Cherubic Hymn and from the commentaries of Maximus and Germanus. We find an even greater devotion shown to the as yet unconsecrated gifts than to the Gospel-book. They are treated no longer as mere bread and wine but already as symbols of Christ and his Passion, and are borne into the church by all the clergy except the patriarch himself.

In the final development, the entry became a purely symbolic circuit wholly within the church. Starting from a prothesis table somewhere to the left of the altar, it merely looped back to the altar via the solea. And, when a solid inconostatis took the place of the original open chancel screen and hid virtually everything that happened inside the sanctuary from those outside it, this Great Entrance became, for most of those present, the spectacular climax of the whole rite.

The impact of a new architectural setting

This, however, is only part of the picture, and probably not even the most important part. For the whole reaction of all present must have been coloured, above all else, by the character of the space they were in.

It would doubtless be an exaggeration to say that, for the second-century experience of shared meditation, prayer, and communion in a setting that in itself counted for nothing, had been substituted an experience of being transported to a heaven-on-earth where God himself must dwell. But the impact of the new interior cannot have been far short of this. In such a setting, it was inevitable that the liturgy would develop into more of a symbolic heavenly drama accompanied by the songs of the cherubim and the angelic hosts.

This, surely, is what underlies later symbolic interpretations of the architecture, and the reaction of the Russian emissaries that was referred to in the Introduction – which, even if historically on a par with Justinian's exclamation to Solomon, must represent a view current at the time when the chronicle was written.

Imperial participation in the liturgy

The important question of imperial participation has been left for separate discussion because virtually all the evidence is to be found in the *Book of Ceremonies* of Constantine Porphyrogenitus, which chiefly describes what was done in the early tenth century, four centuries after Justinian.

According to the *Book of Ceremonies*, the emperor at this time participated formally in the liturgy in Hagia Sophia on seventeen occasions a year, four of them being feasts introduced after the time of Justinian. For most of each service he remained on his throne in the south aisle. The introductory chapter, devoted to the normal procedures for processions to the Great Church, tells us that he participated in the first entrance-procession, and that he subsequently left his throne at three points: at the entrance of the gifts in the offertory procession, at the sharing of the Peace, and at the communion.[40]

Normally, having processed with his guard of honour and members of his court from the palace by way of the Augusteion, he would meet the patriarch and his procession in the narthex. He would first bow to the Gospel, then greet the patriarch, and then they would proceed together into the church with the emperor's guard going ahead to line up on either side of the solea. When they reached the door in the chancel screen, the patriarch would enter first while the emperor remained outside for a while, holding a lighted candle. Then he also would enter without his retinue, leave a gift on the altar, and presently leave by the right-hand door in the screen for his throne in the south aisle.

While the deacons left for the skeuophylakion to fetch the gifts, the emperor would put on a *chlamys* and, accompanied by chamberlains, senators and others, and preceded by sceptre-bearers and banners, would proceed to a point near the ambo to meet the clerical procession as it returned with the gifts. There a lamp would be handed to him and, with the chamberlains and senators, he would walk ahead of the gifts down the solea as far as the chancel door, while the sceptre-bearers and banners again formed a guard of honour.

The clerical procession now, on the evidence of later frescoes, would probably have included candle-bearers, a deacon with a thurifer, a deacon with a *flabellum* or fan, and other deacons bearing the veils of the chalices and patens, the chalices and patens containing the gifts themselves, and the great veil that would be spread over all the gifts on the altar.[41]

At the chancel door, the emperor would greet the patriarch, place the lamp beside the door, and stand there as the archdeacon censed them, and the gifts were presented to the patriarch and taken in to the altar. He would then return to his place.

For the kiss of Peace, he went forward again, this time as far as the chancel screen on the right-hand side of the sanctuary, and presumably to the door there, but remaining just outside. First the patriarch would come up to the screen to exchange the kiss, then the other principal clergy, and then the patriarch again. Subsequently, moving a little away from the screen, the emperor would exchange the kiss with members of the senate presented by the master of ceremonies.

For the communion, it is stated merely that he followed the same route as previously. It is not entirely clear how this was meant to be understood. Mathews has interpreted it as meaning that he went again to the ambo with a large retinue and then walked down the solea to the sanctuary.[42] It seems more likely that he again took the much shorter route to the right-hand side of the sanctuary that had been taken for the kiss of Peace. He certainly received communion, after the clergy but before anyone else, somewhere at this side and not at the altar itself. A later description of the Christmas ceremony adds the information that, on that occasion at least, he mounted a dais (*pulpiton*) to receive it from the hands of the patriarch, and that he again embraced the patriarch before returning to his metatorion.[43]

The liturgy cannot, at this time, always have concluded with a procession out of the church led by the patriarch, because the practice, when the emperor was present, seems to have been for the patriarch and other invited guests to breakfast immediately afterwards with him in the metatorion. The departure was then via the Holy Well situated beside the south-east porch.[44]

The empress, it will be noted, did not participate with the emperor. When she also was present she remained in the gallery, and communion was brought to her there. Also, on those occasions when the emperor was present without participating in the liturgy, he took his place in the enclosure in the south gallery (to which, as we have seen, there was a direct entry from outside) and had communion brought to him there.

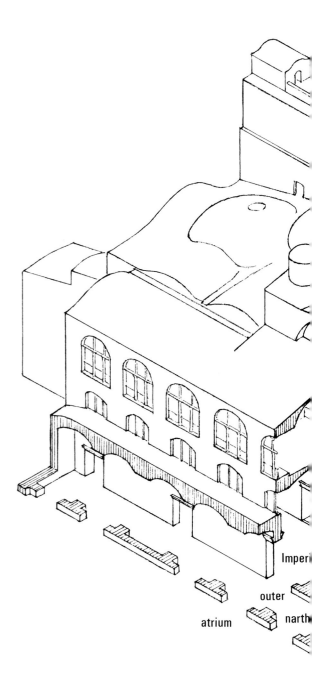

skeuophylakion an

Imperi

outer

atrium narth

252 The probable arrangement of the principal liturgical furnishings and probable location of the imperial metatorion at the time of the second dedication. Near the foot of the drawing may be seen also the location of the screen across the south gallery that is illustrated in plates 246 and 248

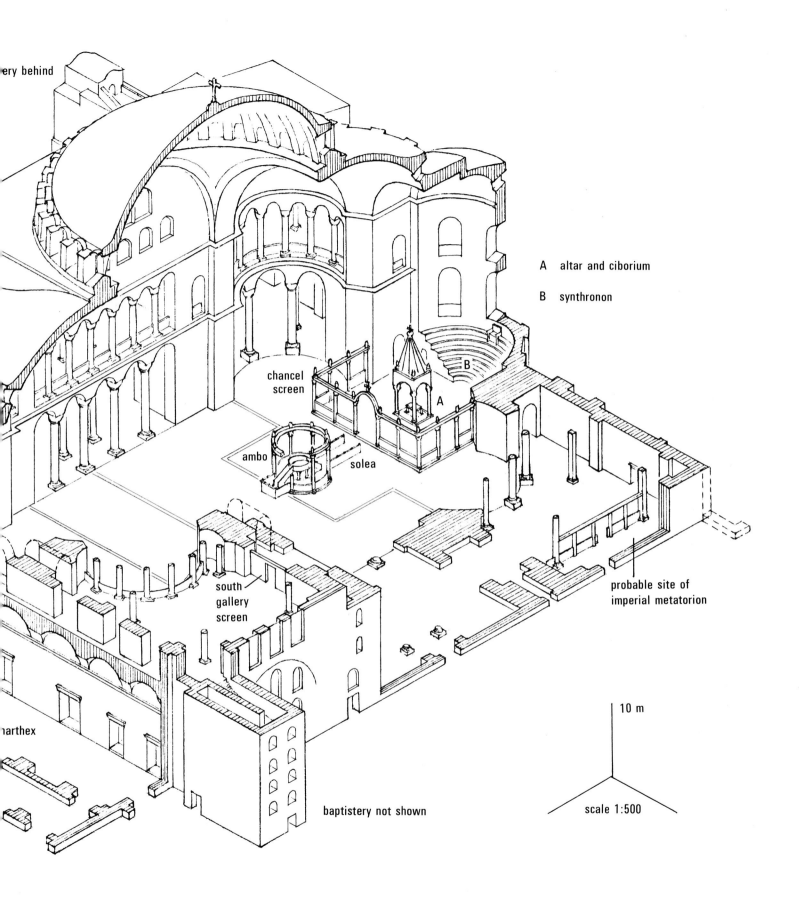

ery behind

A altar and ciborium

B synthronon

chancel
screen

ambo   solea

south
gallery
screen

probable site of
imperial metatorion

narthex

10 m

baptistery not shown

scale 1:500

Furnishing and use: architecture and liturgy   233

253 Justinian and Maximianus. (Mosaic in the apse of San Vitale, Ravenna)

Imperial participation in the sixth century

All we know for certain about the earlier practice is that, from at least the time of the *ekphrasis* of Silentarius, there was the enclosure for the imperial throne in the south aisle, and that, on the occasion of the rededication, the emperor entered the church with the patriarch.

It seems reasonable to set alongside the description of that entry the representation of Justinian with Bishop 253 Maximianus of Ravenna in the apse of San Vitale in Ravenna. This is not a portrayal of an actual ceremony in Ravenna: it must portray the type of ceremonial entrance that would have taken place at the dedication of that church if Justinian had been present, and probably also the type of entrance that did take place at the rededication of Hagia Sophia.

What we see is the procession about to enter the church. Reading from right to left we have the deacon with the Gospel accompanied by another with a thurible, the bishop carrying a jewelled cross, the emperor bearing a golden chalice as a gift, three of the assistant clergy, and finally the emperor's retinue. On the opposite wall the Empress Theodora stands in the atrium surrounded by ladies of her court, and hands another gift to one of the 254 clergy before they enter the church – whose portal is seen, with its curtain drawn aside, at the left.

From this we may conclude that when the emperor was present the entrance probably took place in much the same way in the sixth as in the tenth century.

One further crumb of evidence is a record in Sozomen – dating therefore from about 450 – that from the time of Ambrose and Theodosius it had been agreed that the emperor should no longer sit with the clergy in the sanctuary, as he had apparently sometimes done earlier.[45]

This virtual prohibition from the sanctuary does not exclude his initial entry with the patriarch at the conclusion of the entrance procession, but does raise a slight doubt about it. There is no conflict, however, with the procedures described in the *Book of Ceremonies* for the sharing of the Peace and the communion, so that there is no reason to suppose that these had undergone much change since the sixth century.

Participation in the offertory procession is more doubtful, because of the likelihood that this procession had not yet acquired its tenth-century importance.

254 Theodora and her court. (Mosaic in the apse of San Vitale, Ravenna)

The coronation ritual

As something performed only very occasionally, the coronation rite is one for which special provisions would always have been made. Since it also appears to have been first celebrated in Hagia Sophia for Constans II in 641, it calls only for a much briefer mention.

There are several accounts. The earliest, in the *Book of Ceremonies*, describes the ritual that was followed in the tenth century and a little earlier. The latest describe its final development in the fourteenth century, after it had probably absorbed certain Western elements.[46]

The rite in the tenth century was essentially a vesting and crowning performed either independently of the full liturgy or near its beginning. The new emperor would vest in *divetsion*, *tzitzakion* and *sagion* in a metatorion near the south door of the narthex. He would enter the church with the patriarch, as for the liturgy, pausing to light candles by the Imperial door, and proceeding down the solea to the chancel door. On reaching this he would pray and light other candles before turning back to the ambo and ascending it with the patriarch. There he would be further vested with the *chlamys*, and finally the crown would be placed on his head. After acclamations by the people, he would descend and proceed to a throne in the metatorion, where he would receive the homage of the magistrates, the court, and other civil and military dignitaries. If the full liturgy followed on, it was performed according to the normal practice.

By the fourteenth century two main changes had occurred. The vesting with the *chlamys* in the ambo had been replaced by an anointing. And, after the coronation proper, and after taking part in the Great Entrance procession of the ensuing liturgy, the emperor entered the sanctuary to receive communion at the altar in the same way as a priest.

What is chiefly significant here is the completion of a change from a purely secular ceremony, as the coronation probably remained in Justinian's time, to a rite closely resembling an ordination or the consecration of a bishop. Could this be one more indication of the impact of Hagia Sophia's overwhelming interior?

Opus imitabile: tempus minat' destruere: prohibet aue nostram per curam.
Sed o, rex excelse aperi nobis domum quam tempus non tangit.

ΥΜΟ ΔΟΒΜΙ
ΦΙΑ ΩΝ ΝΨΒΑΩΝ
ΣΤΑ ΤΗΙ ΘΕΑΙ

Almę sophię sapientię ut sacti in bysantio a iustiniano cęsare templum maximum & cIIII porfireis
Serpentinus ac marmoreis columnis diuersorąq nobilcu & cospicuum lapidum in signe antemio tranio
& isidoro milesio nobilibus architectorą principio.

Ab eterna templi & occidua parte figura a qua primu uestibulum atq ingressum habuisse uidetur cuius
amplitudo per lat' cubit' .c. & i. alest' uo cubit' .c.x.x. metita est.

CIVITAS ATHE

Eadem bonos
ciues cora de
corandi p mo
cosuetudinte
introducere d
uobt oscat co
nexis ratuilie
clar pericles
acctendo ca
pu pbabile
instituta sere
sti persona
intueri uelis
na & itutis
uberrimu ali
melt & honos
açpencles ded
set aq rat'
menest dade
potestas caperet

ΔΙΟΙ
ΣΙΟ
ΑΜΜ
ΩΝΙC
ΑΝΑ
ΛΥΤ
Ο
Σ

CHAPTER 10

The sixth-century achievement and its sequels

WHATEVER JUSTINIAN'S REAL OBJECTIVES in undertaking the rebuilding were, his feelings about it towards the end of his long reign must have been a mixture of elation and disillusionment – elation at what his architects had achieved and disillusionment in relation to any hopes he entertained that it would contribute significantly to unity in the Church and the rebirth of a united Empire.

There could be no doubt about the architectural achievement. But wider hopes were to remain unfulfilled, at least in the short term. Partly through his own vacillations, the rift between the Monophysite and Orthodox groups in the Church widened, preparing the ground for the rapid Muslim advance in the following century. And the rapprochement with Persia and military gains in North Africa and Italy proved to be short-lived. Though he gave the State a new sense of identity and a new focus, his military campaigns and financial policies, as well as a serious outbreak of bubonic plague in 541–2, left it economically weakened to an extent from which it never fully recovered.

Even if it had been desired to follow up the new church with others like it in scale and magnificence, there were never again the necessary resources. Indeed the edict limiting the numbers of clergy serving it suggests that its costs alone were already becoming an embarrassment within a few decades of its opening. Justinian's other major church rebuildings – of the churches of Hagia Irene and the Holy Apostles in Constantinople and of St John at Ephesus – were all undertaken less ambitiously, as we saw in Chapter 5. In each of them, several relatively small square-domed bays were simply added to one another, either in line or so as to form a cross-shaped plan.[1]

Nevertheless the influence of the new Hagia Sophia on both the liturgy and subsequent church architecture in the East was more lasting and universal than the comparable influence of any other single building. And it did materially contribute to the later spread of the Orthodox faith, much as Pope Nicholas V hoped that the rebuilding of St Peter's would contribute to the spread of Roman Catholicism.

The direct architectural influence did not end with the Ottoman conquest, but has endured to the present day wherever Orthodox Christianity has survived. Even more significantly, the great domed structure then presented to the conquerors an architectural challenge and exemplar that could not be ignored, and thereby exerted a further influence on a long series of imperial mosques.

The direct influence

We have already seen something of the influence on the liturgy. Some changes along similar lines might have taken place elsewhere even without the impetus given by performance in a new setting. Internal sacristies or prothesis chapels already existed in Syria by the late fifth century for the reception of the offerings of the faithful.[2] With them, naturally, went a much shorter offertory procession following a route more like that of the later Great Entrance. But this was really no more than an example of a different, and perhaps more convenient, way of collecting the gifts and bringing them to the altar. Something more was needed to give the procession a completely new symbolic significance, and the most powerful impetus in this direction must have come from the new setting in Hagia Sophia.

The architectural influence of the great domed interior was no less potent. The dome itself, as the culminating feature of both interior and exterior, was not new, as we have seen. Nor was its natural symbolism of the vault of heaven previously unrecognized. But it can only have been the much more powerful example of the larger church that made the centralized domed form henceforth the only appropriate one for new church buildings throughout the Byzantine Empire and the wider Orthodox world. At the same time, by demonstrating how the dome could be set on only four piers by using pendentives to bridge the spaces between their interconnecting arches, it greatly enlarged the planning options available to the architect. 256–8

In the increasingly straitened circumstances of the Empire it was necessary, however, to evolve plans appropriate to a considerably smaller scale. A common later form was a central domed square set within a larger square. Four tall arms radiating from the central square enlarged this to a cross, and the spaces between the arms of the cross were vaulted at a lower level to give the overall square plan.

In the earlier churches of this kind, the spaces between the arms were relatively small, and tended to be separated from the rest of the interior by the bulk of the main piers. 259a, b, Later, any remaining galleries were eliminated, and these 260 piers were reduced in size, often to no more than single columns in the smaller churches. The whole interior space 259c then became one, except for an apsidal sanctuary and flanking smaller apses which were now usually shut off behind the straight solid screen of a three-doored

255 Copy by Giuliano da Sangallo of interior and exterior elevations of Hagia Sophia by Cyriacus of Ancona. (Vatican Cod. Lat. Barb. 4424, folio 28)

258 Kubelli church, Soganli, Cappadocia – unusual for a rock-cut church in being domed externally as well as internally

261 iconostasis. Thus the earlier distinctions between nave and aisles and nave and galleries disappeared, to be replaced by a sharper distinction between nave and sanctuary.

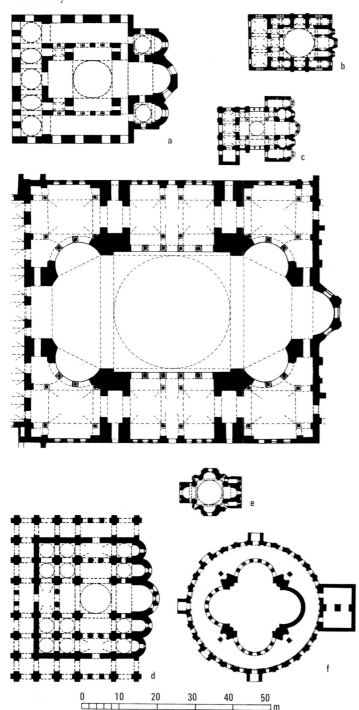

259 Justinian's Hagia Sophia (centre) compared with: **a** Hagia Sophia, Thessaloniki; **b** Daphni monastery church; **c** the original Theotokos church of Constantine Lips (Fenari Isa Camii), Istanbul; **d** Hagia Sophia, Kiev; **e** Holy Cross, Aght'amar; **f** palace chapel, Zvart'nots. (Scale 1:1000)

Since the interiors of these churches had neither the spatial quality nor the vastness of that of Hagia Sophia, they did not in themselves convey the same sense of being a heaven-on-earth. This must have been felt as a serious shortcoming because, after the end of iconoclasm, new ways were found to make it good. On the vaults and walls, cycles of iconic figural mosaics or frescoes took the place of the simple gold mosaic, decorated only with crosses and similar symbols, that had covered the vaults of Hagia Sophia. Arranged in a strictly heirarchic manner, these directly represented the Heavenly Kingdom. Christ looked down as ruler from the dome. Below this were represented those major episodes in his earthly ministry which were commemorated in the church calendar. And in the lowest registers, almost on a level with the worshippers, were portrayed the saints who had themselves more recently walked on earth.[3] 262, 263 262-

At this time, of course, Hagia Sophia received its own figural mosaics. But only the huge Pantocrator in the dome, the Virgin in the apse, and the representations of Christ's earthly ministry on the domical vaults of the side galleries, were strictly analogous.

Outside the Empire there was more variety of form. The earlier domed tetraconch survived for a time. Later the domed cross plan and various multi-domed forms were more usual.[4] 259f, 259e 267

For St Mark's in Venice, Justinian's Church of the Holy Apostles was a more direct prototype, though Hagia Sophia itself must have been the prime stimulus to depart from Italian models and emulate one from Constantinople. Today the interior of this Venetian church, though dependent again on extensive cycles of mosaic decoration for much of its impact, is the best aid to visualizing the lost richness of Hagia Sophia's interior.[5] 268

In Russia, with no tradition of masonry dome-construction, there was no suitable direct prototype for the desired counterparts of the church that was said to have so impressed Prince Vladimir's emissaries. The designers of churches like Hagia Sophia in Kiev and Hagia Sophia in Novgorod therefore attempted to achieve something of the same character, and an approximation to the desired scale, by means of a multiplicity of much smaller square domed bays. A focus was given to the ensemble by varying the sizes of the domes, and by incorporating galleries around the perimeter that left only the slightly wider bays on the central axes open for their full height. Mosaics and frescoes again covered the interiors to enhance the overall impact.[6] 259c 269–

A late extreme example of this form, before Western models largely supplanted it, was St Basil's Cathedral in Moscow.

Later still, we finally see a few attempts to model designs more directly on the single wide-spanning dome of Hagia Sophia – attempts ranging from the Refectory Church of the Pecherska Monastery in Kiev to Frank Lloyd Wright's posthumously completed Church of the Annunciation in Milwaukee.

260 Daphni monastery church from the east

261 Interior of the Holy Apostles, Athens, looking east

Facing page
262 Looking up into the dome (bottom left) and a corner bay of the side chapel, St Mary Pammakaristos (Fethiye Camii), Istanbul

263 Interior detail of Karanlik church, Göreme. The dome is above the arches in the centre. On the far wall, a representation of the Transfiguration

264 Looking up into the dome of Daphni monastery church

265 Holy Cross, Aght'amar, from the south west.

266 Looking from the ambulatory across one of the exedrae towards the altar of the palace chapel, Zvart'nots

267 Looking up into the dome of the church of the Holy Cross, Aght'amar

268 Interior of St Mark's, Venice, looking east

269 Interior of Hagia Sophia, Kiev, looking east from the gallery

270 Hagia Sophia, Novgorod, from the south

Indirect influence in the West

Outside the Empire and independent countries like Russia that had adopted the Orthodox faith, the direct influence so far considered was mostly confined to places like Venice which had close connections with Constantinople.

The fame of Justinian's church travelled further afield, however, much as knowledge of the Church of the Holy Sepulchre had done earlier. Thus we find that Abbot Suger of St Denis was delighted to learn from travellers that the church on whose partial rebuilding he had lavished such care was furnished in a manner that would stand comparison with Hagia Sophia.[7]

As far as is known, reasonably accurate drawings of the church which could serve as architectural models were first brought to the West by Cyriacus of Ancona at about the time of the fall of Constantinople. They had a sufficiently wide circulation to have been known to and copied by Giuliano de Sangallo towards the end of the fifteenth century, and it is through Giuliano's copies that they are known today.[8] Whether these drawings had any significant influence on the development at that time of the fully centralized domed church it is difficult to say, but the possibility cannot be excluded. Giuliano's Church of Sta Maria delle Carceri at Prato was the first to follow the Albertian precepts, and there are hints in his copy of Cyriacus' external elevation of his own 'improvements' to bring it more into line with these precepts. 255 271

The Ottoman sequel

Justinian's church was certainly not unknown to the

Ottomans in the century or so during which they consolidated their power, first in Bursa to the south of Constantinople and then in Edirne to the west. They never attempted then to build anything like it. Their mosques typically still consisted, as earlier Seljuk mosques had done, of a number of linked square bays. But it is noticeable that they did give increasing prominence to one or two domed bays on the main axis, flanked by smaller secondary bays, often in such a way as to give an overall T-shaped plan.

With the fall of Constantinople and the conversion of Justinian's church to serve as the first mosque, they at last had direct experience of its unique interior space, and the merits of its great unobstructed nave for their own simpler type of prayer.

From that time onwards we see them turning progressively towards a complete spatial unification of the interior under a single dominant central dome. In one important respect they went even further towards unification than Anthemius and Isidorus had done. For, having no need for separate aisles, they consciously or unconsciously treated the smaller flanking bays more as these had been treated in the later cross-in-square Byzantine church.[9]

Direct copying from Hagia Sophia initially went no further than a similar use of a semidome to expand the space under the central dome. It was first so used in the new Fatih Mosque, commissioned by Mehmet the Conqueror himself to replace the Church of the Holy Apostles, and begun in 1463. Its dome fell in 1766, and the mosque was subsequently reconstructed to a different design. But the original form is reasonably clear. One semidome only was added to the dome, on the side towards Mecca opposite the main entrance. On each side of the central space covered by dome and semidome were three similar square bays only half as wide, covered by domes at a lower level.[10]

The result cannot have been entirely satisfactory. There was no prelude on the entrance-side to the central dome. And a strong lingering suggestion of nave and aisles must have been accentuated by a huge monolithic column to each side of the central dome to provide the necessary intermediate support for two of the flanking lesser domes.

In the mosque of Mehmet's successor, Beyazit II, the principal defect was remedied by the addition of a second semidome on the entrance side, thus giving a principal vaulting system identical to that of Hagia Sophia but for the lack of smaller semidomes around the main ones. In the absence of these smaller semidomes and the exedrae beneath them, the two large semidomes were brought down to the square corners of the end bays of the 'nave' by means of pendentives. At the two sides there were smaller domed bays, as in the Fatih Mosque, though there were now four each side on account of the extra semidome on the central axis. There was also the same use of large monolithic columns beneath the dome at each side. The scale was more modest. Whereas the Fatih dome probably

271 Sta Maria delle Carceri, Prato

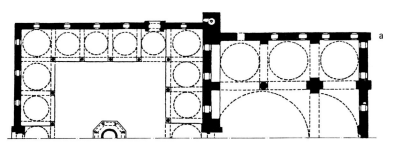

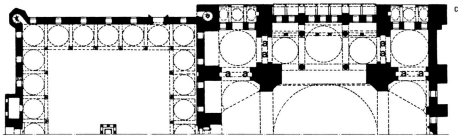

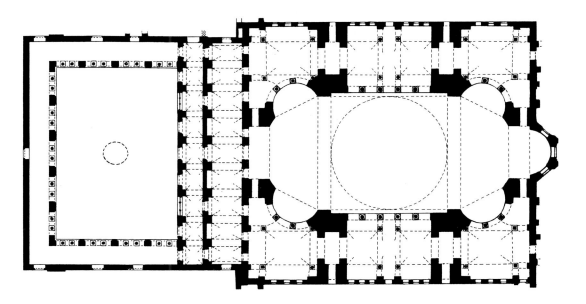

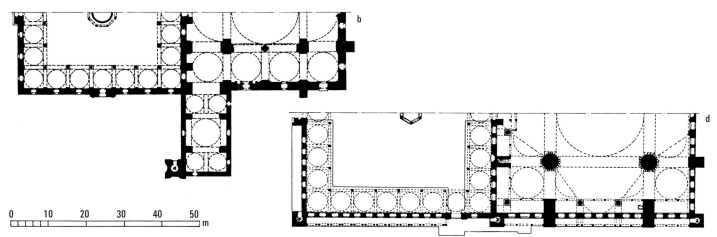

272 Hagia Sophia (centre) compared with Ottoman mosques in Istanbul: **a** the first Fatih Mosque; **b** the Mosque of Beyazit II; **c** the Suleymaniye Mosque; **d** the Mosque of Sultan Ahmet. The projections denoted by the letters a, a in **c** are referred to in the text. (Scale 1:1000)

273 The Suleymaniye Mosque from the east

approached that of Hagia Sophia in size, with a diameter of about 27 m, the Beyazit dome (which twice fell and had to be rebuilt) was little more than 17 m in diameter.

Despite the closer resemblance of the main vaulting system and the plan to those of Hagia Sophia, the design of the Beyazit Mosque nevertheless still betrayed its other origins in the simple additive arrangement of domed bays characteristic of pre-Conquest mosques. Though its interior lacked the crystalline clarity of the Green Mosque in Bursa, all the elements remained sharply distinguished. The broad transverse arches that carry the central dome project well below the semidomes, for instance, isolating and emphasizing them, and isolating in turn the bays beyond them. And there is no continuity of cornice levels, lines of fenestration, or size of arch, to unify the whole.

The full impact of Hagia Sophia becomes apparent only when we turn to the work of Sinan and his successors.[11] In Suleyman the Magnificent, Sinan had a patron who might be compared with Justinian. Of the two major mosques he built for Suleyman in Istanbul, the Sehzade and the Suleymaniye itself, it is the latter, built between 1550 and 1556, that most fully shows this impact.

It is once more on a scale approaching that of Hagia Sophia. Like the Beyazit Mosque it has a central dome with semidomes at the entrance side and at the side towards Mecca, and flanking bays with smaller, lower domes at the remaining sides. Unlike the Beyazit Mosque, however, it has a pair of smaller semidomes rising, like those of Hagia Sophia, into each main semidome. It also has three, not two, bays flanking the dome on each side.

272c, 273

The introduction of the smaller semidomes permitted the same continuity of the cornice at the springing level of the main arches as in Hagia Sophia, and a similar continuity of the lines of fenestration. But the square corners of the bays beneath the semidomes in the Beyazit design were retained, and the absence of exedrae beneath

274

The sixth-century achievement and its sequels   251

274 Interior of the Suleymaniye Mosque

275 Interior of the Suleymaniye Mosque from the corner seen at the top left of plate 272c

276 The Mosque of Sultan Ahmet from the north east

the smaller semidomes called for other transitional elements between their curved springings and the flat surfaces of the walls below. The elements chosen were essentially small pendentives, rather awkwardly related to the arches below. Perhaps to disguise this awkwardness, their surfaces were covered with stalactites, some of which cut into the faces of the arch voussoirs.

A relatively unimportant but nonetheless very telling detail is the exact correspondence of projections from the outer faces of the main piers and from the opposite faces of the answering buttress piers (marked aa on the plan) to the projections that were added to the main and buttress piers

in the aisles and galleries of Hagia Sophia. This correspondence can have resulted only from a copying of the earlier prototypes, presumably in ignorance of their origin.

The slightly earlier Sehzade Mosque, which became the model for most subsequent imperial mosques, including those of Sultan Ahmet, Yeni Valide and the rebuilt Fatih, was the first to have smaller semidomes added to the main semidomes, as in the Suleymaniye. But Sinan's other innovation here – the replacement of the smaller domed bays to each side of the central dome by further large semidome bays identical with those on the main axis – was

simply a further development of the structural system of the Beyazit Mosque. This gave a further expansion of the main central space laterally, and evaded the problems – both aesthetic and structural – of relating different systems on the two axes. It resulted in a form so similar to that of other centralized churches of the Italian Renaissance that there may have been some influence from these.

It is more difficult to say how far a study of Hagia Sophia influenced the structural design of these Ottoman mosques. Certainly there was no direct copying of construction techniques. There was a much more extensive and cautious use of cut stone for arches and vaults in place of the brick used in Hagia Sophia. Iron ties were also consistently used, not only between the springings of the smaller arches but also across the springings of the semidomes. These techniques were, in part, a straightforward continuance of previous Ottoman practice. But it is difficult to believe that good designers would not also have looked closely at the construction of Hagia Sophia and profited by the lessons of any weaknesses that they were able to identify.

Hagia Sophia, the Suleymaniye Mosque and the Mosque of Sultan Ahmet

There is today no more revealing comparison than that between the interior effects achieved by Justinian's architects and those achieved by Sinan in the Suleymaniye Mosque, and by Mehmet Aga in the Mosque of Sultan Ahmet – the two mosques that perhaps best represent the mature Ottoman response.[12] The comparison with the Suleymaniye Mosque is in some ways more telling because the differences there do not result from differences of plan, main vaulting system, and support system. In the comparison with the Mosque of Sultan Ahmet it is necessary to discount the differences stemming from its fully centralized plan, in order to isolate those of primary interest.

Essentially, the differences in architectural expression may be summed up as, first, those leading to different perceived relationships of the central to the peripheral spaces; second, those in the expression of relationships between the constituent structural elements; and, third, those between the treatments of surfaces in relation to the underlying structure. There are also differences in lighting. But these are of less interest because they result to a great extent from the later changes in the lighting of Hagia Sophia that have already been referred to. Differences of furnishing may also be passed over here.

The most striking differences are probably those affecting the perceived relationships of central and peripheral spaces.

Quite deliberately, to meet the requirement for a single large covered prayer hall, the central space in the mosques has been left as open as possible to the peripheral spaces. Thus the only boundary of which one is aware in the Mosque of Sultan Ahmet is the square boundary of the

Facing page

277 Interior of the Mosque of Sultan Ahmet

278 Looking down on the dome of the Mosque of Sultan Ahmet from the central minaret on its north-east side

279 (*Above*) Sta Maria della Consolazione, Todi

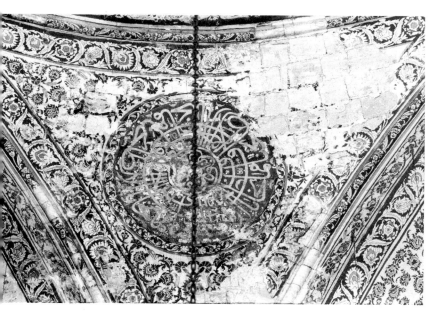

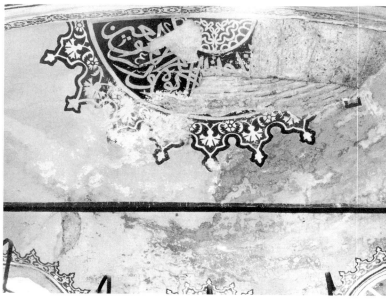

280 (*Above left*) Detail of a pendentive constructed entirely of cut stone in the Mosque of Sultan Ahmet

281 (*Above right*) Detail of a small semidome in the Mosque of Sultan Ahmet, the semidome being of brick but its forward arch of cut stone to minimize deformations due to the compression of mortar in the joints. The iron tie seen near the foot spans between the springings of the arch

282 Other iron tie bars spanning freely across arches and semidomes in the Mosque of Sultan Ahmet

Facing page
283 Looking into the nave of Hagia Sophia from the western bay of the south aisle

284 Looking towards the nave of Hagia Sophia from the western bay of the south gallery

277
274 outer wall, and this is the case, to almost the same extent, in the Suleymaniye Mosque. For this reason the squareness of the ends of the bays under the semidomes can almost escape notice.

38 In Hagia Sophia one is much more aware, when standing in the nave, of the intermediate boundary of the colonnades which mark it off from the flanking aisles and galleries. And this is a very different type of boundary. Not only is it far from square, often receding out of view behind a pier, but, where it is visible, it is far from impenetrable and somewhat ambiguous. One is always also conscious of the spaces beyond it, without being able to identify clearly their outer boundaries. In the aisles and galleries one is correspondingly aware of being outside the
39,
283–4 nave, yet never completely shut out.

Back in the nave, one is next chiefly conscious of the continuity of colonnades, arcades and cornices, and of the
38, 40 continuous sweep of the vaults high above. They are each made up of individual elements, but these elements are so related to one another as to emphasize the continuity and unity of the whole, rather than the individuality of each one.

In the mosques there is no such continuity. The elements are sharply distinguished from one another, as we saw in the earlier Beyazit Mosque. And this distinction is accentuated by differences in spans, heights and even arch profiles, where in Hagia Sophia there are no such differences, and by such juxtapositions as that of the stalactite pendentives and the smoothly curved semidomes which rise from them. Overall unity in the mosques is achieved partly, as in Hagia Sophia, by the organization of the plan, by the overall geometry of the high vaults, and by the continuous cornice at the main springing level. But, beyond this, it is achieved very differently by the symmetrical repetition of dissimilar elements.

Finally, there is the very different treatment of surfaces in relation to the underlying structure.

In the mosques, the structure is openly expressed. This is nowhere more obvious than in the great 'elephant's feet' 287 that support the central dome of the Mosque of Sultan Ahmet. But it is typical also of the entire treatment of the interiors. There is never any doubt about what is carrying what. The window-filled tympana beneath the principal lateral arches that help to carry the central dome of the Suleymaniye Mosque are, for instance, set well back from the inside faces of the arches. Their soffits are thereby 274 exposed and their structural role is emphasized.

In Hagia Sophia, on the contrary, everything seems to

285 (*Top right*) Looking up from the western bay of the north gallery of Hagia Sophia. The dome is seen beyond the exedra semidome at the right

286 (*Above*) Detail in the south-east exedra of Hagia Sophia, showing the way in which marble and mosaic are fitted to arch, wall and vault as a continuous skin

be done to hide the structure. The mass of the piers is lost in the continuity of their faces with those of the adjacent open colonnades, and the ambiguous relationship with their arcades that was noted in Chapter 2. The tympanum walls are flush with the inside faces of the main north and south arches, whose soffits are invisible internally and whose presence is therefore unsuspected. Vault similarly flows into vault without any discontinuity, 'fitted together with great skill in mid air, one floating off from another and resting only on the adjacent parts'.[13]

The manner of cutting and fitting of the marble facings of the piers, walls and arches further takes away any sense of load-bearing, as originally the continuous mosaic coverings of the vaults must also have done. Even the load-bearing function of the columns in the colonnades is played down by the failure of those at gallery level to answer to those below.

Thus the impression everywhere is not of solid structure but of continuously flowing surfaces interrupted only by seemingly insubstantial open screens.

The sixth-century achievement

This quality was summed up by Procopius when, in seeking to describe the floating impression created by the first dome, he echoed Homer's vision of Zeus suspending the whole earth from Mount Olympus:

> It seems not to rest upon solid masonry but to cover the space as if suspended from heaven by a golden chain.[14]

It is virtually unique in the great buildings that have come down to us from the past. To men unaccustomed to the feats of modern engineering – though more familiar than we are with the emphasis on the surface and the use of colour and light – it must have been all the more astounding.

It must, however, be concluded from the preceding analysis of the design and construction that the final form was not wholly intended at the outset. The basic concept of Anthemius and Isidorus was a purely geometric one – combining arched and part-spherical forms and supporting them with normal classical propriety. Changes had to be made, and with them the classical expression of the relationship of load and support that had been usual hitherto gave way to something new and very unclassical. The opportunities presented were seized to the full. And what might have been chiefly a geometric and structural *tour de force* became also something much greater. Such can be the strange alchemy of artistic creation.

287 An 'elephant's foot' pier in the Mosque of Sultan Ahmet

288 (*Facing page*) Looking across the nave of Hagia Sophia from the north west. The impression of continuity of surface would be even greater without the caesuras created by the nineteenth-century plaques with Arabic inscriptions

List of Abbreviations

AARP	*Art and archaeology research papers*
AB	*Art Bulletin*
Agathias	Agathias, *Historiae, PG*, vol. 88
AF	*Architectural Forum*
AJA	*American Journal of Archaeology*
AH	*Architectural History*
AMY	*Ayasofya Muzesi Yilligi (Annual of the Ayasofya Museum)*
Antoniades	Antoniades, E., *Ekphrasis tes Hagias Sophias*, 3 vols, Athens, 1907–9
AR	*Architectural Review*
BBI	*Bulletin of the Byzantine Institute*
Byz	*Byzantion*
BZ	*Byzantinische Zeitschrift*
CA	*Cahiers archéologiques*
CCRB	*Corsi di cultura Ravennate e Bizantina*
Cedrenus	Georgius Cedrenus, *Compendium historiarum, PG*, vol. 121
Chronicon Paschale	*Chronicon Paschale, PG*, vol. 92
De ceremoniis	Constantine Porphyrogenitus, *De ceremoniis, PG*, vol. 112. Revised edition with French translation, A. Vogt, *Le livre des cérémonies*, 2 vols, Paris, 1935
DOP	*Dumbarton Oaks Papers*
Ebersolt, *Sainte Sophie*	Ebersolt, J., *Sainte Sophie de Constantinople, Étude de topographie d'après les cérémonies*, Paris, 1910
Emerson and Van Nice *Preliminary report*	Emerson, W. and R. L. Van Nice, 'Hagia Sophia, Istanbul: preliminary report of a recent examination of the structure', *AJA*, vol. 47, 1943, pp. 403–36
Eusebius, *Historia*	Eusebius, *Historia ecclesiastica, PG*, vol. 20. Revised edition with English translation, K. Lake et al., *LCL*, 2 vols, 1926, 1932
Eusebius, *Vita*	Eusebius, *Vita Constantini, PG*, vol. 20. English translation, E. C. Richardson, *SLNPNF*, vol. 1, 1890, reprinted 1982
Evagrius	Evagrius Scholasticus, *Historia ecclesiastica, PG*, vol. 86
Fossati	Fossati, G., *Aya Sofia, Constantinople, as recently restored by order of H.M. the Sultan Abdul Mediid*, London, 1852
Germanus	Germanus Constantinopolitanus, *Historia ecclesiastica, PG*, vol. 98
Grelot	Grelot, G. J., *Relation nouvelle d'un voyage de Constantinople*, Paris, 1860
IF	*Istanbuler Forschungen*
IM	*Istanbuler Mitteilungen*
Janin	Janin, R., *Le géographie ecclésiastique de l'empire byzantine: Constantinople, les églises et les monastères*, Paris, 1969
JOB	*Jahrbuch der Osterreichischen Byzantinistik*
JRIBA	*Journal of the Royal Institute of British Architects*
JRS	*Journal of Roman Studies*
JSAH	*Journal of the Society of Architectural Historians*
LCL	*Loeb Classical Library*, London and Cambridge, Mass.
Lethaby and Swainson	Lethaby, W. R., and H. Swainson, *The church of Sancta Sophia, Constantinople*, London, 1894
Mainstone, *Developments*	*Developments in structural form*, London and Cambridge, Mass., 1975, reprinted 1983
Mainstone, *Repair and strengthening*	Mainstone, R. J. (for Working Group F of UNIDO/UNDP Project RER/79/015), *Repair and strengthening of historical monuments and buildings in urban nuclei. Building construction under seismic conditions in the Balkan region*, vol. 6, Vienna, 1984
Malalas	Ioannes Malalas, *Chronographia, PG*, vol. 97
Mango, *Documents*	Mango, C., *The art of the Byzantine empire 312–1453*, Englewood Cliffs, 1972
Mango, *Materials*	Mango, C., *Materials for the study of the mosaics of St. Sophia at Istanbul*, Washington, DC, 1962
Mathews, *Churches*	Mathews, T. F., *The Byzantine churches of Istanbul*, University Park, 1976
Mathews, *Early churches*	Mathews, T. F., *The early churches of Constantinople; architecture and liturgy*, University Park, 1971
Maximus Confessor	Maximus Confessor, *Mystagogia, PG*, vol. 91

Narratio	*Narratio de structura templi S. Sophiae*, in Preger, T., *Scriptores originum Constantinopolitanarum*, Leipzig, 1901, vol. 1, pp. 74–108. Partial translation in Mango, *Documents*, pp. 96–102
OCP	*Orientalia Christiana Periodica*
Palladius	Palladius, *Dialogus de vita Ioannes Chrysostom*, *PG*, vol. 47
PBA	*Proceedings of the British Academy*
PBSR	*Papers of the British School at Rome*
PG	*Patrologia Graeca*, ed. J.-P. Migne, Paris, 1844–66
Procopius	Procopius, *De aedificiis*, *PG*, vol. 87. Revised edition with English translation, H. B. Dewing and G. Downey, *LCL*, 1959
RAC	*Rivista di archeologia cristiana*
REB	*Revue des études byzantines*
RK	*Repertorium für Kunstwissenschaft*
Salzenberg	Salzenberg, W., *Altchristliche Baudenkmale von Constantinopel vom V bis XII Jahrhundert*, Berlin, 1854
Sanpaolesi, *Hagia Sofia*	Sanpaolesi, P., *Sancta Sofia a Constantinopoli*, series *Forma e colore*, Florence, 1965
Schneider, *Grabung*	Schneider, A. M., *Die Grabung in Westhof der Sophienkirche zu Istanbul*, *IF*, vol. 12, Berlin, 1941
Silentarius, *ecclesia*	Paulus Silentarius, *Descriptio ecclesiae*
Silentarius, *ambon*	*sanctae Sophiae et ambonis*, *PG*, vol. 86. Revised edition with German translation, P. Friedlander, *Johannes von Gaza und Paulus Silentarius*, Leipzig and Berlin, 1912. Partial translation in Mango, *Documents*, pp. 80–96
SLNPNF	*Select library of Nicene and post-Nicene fathers of the Christian Church*, 2nd series, edited P. Schaff and H. Wace, reprinted Grand Rapids, Mich.
Socrates	Socrates, *Historia ecclesiastica*, *PG*, vol. 67. English translation, A. C. Zenos, *SLNPNF*, vol. 2, reprinted 1979, pp. 1–178.
Sozomen	Sozomen, *Historia ecclesiastica*, *PG*, vol. 67. English translation, C. D. Hartranft, *SLNPNF*, vol. 2, reprinted 1979, pp. 239–427
Strube, *Eingangsseite*	Strube, C., *Die westliche Eingangsseite der Kirchen von Konstaninopel in justinianscher Zeit*, Wiesbaden, 1973, pp. 13–105
Survey	Van Nice, R. L., *St Sophia in Istanbul; an architectural survey*, Washington, 1st instalment 1965, 2nd instalment due 1986
Swift, *Hagia Sophia*	Swift, E. H., *Hagia Sophia*, New York, 1940
TAD	*Turk Arkeoloj Dergisi*
Theophanes	Theophane, *Chronographia*, *PG*, vol. 108

Notes on the Text

1 Introduction

1 *Narratio*, 27.
2 *Procopius*, I, i, 27–30.
3 *Procopius*, I, i, 34.
4 *Procopius*, I, i, 54–61.
5 *The Russian Primary Chronicle*, translated and edited by S. H. Cross and O. P. Sherbowitz-Wetzor, Cambridge, Mass., 1953, p. 111.
6 Clemens, S. L., *The Innocents Abroad*, Hartford, Conn., 1869.
7 *Survey* and other publications referred to in Chapters 3, 4, 5, 7 and 8.
8 In drawing on these resources it is important to remember that a masonry structure like Hagia Sophia does not behave in the same manner as most modern structures of steel and concrete, and that the interpretation of what has happened in the past calls for a different approach from that appropriate to the design of a new structure. These factors have not been sufficiently recognized in much recent literature. My own views were presented at the 1973 Joint Meeting of the Societies of Architectural Historians of the USA and Great Britain (Mainstone, 'Structural analysis and historical interpretation', abstract in *JSAH*, vol. 33, 1974, p. 166) and full publication is intended shortly. A summary of the present possibilities for the analysis of seismic response is given in Mainstone, *Repair and strengthening*, 89–95.

2 The church today: exterior and interior

1 For these bronze doors see Bertelli, C., 'Notizia preliminare sul restauro di alcune porte di S. Sofia a Istanbul', *Bolletino dell' Istituto Centrale de Restauro*, vol. 34/35, 1958, pp. 95/115.
2 Swift, E. H., 'The bronze doors of the Gate of the Horologion at Hagia Sophia', *AB*, vol. 19, 1937, pp. 137–47.
3 Fully illustrated descriptions of this and the other mosaics mentioned below will be found in the works cited under the heading 'mosaics' in the Bibliography.
4 For fuller descriptions of the marble columns, capitals, facings and other details see Lethaby and Swainson, *Sancta Sophia*; Swift, *Hagia Sophia*; and Hawkins, E. J. W., 'Plaster and stucco cornices in Hagia Sophia, Istanbul', *12ᵉ Congrès internationale des études byzantines*, 1964, vol. 3, pp. 131–5. See also, now, Strube, *Polyeuktoskirche und Hagia Sofia: umbildung und Anflösung antiker Formen, Entstehen des Kämpferkapitells*, Munich, 1984.
5 These rooms are described further in Cormack, R. and E. J. W. Hawkins, 'The mosaics of St Sophia at Istanbul: the rooms above the southwest vestibule and ramp', *DOP*, vol. 31, 1977, pp. 175–251, and in Mango, *Mosaics*, pp. 44–6.
6 Mango, op. cit., pp. 38–9.

3 The church today: materials and structural systems

1 For the available information on the geology of the site see Chaput, E., *Voyages d'études géologiques et géomorphique en Turquie*, Paris, 1936, and Sayar, M. and C., *The geology of the area within the ancient walls of Istanbul, Turkey*, Istanbul, 1962.
2 For further details of the marbles used see Lethaby and Swainson, *Sancta Sophia*, pp. 234–63, and for the brickwork Emerson and Van Nice, *Preliminary Report*, pp. 416–23.
3 See also Emerson, W. and R. L. Van Nice, 'Hagia Sophia: The construction of the second dome and its later repairs', *Archaeology*, vol. 4, 1951, p. 169, fig. 13, for the reconstructed eastern arch.
4 *Narratio*, 14.
5 This has been shown most recently in tests by Professor Penelis at the Aristotelis University of Thessaloniki.
6 Choisy, A., *L'art de bâtir chez les Byzantines*, Paris, 1883, pp. 121–2.

4 Looking back

1 Goodyear, W. H., *Vertical curves and other architectural refinements in the Gothic cathedrals and churches of northern France and in early Byzantine churches at Constantinople*, New York, 1904.
2 Notably Conant, K. J., 'The first dome of St Sophia and its rebuilding', *BBI*, vol. 1, 1946, pp. 71–8; and Warren, J., 'Greek mathematics and the architects to Justinian', *AARP*, December 1976.
3 The most relevant C14 dates are those for specimens UCLA 562–564 (*Radiocarbon*, vol. 7, 1965, p. 351), M 1942–1945 (*Radiocarbon*, vol. 10, 1968, p. 109), and SI 778–782 (*Radiocarbon*, vol. 15, 1973, p. 399), though it is important to remember that the dates are subject to considerable margins of uncertainty, and give directly only ages of the timber and not dates of insertion in the structure. It may in future be possible to supplement them by more precise ages obtained from dendrochronological studies now in progress. See, in this connection, Kuniholm, P. I. and C. L. Striker, 'Dendrochronological investigations at St Sophia in Istanbul: a preliminary report', *AMY*, vol. 10, in the press (due for publication in 1985).
4 Agathias, *PG*, vol. 88, cols 1556–7.
5 Malalas, *PG*, vol. 97, cols 708–9 and 716 (the mention of '30 feet higher' in the latter reference being presumably a copyist's slip, substituting λ for κ).
6 Theophanes, *PG*, vol. 108, col. 509.
7 Cedrenus, *PG*, vol. 121, col. 737.
8 The extensive and sometimes contradictory documentary evidence for these collapses and the subsequent reconstructions is cited and elucidated in Mango, *Materials*, pp. 76–7 and 66–7, and, for the latter only, in Sevcenko, I., 'Notes on Stephen, the Novgorodian pilgrim to Constantinople in the XIV century', *Südost-Forschungen*, vol. 12, 1953, pp. 165–75.
9 These sections were first clearly identified by Van Nice, as reported in Emerson and Van Nice, *Preliminary Report*, pp. 423–36.
10 Sevcenko, I., op. cit., note 8.
11 Underwood, P. A. and E. J. W. Hawkins, 'The mosaics of Hagia Sophia at Istanbul 1959–60. The portrait of the Emperor Alexander', *DOP*, vol. 15, 1961, pp. 212–13.
12 These and the full subsequent investigation are described in Mainstone, R. J., 'The reconstruction of the tympana of St Sophia at Istanbul', *DOP*, vol. 23/24, 1969–70, pp. 355–68.
13 Quoted by Emerson, W. and R. L. Van Nice, 'Hagia Sophia and the first minaret erected after the conquest of Constantinople', *AJA*, vol. 54, 1950, pp. 33–4.
14 Mango, *Materials*, pp. 11–16.
15 Nicephorus Gregoras, *PG*, vol. 148, col. 448.
16 Swift, E. H., 'The Latins at Hagia Sophia', *AJA*, vol. 39, 1935, pp. 458–74, and *Hagia Sophia*, pp. 87–8, 117–19.
17 Plan no. [29] 6 and sectional elevations nos [29] 18 and 19 in the forthcoming final (T–Z) volume of the RIBA Drawings Catalogue.
18 Text reproduced in Mango, *Materials*, pp. 107–12.
19 Text reproduced in Mango, *Materials*, pp. 112–16.
20 Janin, R., 'Le palais patriarcal de Constantinople byzantine', *REB*, vol. 20, 1962, pp. 131–155.
21 Dirimtekin, F., 'Le local du Patriarcat à Sainte Sophie', *IM*, vol. 13/14, 1963–4, pp. 113–27.
22 Cormack, R. and Hawkins, E. J. W., 'The mosaics of St Sophia at Istanbul: the rooms above the southwest vestibule and ramp', *DOP*, vol. 31, 1977, pp. 175–251.

23 Mango, C., *The Brazen House*, Copenhagen, 1959, pp. 60–72.
24 Schneider, A. M., *Grabung*.
25 Emerson, W. and R. L. Van Nice, 'Hagia Sophia and the first minaret erected after the conquest of Constantinople', *AJA*, vol. 54, 1950, pp. 28–40.
26 Goodwin, G., *A history of Ottoman architecture*, London, 1971, pp. 280–1.
27 Eyice, S., 'Le baptistère de Sainte Sophie d'Istanbul', *9° Congresso di Archeologia Cristiana*, 1975, vol. 2, pp. 270–1.
28 Hawkins, E. J. W., 'Plaster and stucco cornices in Hagia Sophia, Istanbul', *12ᵉ Congrès internationale des études byzantines*, 1964, vol. 3, pp. 131–35.
29 Cormack, R. and E. J. W. Hawkins, 'The mosaics of St Sophia at Istanbul: the rooms above the southwest vestibule and ramp', *DOP*, vol. 31, 1977, pp. 175–251.
30 Mango, *Materials*, is the best reference for the history as a whole. Cormack, R., 'Interpreting the mosaics of S. Sophia at Istanbul', *Art History*, vol. 4, 1981, pp. 131–49 is a more recent critical appraisal. Only the principal publications devoted to particular mosaics are referred to in the following notes.
31 Mango, C. and E. J. W. Hawkins, 'The apse mosaic of St Sophia at Istanbul', *DOP*, vol. 19, 1965, pp. 11–51.
32 Mango, C. and E. J. W. Hawkins, 'The mosaics of St Sophia at Istanbul. The church fathers in the north tympanum', *DOP*, vol. 26, 1972, pp. 1–41.
33 Whittemore, T., *The mosaics of St Sophia at Istanbul 1931–2. The mosaics of the narthex*, Oxford, 1933; Oikonomides, N., 'Leo VI and the narthex mosaic of Saint Sophia', *DOP*, vol. 30, 1976, pp. 151–72; and Brekenridge, J. D., 'Christ on the lyre-backed throne', *DOP*, vol. 34/35, 1980–1, 247–60.
34 Whittemore, T., *The mosaics of St Sophia at Istanbul 1933–4. The mosaics of the southern vestibule*, Oxford, 1936.
35 Underwood, P. A. and E. J. W. Hawkins, 'The mosaics of Hagia Sophia at Istanbul 1959–60. The portrait of the Emperor Alexander', *DOP*, vol. 15, 1961, pp. 187–217; and Whittemore, T., *The mosaics of St Sophia at Istanbul 1935–8. The imperial portraits of the south gallery*, Oxford, 1942.
36 Whittemore, T., *The mosaics of St Sophia at Istanbul, 1934–8. The Deisis panel of the south gallery*, Oxford, 1952. A further study by Cormack is in the press (see Bibliography).
37 Mango, *Materials*, pp. 13–15.
38 Silentarius, *ecclesia*, lines 590–616.
39 op. cit., note 24. There is a view of a part of the colonnade, since disappeared, in Wulff, O., *Altchristliche und Byzantinische Kunst*, vol. 2, Berlin, 1914, figure 327.
40 Silentarius, *ecclesia*, lines 563–6.
41 *De ceremoniis*, II, 22 and Ebersolt, *Sainte Sophie*, pp. 33–35.
42 Silentarius, *ecclesia*, lines 533–7.
43 op.cit., note 12.
44 op.cit., note 2.
45 Silentarius, *ecclesia*, lines 810–38.
46 Silentarius, *ecclesia*, lines 884–7.
47 Silentarius, *ecclesia*, lines 668–70.
48 Silentarius, *ecclesia*, lines 506–8.
49 Procopius, I, i, 54.
50 Procopius, I, i, 56.
51 Procopius, I, i, 54.
52 Downey, G., 'The composition of Procopius, De aedificiis', *Transactions of the American Philological Association*, vol. 78, 1947, pp. 171–183; idem, 'Notes on Procopius, De aedificiis, Book I', *Studies presented to D. M. Robinson on his seventieth birthday*, vol. 2, St Louis, 1953, pp. 719–25.
53 Traquair, R., 'The origin of the pendentive', *JRIBA*, vol. 35, 1927–28, pp. 185–7.
54 Procopius, I, i, 41–5.
55 Antoniades, vol. 3, pp. 99–104.
56 op.cit., note 2.

5 The church before Justinian

1 Barnes, T. D., *The new empire of Diocletian and Constantine*, Cambridge, Mass., 1982, chapter V, lists the known imperial residences and journeys.

2 Baynes, N. H., *Constantine the Great and the Christian Church*, 2nd edn., London, 1972, is the best analysis of this complex subject and includes very full references to the relevant sources. Barnes, T. D., *Constantine and Eusebius*, Cambridge, Mass., 1981, deals more specifically with Constantine's relations with the Eastern Church. See also Shepherd, M. H., 'Liturgical expressions of the Constantinian triumph', *DOP*, vol. 21, 1967, pp. 59–78.
3 Krautheimer, R., *Rome. Profile of a city, 312–1308*, Princeton, NJ, 1980, pp. 3–31. See also Krautheimer, R., S. Corbett and A. K. Frazer, *Corpus Basilicarum Christianarium Romae*, vol. 5, Vatican City, 1977; and Krautheimer, R., *Three Christian Capitals*, Berkeley, 1983.
4 Eusebius, *Vita*, III, xxv–xlii, xlviii, l–liii and lviii–lx.
5 Dagron, G., *Naissance d'une capitale. Constantinople et ses institutions de 330 à 451*, Paris, 1974, is the principal recent source for the early history of the city. But now *see also* Mango, C., *Le développement urbain de Constantinople (IVᵉ–VIIᵉ siècles)*, Paris, 1985, which appeared only after the present text was completed.
6 Eusebius *Vita*, III, xlviii.
7 Eusebius *Vita*, III, lviii–lx.
8 Socrates, I, xvi.
9 Socrates, I, xxxvii and II, vi.
10 Socrates, II, xvi.
11 Socrates, II, xliii.
12 *Chronicon Paschale*, *PG*, vol. 92, col. 737.
13 Notably by Millet, G., 'Sainte-Sophie avant Justinian', *OCP*, vol. 13, 1947, pp. 597–612.
14 Cedrenus, *PG*, vol. 121, cols 544, 577.
15 Zosimus, *Historia Nova*, II, xxxii.
16 Cedrenus, *PG*, vol. 121, col. 561.
17 Cedrenus, *PG*, vol. 121, col. 569.
18 Cedrenus, *PG*, vol. 121, cols 577–80.
19 Downey, G., 'The name of the church of St Sophia in Constantinople', *Harvard Theological Review*, vol. 52, 1959, pp. 37–41; Cameron, A., 'Procopius and the church of St Sophia', *ibid.*, vol. 58, 1965, pp. 161–3: and Janin, *Églises*, pp. 455–6.
20 Percival, H. R., *The seven ecumenical councils*, SLNPNF, vol. 14, 1899, pp. 178–9. See also Honigman, E., 'Juvenal of Jerusalem', *DOP*, vol. 5, 1950, pp. 272–4, on the introduction of the patriarchates.
21 Socrates, VI, xv–xviii, and Sozomen, VIII, xvii–xxii.
22 *Chronicon Paschale*, *PG*, vol. 92, col. 788.
23 *Chronicon Paschale*, *PG*, vol. 92, col. 784.
24 Procopius, *Wars*, I, xxiv; Malalas, *PG*, vol. 97, col. 689–92. See also Bury, J. B., *A history of the later Roman Empire*, vol. 2, London, 1923, pp. 39–48; and Stein, E., *Histoire du Bas-Empire*, Paris, Brussels and Amsterdam, vol. 2, 1959, pp. 449–54.
25 Procopius, I, i, 20–2.
26 *Narratio*, 1, and Nicephorus Callistus, *Ecclesiastica historia*, XVII, x, *PG*, vol. 147, col. 244.
27 Eusebius, *Historia*, X, iv.
28 Procopius, I, i, 22.
29 Procopius, I, ii, 13.
30 Procopius, V, i, 6.
31 *Chronicon Paschale*, *PG*, vol. 92, col. 876 and Theophanes, *PG*, vol. 108, col. 425.
32 Palladius, *De vita S. Joannis Chrysostomi*, *PG*, vol. 47, cols. 35–6.
33 Socrates, VI, v, and Sozomen, VIII, v.
34 Joannis Chrysostom, *In psalmum XLVIII*, *PG*, vol. 55, col. 508. See also Symeon Metaphrastes, *Vita S. Joannis Chrysostomi*, *PG*, vol. 114, col. 1113.
35 loc.cit., note 12.
36 Schneider, *Grabung*.
37 Then briefly reported only in Mamboury, E., 'Les fouilles Byzantines à Istanbul: les sondages à l'intérieur de Ste-Sophie', *Byz*, vol. 21, 1951, pp. 437–8, and illustrated in idem, *The tourist's Istanbul*, Istanbul, 1953, p. 280. See now *Survey*, plates 9 and 10.
38 Schneider's view was first challenged in a review by A. S. Keck of Swift, *Hagia Sophia* in *AB*, vol. 23, 1941, pp. 237–40.
39 For the Church of the Holy Sepulchre, Corbo, V. C., *Il Santo Sepulcro di Gerusaleme*, Jerusalem, 1981, supersedes all previous studies. It should be noted, however, that the front of the Theodosian church was not necessarily parallel to that of the present church. The remains of foundation walls beneath the present nave floor (which are referred to below) are equally consistent with alignments corresponding closely to

that of the colonnade. Such alignments are also suggested by the alignments of several of the surviving peripheral structures of Justinian's church – notably those of the north-west ramp, of the eastern terminations of the north-east ramp and the eastern porches, and of the baptistery.

40   Turkoglu, S., 'Ayasofya skevophilakionu kazisi', *AMY*, vol. 9, 1983, pp. 25–35. The evidence for identification is discussed by various authors including Ebersolt, *Saint Sophie*, pp. 32–5 and, most recently, Mathews, *Early churches*, pp. 158–60.

41   Dirimtekin, F., 'Le skeuophylakion de Sainte-Sophie', *REB*, vol. 19, 1961, pp. 390–400.

42   Pallas, D., *Les monuments paléochrétiens en Grèce découverts de 1959 à 1973*, Rome, 1977; Mentzos, A., *Symbole sten ereuna tou archaioterou naou tes Agias Sophias Thessalonikes*, Thessaloniki, 1981.

6   Justinian's church: his objectives and the architectural brief

1   Krautheimer, R., S. Corbett and A. K. Frazer, *Corpus Basilicarum Christianarum Romae*, vol. 5, Vatican City, 1977, pp. 104–5, 145–6.

2   Sotiriou, G. and M., *Hi basiliki tou Hagiou Dimitriou tis Thessalonikis*, Athens, 1952.

3   op.cit., chapter 5, note 31.

4   Manetto, J., *Vita Nicolai summi pontificis*, III, in Muratoris, L. A., *Rerum italicarum scriptores*, vol. 3, part 2, Milan, 1734, pp. 949–50 (free translation of part of a considerably longer text).

5   For Justininan generally and the historical background see Browning, R., *Justinian and Theodora*, London, 1971; Bury, J. B., *A history of the later Roman Empire from the death of Theodosius I to the death of Justinian*, 2 vols, London, 1923, Stein, E., *Histoire du Bas-Empire*, Paris, Brussels, Amsterdam, 2 vols, 1949–59; and Ure, P. N., *Justinian and his age*, Harmondsworth, 1951. Also Procopius, *Secret History*, *LCL*, 1935.

6   Downey, G., *Constantinople in the age of Justinian*, Norman, Oklahoma, 1960.

7   Meyendorf, J., 'Justinian, the empire and the church', *DOP*, vol. 22, 1968, pp. 45–60.

8   A series of preliminary reports by Professor Harrison, 'Excavations at Sarachane in Istanbul', *DOP*, vol. 19, 1965, pp. 230–6; vol. 20, 1966, pp. 222–38; and vol. 21, 1967, pp. 273–8, will shortly be superseded by the definitive publication now in the press (see Bibliography). See also Mango, C. and I. Sevcenko, 'Remains of the church of St Polyeuktos at Constantinople', *DOP*, vol. 15, 1961, pp. 243–7.

9   As suggested in Harrison, M., 'Solomon's Temple and excavations in Byzantium', *New Scientist*, 10 February 1983, 388–9.

10   For Justinian's building activities generally see Downey, G., 'Justinian as builder', *AB*, vol. 32, 1950, pp. 262–6; and for Procopius' account of them, idem, 'Notes on Procopius, *De aedificiis*, Book I', *Studies presented to D. M. Robertson on his seventieth birthday*, vol. 2, St Louis 1953, pp. 719–25. The Holy See's counterpart to the accounts of Justinian's buildings by Procopius and Silentarius was Costaguti, G. B. and M. Ferabosco, *Libro de l'architettura di San Pietro in Vaticano finito col disegno di Michel Angelo Bonaroto et d'altri architetti espressa in piu tavole da Martino Ferabosco*, Rome, 1st edn, 1620, 2nd edn, 1684.

11   For these churches see Krautheimer, R., S. Corbett and A. K. Frazer, op.cit.; and Corbo, V. C., *Il Santo Sepulcro di Gerusaleme*, Jerusalem, 1981. For the Constantinian basilica generally see Krautheimer, R., 'The Constantinian basilica', *DOP*, vol. 21, 1967, pp. 117–40; idem, 'Constantine's church foundations', *Akten des VII International Kongresses für Christliche Archäologie Trier 1965*, 1969, pp. 237–55; and Ward-Perkins, J. B., 'Constantine and the origins of the Christian basilica', *PBSR*, vol. 22, 1954, pp. 69–90.

12   Eusebius, *Vita*, III, 1.

13   Evagrius, VI, viii.

14   For tentative reconstructions see Birnbaum, A., 'Die Oktagon von Antiochia, Nazianz und Nyssa', *RK*, vol. 36, 1913, pp. 181–209; and Dynes, W., 'The first Christian palace church type', *Marsyas*, vol. 11, 1964, pp. 1–9. See also Downey, G., *A history of Antioch in Syria from Seleucus to the Arab conquest*, Princeton, NJ, 1961, pp. 342–9.

15   Smith, E. B., *The dome: a study in the history of ideas*, Princeton, 1950; Lehmann, K., 'The dome of heaven', *AB*, vol. 27, 1945, pp. 1–27; and, as a partial corrective to Lehmann, Mathews, T. F., 'Cracks in

Lehmann's "Dome of Heaven"', *Source notes in the history of art*, vol. 1, 1982, pp. 12–16.

16   The possibility is discussed more widely in Lavin, I., 'The house of the Lord: aspects of the role of palace triclinia in the architecture of Late Antiquity and the Early Middle Ages', *AB*, vol. 44, 1962, pp. 1–27.

17   The principal publication on the original church is Calderini, A., G. Chierici and C. Cecchelli, *La basilica di S. Lorezno Maggiore in Milano*, Milan, 1951. Of the proposed reconstructions of the superstructure I prefer that of Kleinbauer, W. E., '"Aedita in turribus": The superstructure of the early Christian church of S. Lorenzo in Milan', *Gesta*, vol. 15, 1976, pp. 1–9.

18   See, for instance, Crowfoot, J. W., *Churches at Bosra and Samaria-Sebaste*, London, 1937, British School of Archaeology in Jerusalem Supplementary Paper 4; idem, *Early churches in Palestine*, London, 1941; and Kleinbauer, W. E., 'The origin and functions of the aisled tetraconch churches in Syria and northern Mesopotamia', *DOP*, vol. 27, 1973, pp. 91–114.

19   Sisson, M. 'The Stoa of Hadrian at Athens; Pt IV: The central building in the court', *PBSR*, vol. 11, 1929, pp. 66–71.

20   For the latter see Grabar, A., *Martyrium: recherches sur le culte des reliques et l'art chrétien antique*, 2 vols plus 1 vol. plates, Paris, 1943–6; Verzone, P., 'Il martyrium ottagono a Hierapolis di Frigia: relazione preliminare', *Palladio*, NS, vol. 10, 1960, pp. 1–20; idem, 'Hierapolis Christiana', *CCRB*, vol. 12, 1965, pp. 613–27; and Krencker, D. and R. Naumann, *Die Wallfahrtskirche des Simeon Stylites in Kal'at Sim'an*, Berlin, 1939, Abhandlungen der Preussischen Akademie der Wissenschaften.

21   Krautheimer, R., *Rome. Profile of a city, 312–1308*, Princeton, NJ, 1980, pp. 33–45.

22   Eubesius, *Vita*, III, xxxi–xxxii.

23   Agathias, *PG*, vol. 88, col. 1556.

24   For these see, for instance, Licht, K. de F., *The Rotunda in Rome*, Copenhagen, 1968, Jutland Archaeological Society Publications VIII; Minoprio, A., 'A restoration of the Basilica of Constantine, Rome', *PBSR*, vol. 12, 1932, pp. 1–25; and Palladio, A., *Fabbriche antiche disegnate da Andrea Palladio Vicentino e date in luce da Riccardo Conte di Burlington*, London, 1730. Also, passim, Nash, E., *Pictorial dictionary of ancient Rome*, 2 vols, London, 2nd edn, 1968; and Ward-Perkins, J. B., *Roman imperial architecture*, Harmondsworth, 2nd edn, 1981.

25   McVey, K. E., 'The domed church as microcosm: literary roots of an architectural symbol', *DOP*, vol. 37, 1983, pp. 91–121, gives the full text with translation.

26   The fullest publication remains that of Sanpaolesi, P., 'La chiesa di SS. Sergio e Bacco a Constantinopoli', *Rivista dell'Istituto Nazionale d'Archeologia e Storia dell'Arte*, NS vol. 10, 1961, pp. 116–80, though the structure still waits a full investigation and several of Sanpaolesi's conclusions are questionable.

27   The most recent publication is Mango, C., 'The church of Sts Sergius and Bacchus once again', *BZ*, vol. 68, 1975, pp. 385–92, which contains a more comprehensive summary of the known facts than can be given here. Mango argues for a later foundation than I am suggesting.

28   Procopius, I, i, 24 and I, i, 50; Agathias, *PG*, vol. 88, cols 1549, 1552.

29   Downey, G., 'Byzantine architects, their training and methods', *Byz*, vol. 18, 1946–8, pp. 99–118.

30   See also Huxley, G. L., *Anthemius of Tralles: a study in later Greek geometry*, Cambridge, Mass., 1959; and Downey, G., 'Pappus of Alexandria on architectural studies', *Isis*, vol. 38, 1948, pp. 197–200.

31   Procopius, II, iii, 6–13.

32   *Narratio*, 7. For the parallel with Brunelleschi see Mainstone, R. J., 'Brunelleschi's dome', *AR*, vol. 162, 1977, pp. 156–66.

7   Justinian's church: the initial development of the design

1   There may, nevertheless, still be difficulties, in arranging the drawings in correct sequence and assessing their relative significance. For St Peter's the principal successive plans were published in Letarouilly, P. *Le Vatican et la basilique de Sainte-Pierre de Rome*, vol. 1, Paris, 1883, and for St Paul's the majority of the drawings now known were reproduced in *The Wren Society*, vols 1–3 and 13, London 1924–6 and 1936, with a catalogue in vol. 20, 1943. There are also, for St Peter's, numerous drawings of the church under construction reproduced in Egger, H., *Römische Veduten*, vol. 1, Vienna and Leipzig, 1911, and Huelsen, C. and H. Egger, *Die römischen Skizzenbücher von Martin van Heemskerck*, 2 vols, Berlin, 1913–16.

2 I have attempted to analyse part of the process in a number of previous publications including Mainstone, R. J., 'The springs of structural invention', *JRIBA*, vol. 70, 1963, pp. 57–71 (revised version 'Intuition and the springs of structural invention', *VIA*, vol. 2, 1973, pp. 42–63) and idem, *Developments*.

3 See especially Forsyth, G. H., 'Architectural notes on a trip through Cilicia', *DOP*, vol. 11, 1957, pp. 223–36; and Herzfeld, E. and S. Guyer, *Meriamlik and Korykos*, Manchester, 1930, Monumenta Asiae Minoris Antiqua, vol. II.

4 Most of the relevant structures are described in Swift, E. H., *Roman sources of Christian art*, New York, 1951, pp. 111–25: and Creswell, K. A. C., *Early Muslim architecture*, vol. 1, part 2, 2nd edn, Oxford, 1969, pp. 450–71, though with excessively polarized attributions of the basic idea to West and East respectively and a highly questionable analysis of the dimensions of the pendentives of Hagia Sophia by Creswell.

5 Creswell, K. A. C., *Early Muslim architecture*, vol. 2, Oxford, 1940, pp. 101–18, similarly describes the principal structures that exhibit early squinches. For Firuzbad and Sarvistan, see also Dieulafoy, M., *L'art antique de la Perse*, vol. 4: *Les monuments voutés de l'époque achéménide*, Paris, 1885; and, on the matter of definition, Mainstone, R. J., 'Squinches and pendentives: comments on some problems of definition', *AARP*, vol. 4, 1973, pp. 131–7 (with an unfortunate omission of one line on p. 131).

6 This review is amplified in some respects in Mainstone, *Developments*, and idem, *Repair and strengthening*, pp. 17–77.

7 Archimedes, *On the equilibrium of planes*, in Heath, T. L., *The works of Archimedes*, Cambridge, 1897, pp. 189–220. See also Heath, T. L., *A manual of Greek mathematics*, Oxford, 1931.

8 See again the works cited in note 2, and Mainstone, R. J., 'Structural theory and design before 1742', *AR*, vol. 143, 1968, pp. 303–10.

9 The evidence is discussed further with fuller references in the first work cited in note 6, especially pp. 99–104, 113–28, 168–9 and 194–206. The principal references only are repeated here. For Roman precedents generally see Choisy, A., *L'art de bâtir chez les Romains*, Paris, 1872; Blake, M. E., *Ancient Roman construction in Italy from the prehistoric period to Augustus*, Washington, DC, 1947; idem, *Roman construction in Italy from Tiberius through the Flavians*, Washington, DC, 1959; idem and D. T. Bishop, *Roman construction in Italy from Nerva through the Antonines*, Philadelphia, 1973; and Lugli, G., *La tecnica edilizia romana con particolare riguardo a Roma e Lazio*, 2 vols, Rome, 1957. MacDonald, W., 'Some implications of later Roman construction.', *JSAH*, vol. 17, 1958, pp. 2–8; and Ward-Perkins, J. B., 'Notes on the structure and building methods of early Byzantine architecture' in *The Great Palace of the Byzantine Emperors*, ed. D. Talbot Rice, Edinburgh, 1958, pp. 52–104, continue the story and include precedents outside Italy.

10 Numerous examples of comparatively recent date are illustrated and discussed together with a discussion of construction procedures in Séjourné, P., *Grandes voûtes*, vol. 5, Bourges, 1914, 132–77.

11 Terenzio, A., 'La restoration du Pantheon de Rome', *Museion*, vol. 20, 1932, pp. 52–7; and Licht, K. de F., *The Rotunda in Rome*, Copenhagen, 1968, Jutland Archaeological Society Publications VIII; pp. 133–46.

12 Maiuri, A., 'Il restauro di una sala termale a Baia', *Bolletino d'Arte*, vol. 10, 1930, pp. 241–53.

13 Caraffa, G., *La cupola della sala decagona degli Horti Linciani restauri 1942*, Rome, 1944.

14 Bovini, G., 'L'impiego dei tubi fittili nelle volte degli edifici ravennati', *Felix Ravenna*, vol. 81, 1959–60, pp. 78–99; and Kostof, S., *The Orthodox Baptistery in Ravenna*, New Haven and London, 1965.

15 Penelis, G. et al., *Restoration and strengthening of the Rotonda*, Thessaloniki, 1980.

16 Naumann, R., 'Der antike Rundbau beim Myrelaion und der Palast Romanos I. Lekapenos', *IM*, vol. 16, 1966, pp. 199–216.

17 Sanpaolesi, P., 'Strutture a cupola autoportante', *Palladio*, vol. 21, 1971, pp. 3–64, is a wider-ranging tentative exploration of the possibilities. But it is open to a number of criticisms.

18 Gregory of Nyssa, Epistola XXV, *PG*, vol. 46, col. 1097. Choisy, A., *L'art de bâtir chez les Byzantines*, Paris 1883, pp. 59–72, describes

some of the procedures used.

19 See for instance, Butler, H. C., *Early churches in Syria*, Princeton, 1929.

20 By the author – as yet unpublished.

21 Examples of the most relevant types of construction are described and illustrated more fully in Ward-Perkins, op.cit., note 9.

22 Wilcox, R. P., *Timber and iron reinforcement in early buildings*, London, 1981, merely collects some of the scattered references in the literature. Much more investigation is called for.

23 See for instance, Balanos, N. M., *Les monuments de l'Acropole*, Paris, 1938; Livadefs, C. J., 'The structural iron of the Parthenon', *Journal of the Iron and Steel Institute*, vol. 182, 1956, pp. 49–66; and Lugli, op.cit., note 9, pp. 239–41.

24 It is also in sharp contrast to the wide deviations found in the leading dimensions of Sts Sergius and Bacchus. See Underwood, P., 'Some principles of measure in the architecture of the period of Justinian', *CA*, vol. 3, pp. 64–74.

25 Evagrius, *PG*, vol. 86, cols. 2760–1.

26 This differs slightly from the figure of 0.3123 metres previously derived by Antoniades, E., *Ekphrasis tes Hagias Sophias*, vol. 1, Athens, 1907, p. 77. See also Schilbach, E., *Byzantinische metrologie*, Munich, 1970, pp. 13–16.

27 loc.cit., note 25.

28 The likelihood that the columns were reused stems partly from the variations in size and the apparently damaged state of some of them, and partly from descriptions of imperial sarcophagi which suggest that porphyry ceased to be quarried in about the middle of the previous century (Mango, C., *Byzantine architecture*, New York, 1976, p. 24). The *Narratio*, 2, states that they came from Aurelian's Temple of the Sun. A drawing by Palladio reproduced in Zorzi, G., *I disegni delle antichita di Andrea Palladio*, Venice, 1958, fig. 68, shows, in the centre of a large rectangular court, a round temple surrounded by sixteen columns whose size and spacing do correspond fairly closely to those of the exedrae columns in Hagia Sophia, and shows further columns of similar size in an outer court. Most would have been taken away by the time that Palladio saw the temple in the sixteenth century, and it is by no means impossible that some did find their way to Constantinople.

8 Justinian's church: further development of the design, construction and first partial reconstruction

1 Cedrenus, *PG*, vol. 121, col. 712, records the start. See below for the dedication.

2 By Curtis and Aristaches, as noted in Lethaby and Swainson, p. 296.

3 *Narratio*, 8.

4 Emerson and Van Nice, *Preliminary report*, pp. 407–11.

5 Procopius, I, i, 51–53.

6 Silentarius, *ecclesia*, lines 476–80.

7 Silentarius, *ecclesia*, lines 454–6.

8 Hormann, H., et al., 'Die Johanneskirche', *Forschungen in Ephesos*, vol. 4, pt. 3, Vienna, 1951.

9 For marble quarrying generally see Ward-Perkins, J. B., 'Tripolitania and the marble trade', *JRS*, vol. 41, 1951, pp. 89–104; and Mango, C., *Byzantine architecture*, New York, 1976, p. 24.

10 Silentarius, *ecclesia*, lines 392–4.

11 *Narratio*, 11.

12 Emerson and Van Nice, *Preliminary report*, p. 420.

13 Procopius, I, i, , 68–74.

14 Robertson, D. S., 'The completion of the Loeb Procopius', *Classical Review*, vol. 55, 1941, pp. 79–84. Dewey and Downey suggested the translation 'props' in the second reference only.

15 Procopius, I, i, 37.

16 Procopius, I, i, 74–7.

17 Choisy, A., *L'art de bâtir chez les Byzantines*, Paris 1883, pp. 61–4, 72–3.

18 See Chapter 4.

19 Mundell, M., 'Monophysite church decoration', *Iconoclasm*, ed. A. Bryer and J. Herrin, Birmingham, 1977, p. 70.

20 Theophanes, *PG*, vol. 108, col. 480.

21 *Narratio*, 27.

22 Malalas, *PG*, vol. 97, cols 705–8.

23 Malalas, *PG*, vol. 97, cols 708–9; Theophanes, *PG*, vol. 108, col.

509; Cedrenus, *PG*, vol. 121, col. 737. For the Isaurians see Mango, C., 'Isaurian builders', *Polychronion. Festschrift F. Dolger*, Heidelberg, 1966, pp. 358–65.

24 op.cit., note 20; and Downey, G., 'Earthquakes at Constantinople and vicinity AD 342–1454', *Speculum*, vol. 30, 1955, p. 598.

25 The data have mostly been published in reports intended only for limited circulation or in specialist journals. An important general study, now somewhat outdated, is Gutenberg, B. and C. F. Richter, *Seismicity of the earth and associated phenomena*, Princeton, NJ, 1954. Data up to 1964 are tabulated and plotted in Ergin, K., U. Guclu, and Z. Uz, *A catalogue of earthquakes for Turkey and surrounding area*, Istanbul, 1967. Recent assessments are Ambraseys, N. N., 'Value of historical records of earthquakes', *Nature*, vol. 232, 1971, pp. 375–9; idem, *Studies in historical seismicity and tectonics*; and Yara, R., O. Ergunay, M. Erdik and F. Gulkan, 'A preliminary probablistic assessment of the seismic hazard in Turkey', *Proceedings of the seventh world conference of earthquake engineering, Istanbul, 1980*, vol. 1, pp. 309–16.

26 Mainstone, *Repair and strengthening*, pp. 17–77.

27 Silentarius, *ecclesia*, lines 186–204.

28 Agathias, *PG*, vol. 88, col. 1556. See also Chapter 4 p. 90.

29 *Narratio*, 28.

30 Cedrenus, *PG*, vol. 121, col. 737.

9 Furnishings and use: architecture and liturgy

1 Theophanes, *PG*, vol. 108, col. 520. (I have given the version of the Psalm which appears in the Vulgate because this seems to correspond better to the Greek, though less faithful to the original Hebrew.)

2 Silentarius, *ecclesia*, lines 286–95.

3 Silentarius, *ecclesia*, lines 319–49.

4 Silentarius, *ecclesia*, lines 362–8.

5 Silentarius, *ecclesia*, lines 682–719 and 871–83.

6 Silentarius, *ecclesia*, lines 720–51.

7 Silentarius, *ecclesia*, lines 752–805.

8 Silentarius, *ambon*, lines 50–231.

9 Silentarius, *ambon*, lines 232–96.

10 Initially, in Xydis, S. G., 'The chancel barrier, solea and ambo of Hagia Sophia', *AB*, vol. 29, 1947, pp. 1–24.

11 Majeska, G. P., 'Notes on the archeology of St Sophia at Constantinople: the green marble bands on the floor', *DOP*, vol. 32, 1978, pp. 299–308. See also Mathews, *Early churches*, pp. 96–98.

12 Naumann, R. and H. Belting, 'Die Euphemia-Kirche am Hippodrom zu Istanbul und ihre Fresken', *IF*, vol. 25, 1966.

13 Mathews, op.cit., pp. 23–7.

14 *De ceremoniis*, I, 1, Vogt, vol. 1, pp. 18, 27. See also ibid., 1, 9, Vogt, vol. 1, p. 59.

15 Silentarius, *ambon*, lines 224–36.

16 Silentarius, *ecclesia*, lines 580–5.

17 Mathews, op.cit., p. 134.

18 Strube, C., Review of Mathews, *Early churches*, *BZ*, vol. 67, 1974, p. 412.

19 Mathews, op.cit., pp. 38–9.

20 Dix, G. *The shape of the liturgy*, London, 2nd end, 1945, pp. 36–155.

21 Shepherd, M. H., 'Liturgical expressions of the Constantinian triumph', *DOP*, vol. 21, 1967, pp. 59–78.

22 See especially Taft, R., 'The liturgy of the Great Church: an initial synthesis of structure and interpretation on the eve of iconoclasm', *DOP*, vol. 34/35, 1980–1, pp. 45–75, citing all relevant sources.

23 Discussed in more detail in Mathews, op.cit.; Mateos, J., *Célébration de la parole dans la liturgie byzantine*, Rome, 1971, Orientalia Christiana Analecta, p. 191; and Strube, *Eingangsseite*.

24 Maximus Confessor, *Mystagogia*, XIV, XV, *PG*, vol. 91, cols. 692–3.

25 Cedrenus, *PG*, vol. 121, col. 748. For the entrance generally see Taft, R., *The Great Entrance*, Rome, 1975, Orientalia Christiana Analecta, 200, 1978.

26 *Justinian novellae*, ed. R. Schoell and W. Kroll, Berlin, 1928, iii, 1.

27 Notably in Mathews, op.cit., pp. 117–25, though his views have been challenged in more detail by Mathews and Strube, op.cit., and that relating to the place of women and catechumens has more recently been

28 Silentarius, lines 247–51.

29 Majeska, op.cit., note 11.

30 The evidence is discussed by Mathews and Strube, op.cit., and that relating to the place of women and catechumens has more recently been well summarised and analysed by Taft in a review of Strube, *Eingangsseite, OCP*, vol. 42, 1976, pp. 296–303.

31 Procopius, I, i, 55–8.

32 Evagrius, *PG*, vol. 86, col. 2760.

33 Silentarius, *ecclesia*, lines 389, 537–41, 562, 586–9.

34 Mathews, op.cit., pp. 125–30.

35 See also Taft, op.cit., note 30, p. 302.

36 *De ceremoniis*, I, 1, Vogt, vol. 1, pp. 12–13.

37 This procession is a common theme of the mosaic or fresco decoration of the walls of the apse above the altar. There are (or were until recently) good surviving examples of the former in Hagia Sophia and the Church of the Archangel Michael in Kiev, and of the latter in churches such as Sopocani at Mistra, the Perebleptos at Mistra and the Assumption at Volotovo. Earlier representations, almost contemporary with Justinian, occur on the Riha and Stuma patens.

38 Taft, R., 'How liturgies grow', *OCP*, vol. 43, 1977, pp. 355–78.

39 Mateos, op.cit., note 23; and Taft, op.cit., note 25.

41 The lack of earlier representations paralleling the earlier ones of the communion is probably a reflection of the late growth of emphasis on the entrance. There are later representations in the Perebleptos at Mistra, in several churches on Mount Athos, and in the main church at Gelati in Georgia.

42 Mathews, op.cit., pp. 172–3.

43 *De ceremoniis*, I, 32, Vogt, vol. 1, p. 124.

44 *De ceremoniis*, I,1, Vogt, vol. 1, pp. 13–14.

45 Sozomen, VII, xxv.

46 *De ceremoniis*, II, 47, Vogt, vol. 2, pp. 1–5; and, among the later sources, especially Ioannes VI Cantacuzenus, *Historia*, I, xli, *PG*, vol. 153, cols 276–90. See also, for the later ceremony, G. P. Majeska, 'St Sophia and the liturgy of imperial coronation', a contribution to the 1979 Dumbarton Oaks Symposium.

10 The sixth-century achievement and its sequels

1 For Hagia Irene see also Peschlow, U., *Die Irenenkirche in Istanbul: untersuchungen zur Architektur*, Tubingen, 1977; and for St John, Hormann, H., et al., 'Die Johanneskirche', *Forschungen in Ephesos*, vol. 4, part 3, Vienna, 1951.

2 Butler, H. C., *Early churches in Syria*, Princeton, 1929; and Mathews, *Early churches*, p. 106.

3 Demus, O., *Byzantine mosaic decoration*, London, 1947.

4 See for instance, Kleinbauer, W. E., 'Zvart'nots and the origins of Christian architecture in Armenia', *AB*, vol. 54, 1972, pp. 245–62; and Der Nersessian, S., *Aght'amar*, Cambridge, Mass., 1965. Krautheimer, R., *Early Christian and Byzantine architecture*, Harmondsworth, 3rd edn, 1979; and Mango, C., *Byzantine architecture*, New York, 1976, describe more fully the whole development both inside and outside the empire.

5 Demus, O., *The church of San Marco*, Washington, DC, 1960.

6 Hamilton, G. H., *The art and architecture of Russia*, Harmondsworth, 1954; Faenson, H. and V. Ivanov, *Early Russian architecture*, London, 1975.

7 Panofsky, E., *Abbot Suger on the Abbey Church of St-Denis and its treasures*, Princeton, NJ, 2nd edn, 1979, pp. 64–5.

8 Huelsen, C., *Il libro di Giuliano da Sangallo*, Leipzig, 1910, pp. 37–9. See also Lotz, W., *Studies in Italian Renaissance architecture*, Cambridge, Mass., 1977, p. 6.

9 Goodwin, G., *A history of Ottoman architecture*, London, 1971, is the best overall account, without, however, much reference to the influence of Hagia Sophia. See also Vogt-Goknil, U., *Les mosques turques*, Zurich, 1953.

10 Aga-Oglu, M., 'The Fatih mosque at Constantinople', *AB*, vol. 12, 1930, pp. 179–95; Kunter, H. and A. S. Ulgen, *Fatih Camii ve Bizans Sarnici*, Istanbul, 1939.

11 Egli, E., *Sinan, der Baumeister osmanischer Glanzeit*, Zurich, 1954; and Corbett, S., 'Sinan', *AR*, vol. 113, 1953, pp. 290–7. For the mosques discussed here see Vogt-Goknil and Goodwin, op.cit.

12 Charles, M. A., Hagia Sophia and the great imperial mosques', *AB*, vol. 12, 1930, pp. 321–45, gives a very perceptive account of the principal differences, broadly on the same lines as here.

13 Procopius, I, i, 47.

14 Procopius, I, i, 46, echoing the *Iliad*, VIII, 19 (edited with English translation, A. T. Murray, *LCL*, London, 1924, pp. 338–40).

Appendix: Plans, Elevations and Sections

(Scale 1mm: 2 Byzantine ft)

The Theodosian church

A1 Plan of the known earlier remains (shown in heavy line) at the west end of Justinian's church (shown stippled).

Justinian's church

A2 Plan of Justinian's church at ground level.
A3 Plan of Justinian's church at gallery level.
A4 Part-plans of Justinian's church at the levels of the upper cornice and, inset in the lower half, the dome cornice.
A5 South elevation of Justinian's church and longitudinal section through the south aisle, looking north.
A6 Further longitudinal sections of Justinian's church, looking north. These sections are taken on the longitudinal centre-line and through the north aisle.
A7 Partial west elevation of Justinian's church and transverse sections of the west end, including the baptistery, looking east.
A8 Further transverse sections of Justinian's church looking east. These sections are taken on the transverse centre-line, through the eastern bay of the north aisle and the skeuophylakion, and through the eastern main and buttress piers.

In all these drawings the church is shown, as far as possible, as it may be assumed that it was intended to appear immediately after the first partial reconstruction. Thus it is shown with the rebuilt dome and heightened dome base, but without any of the unintended distortions that permitted the collapse, and necessitated the adoption of a slightly non-circular plan for the rebuilt dome, as described in Chapter 8.

In the plans and sections, the materials of the piers, walls, arches and vaults are indicated by hatching. In the plans, the principal known ties are also shown, including some probably original ones below the floor of the west gallery whose end-anchorages only are now visible, and the probably very early added ties around the upper cornices of the western exedrae. Other original ties which may exist within the masonry at the levels of the cornices, or as continuations of the visible ties at springing levels, are not shown because there is no visible evidence of their presence. Reflected plans of arches and vaults are shown in light dashed lines. Features whose form can be shown only somewhat speculatively on account of subsequent changes are distinguished by being shown in broken outline where this would not merely lead to confusion.

Later changes and additions to Justinian's church

A9 Plan of principal changes and additions at ground level.
A10 Plan of principal changes and additions at gallery level.

In these plans Justinian's church is shown in light outline and the principal changes and additions are superimposed in heavy outline, the fillings of openings in the piers and walls being also marked by hatching, as are the minaret bases. Not all the minor Turkish structures built against the exterior are included. Those that are are shown in light outline, like the church itself. They are shown more fully in Plates 1 and 2 of Van Nice, *Survey*, which were the principal source for their depiction here.

Mosaics

A11 Plan at ground level with reflected plans of the arches and vaults, showing the extent of surviving non-figural mosaic decoration of these arches and vaults, and the locations of surviving later figural mosaics in the lunettes above two of the entrance doors.
A12 Plan at gallery level with reflected plans of the arches and vaults there, and of the higher vaults and with inset details of three niches at the foot of the north tympanum, showing the extent of the principal surviving non-figural mosaic decoration of the arches and vaults, and the locations of surviving later figural mosaics and of some others now lost.

The church as shown here is essentially Justinian's church, but with the later Byzantine changes and additions at the south west that provided the settings for some of the decorations.

Not all the survivals shown are complete and fully exposed, and there are more fragmentary survivals not shown – for instance in the room opening off the western gallery and containing the smaller Deisis, and in the small chapel entered from the gallery through the south-west buttress pier. Other figural mosaics, now lost or not yet re-exposed, are recorded as having existed on the tympanum walls and on the main eastern and western arches that carry the dome.

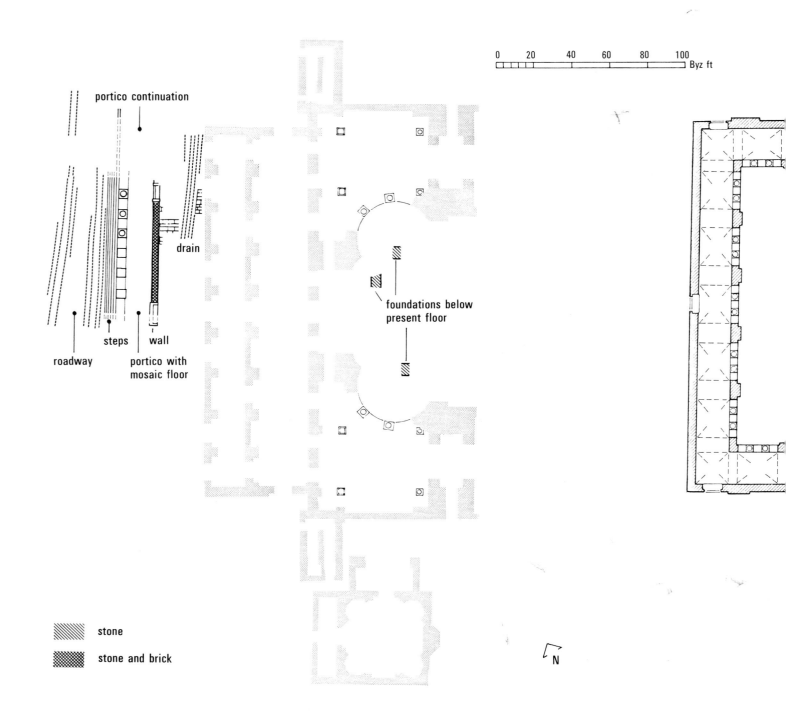

A1 Plan of the known earlier remains (shown in heavy line) at the west end of Justinian's church (shown stippled)

Within the figure:

portico continuation

drain

steps

wall

roadway

portico with mosaic floor

foundations below present floor

0 20 40 60 80 100 Byz ft

stone

stone and brick

N

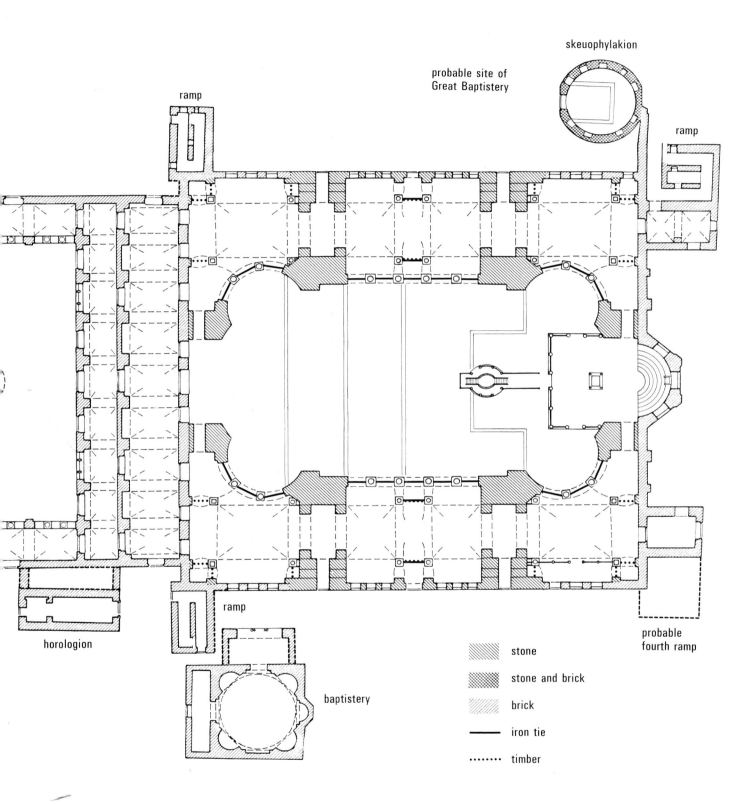

skeuophylakion

probable site of
Great Baptistery

ramp

ramp

ramp

horologion

ramp

baptistery

probable
fourth ramp

	stone
	stone and brick
	brick
	iron tie
....	timber

A2 Plan of Justinian's church at ground level

271

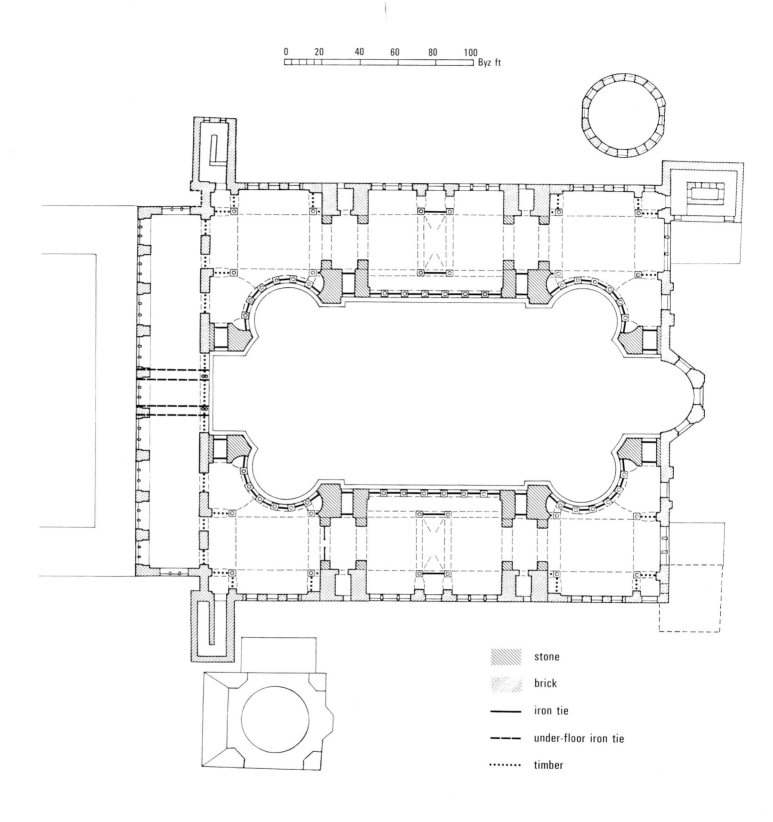

A3 Plan of Justinian's church at gallery level

stone

brick

———— iron tie

– – – – under-floor iron tie

········ timber

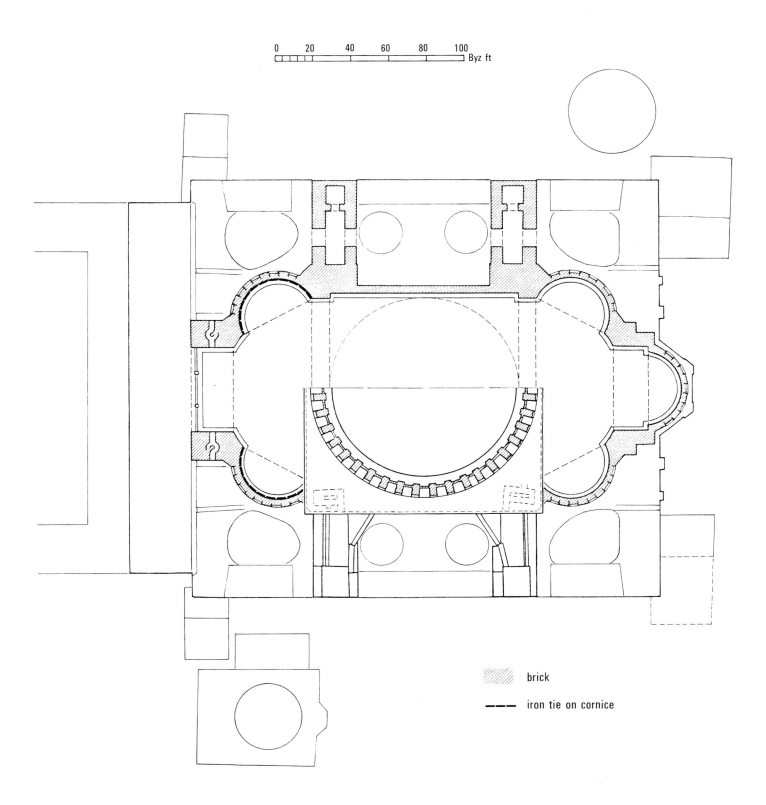

A4 Part plans of Justinian's church at the levels of the upper cornice and, inset in the lower half, the dome cornice

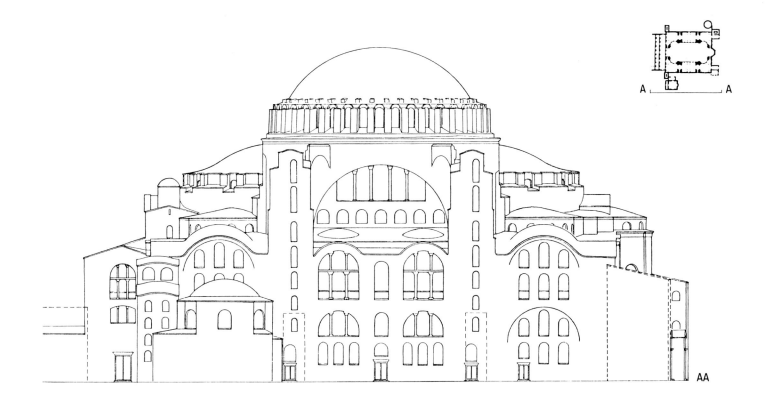

0   20   40   60   80   100
                              Byz ft

▨ stone

▨ brick

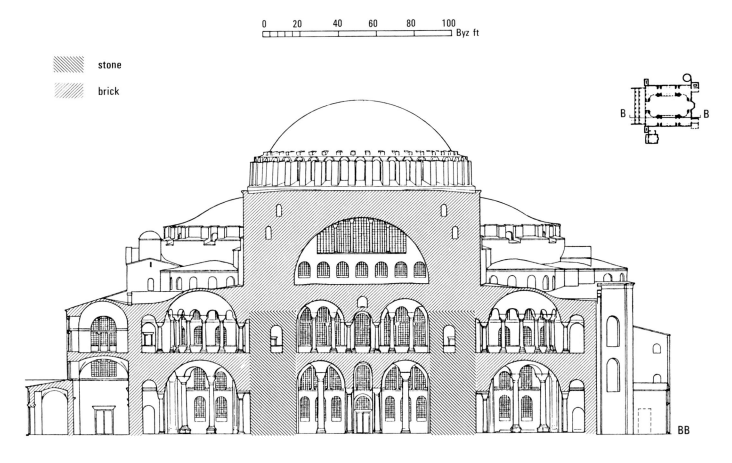

A5 South elevation of Justinian's church and longitudinal section through the south aisle, looking north

0 20 40 60 80 100
Byz ft

stone

brick

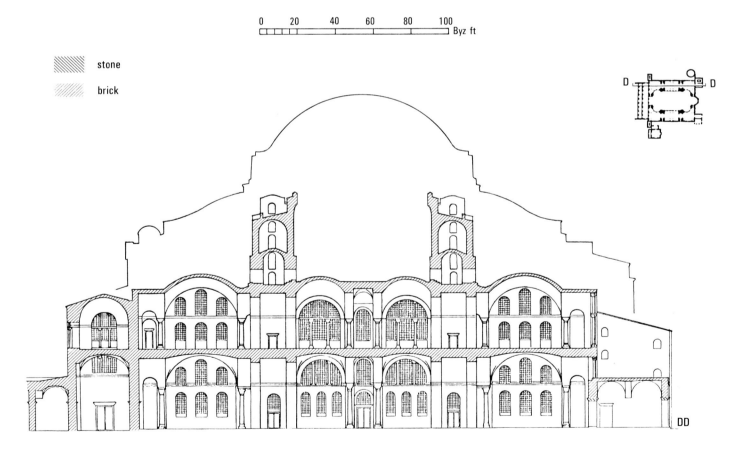

A6 Further longitudinal sections of Justinian's church, looking north

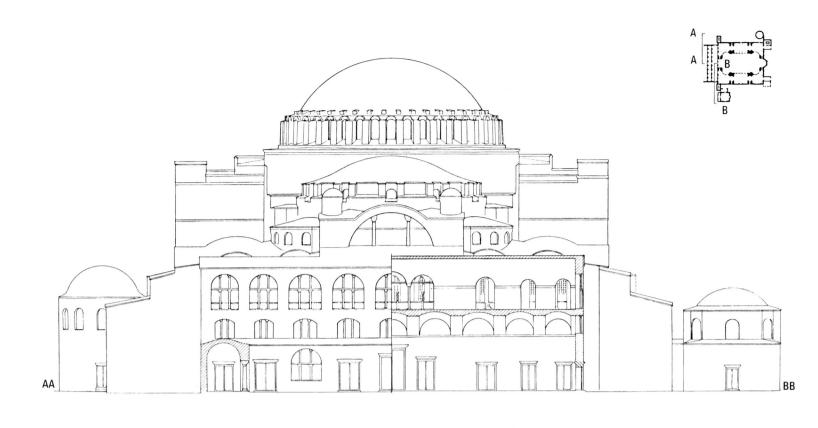

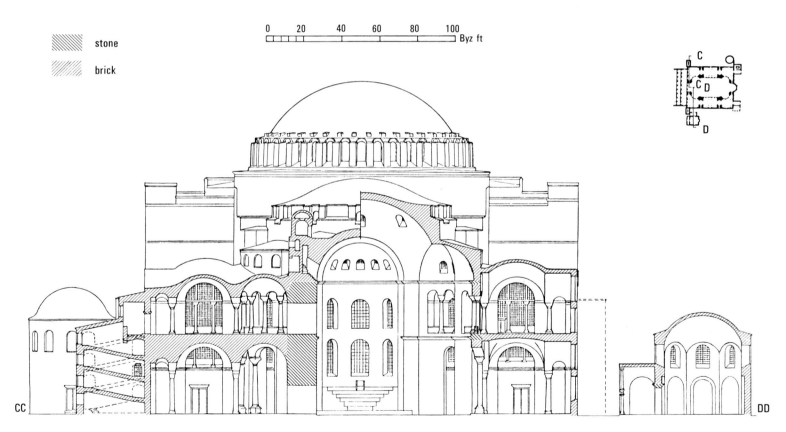

stone

brick

0 20 40 60 80 100
Byz ft

A7 Partial west elevation of Justinian's church and transverse sections of the west end, looking east

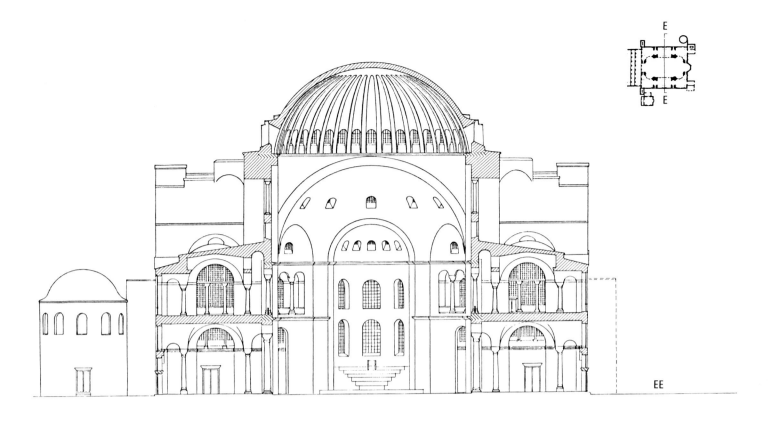

stone

brick

0 20 40 60 80 100
└────────────────────┘ Byz ft

EE

GG

FF

A8 Further transverse sections of Justinian's church looking east

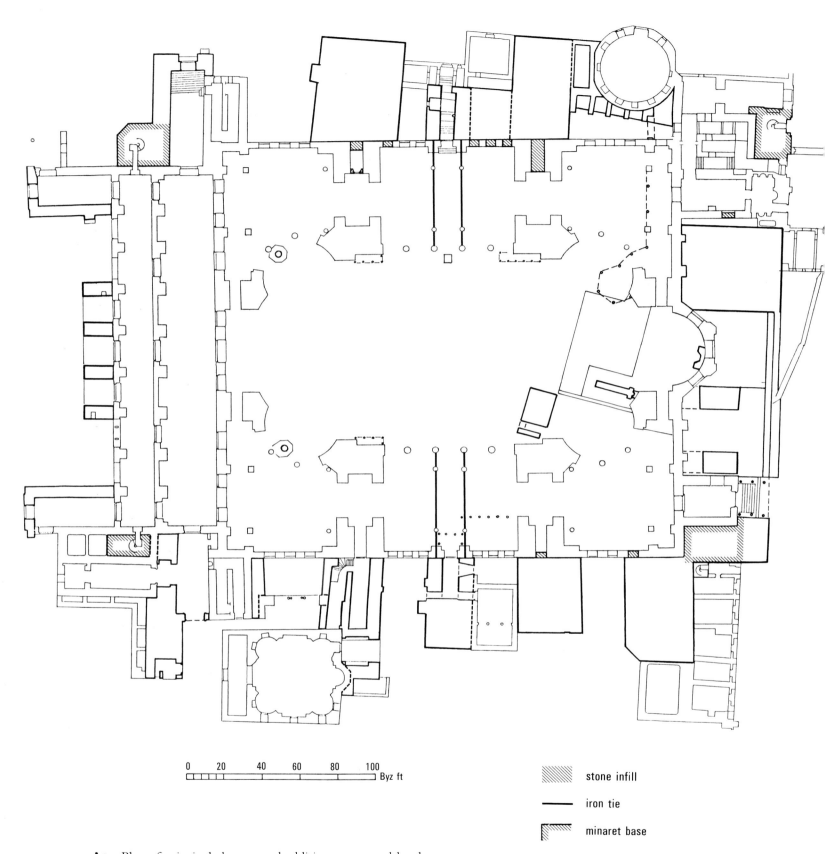

0 20 40 60 80 100 Byz ft

▨ stone infill

━ iron tie

▨ minaret base

A9 Plan of principal changes and additions at ground level

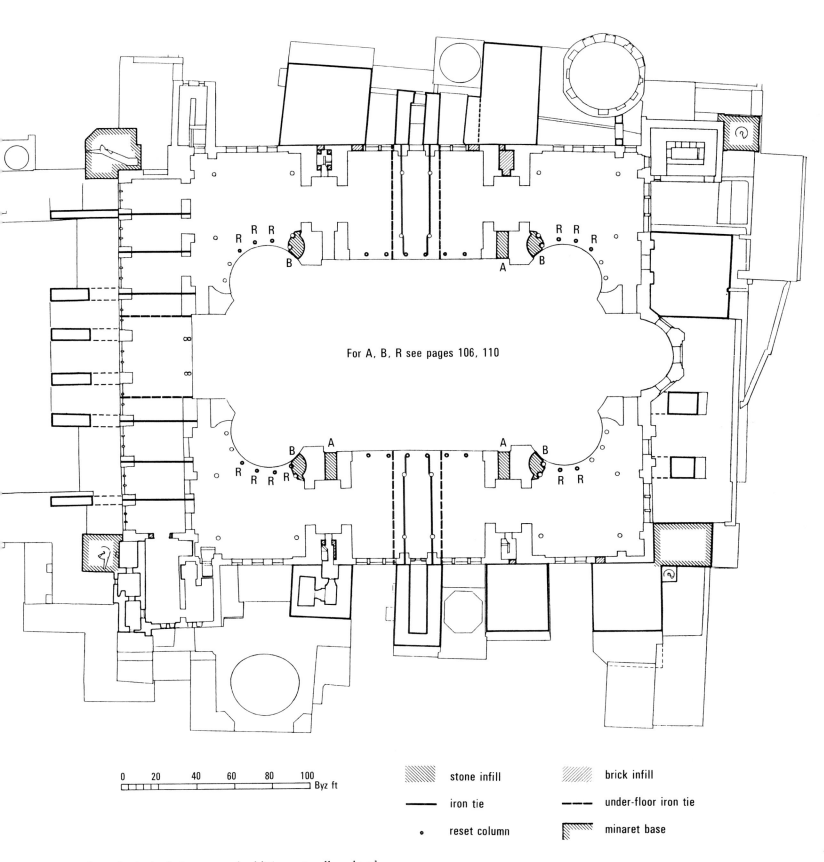

For A, B, R see pages 106, 110

▨	stone infill	▨ brick infill
—	iron tie	- - - under-floor iron tie
∘	reset column	minaret base

A10 Plan of principal changes and additions at gallery level

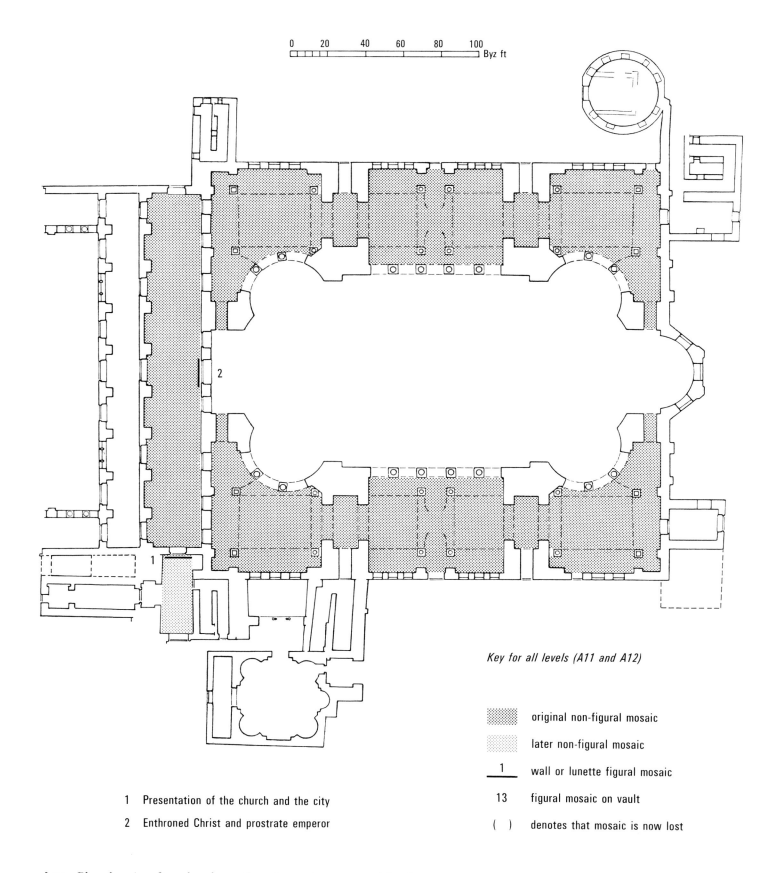

0 20 40 60 80 100
Byz ft

Key for all levels (A11 and A12)

	original non-figural mosaic
	later non-figural mosaic
<u>1</u>	wall or lunette figural mosaic
13	figural mosaic on vault
( )	denotes that mosaic is now lost

1 Presentation of the church and the city

2 Enthroned Christ and prostrate emperor

A11 Plan showing figural and non-figural mosaics at ground level

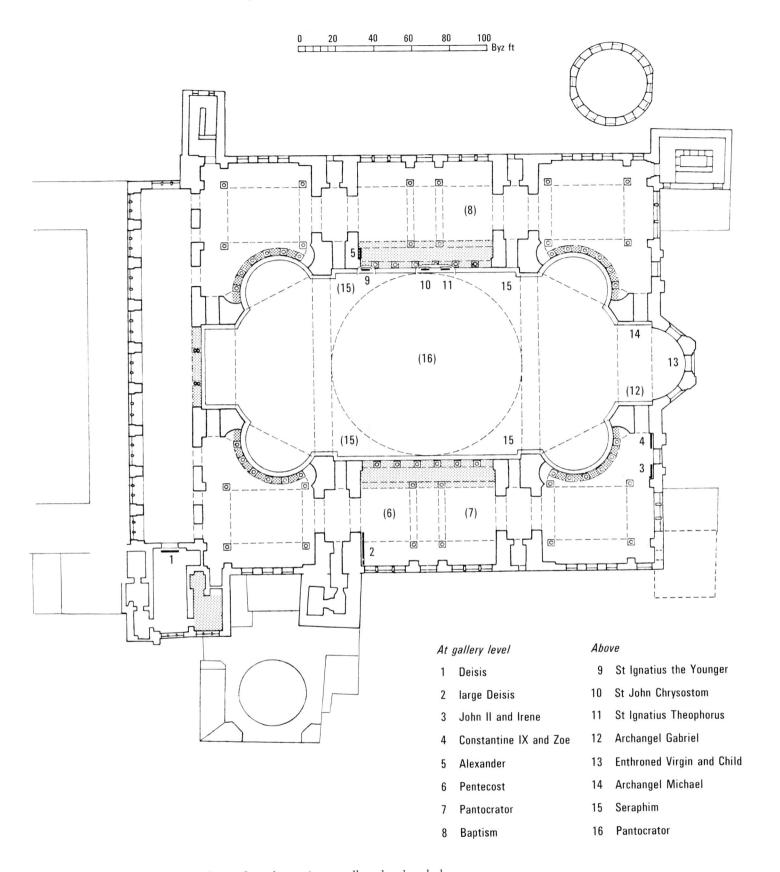

Scale: 0 20 40 60 80 100 Byz ft

At gallery level		Above	
1	Deisis	9	St Ignatius the Younger
2	large Deisis	10	St John Chrysostom
3	John II and Irene	11	St Ignatius Theophorus
4	Constantine IX and Zoe	12	Archangel Gabriel
5	Alexander	13	Enthroned Virgin and Child
6	Pentecost	14	Archangel Michael
7	Pantocrator	15	Seraphim
8	Baptism	16	Pantocrator

A12 Plan showing figural and non-figural mosaics at gallery level and above

Selected Bibliography

The literature on the church is vast, and that on the background to its design, construction and use, vaster still. The most relevant works are cited in the notes. The more important ones only are listed here. Swift gives a more comprehensive listing up to 1939. For a fuller listing of later publications see W. Muller-Weiner, *Bildlexikon zur Topographie Istanbuls*, Tubingen, 1977, pp. 94–6.

Documentary sources

Mango, C., *The art of the Byzantine empire, 312–1453*, Englewood Cliffs, 1972, includes partial translations of some of the most important sources.

The principal sources themselves are included in the list of abbreviations (page 262).

The church before Justinian

Antoniades, E., *Ekphrasis tes Hagias Sophias*, vol. 1, Athens, 1907.

Dirimtekin, F., 'Le skeuophylakion de Sainte-Sophie', *REB*, vol. 19, 1961, pp. 390–400.

Mathews, T. F., *The early churches of Constantinople: architecture and liturgy*, University Park, 1971, pp. 11–19.

Millet, G., 'Sainte-Sophie avant Justinian', *OCP*, vol. 13, 1947, pp. 597–612. (More valuable for its collation of the relevant documents than for its conclusions.)

Schneider, A. M., 'Die Grabung im Westhof der Sophienkirche zu Istanbul', *IF*, vol. 12, Berlin, 1941.

Turkoglu, S., 'Ayasofya skevophilakionu kazisi', *AMY*, vol. 9, 1983, pp. 25–35.

Justinian's church and its later history

Antoniades, E., *Ekphrasis tes Hagias Sophias*, 3 vols., Athens, 1907–9.

Conant, K. J., 'The first dome of St Sophia and its rebuilding', *BBI*, vol. 1, 1946, pp. 71–8.

Dirimtekin, F., 'The baptistery of Saint Sophia', *TAD*, vol. 12, 1963, pp. 65–87 (Turkish text pp. 54–64).

——, 'Le local du Patriarcat à Sainte Sophie', *IM*, vol. 13/14, 1963–4, pp. 113–27.

Ebersolt, J., *Sainte Sophie de Constantinople, Étude de topographie d'après les cérémonies*, Paris, 1910.

Emerson, W. and R. L. Van Nice, 'Hagia Sophia, Istanbul: preliminary report of a recent examination of the structure', *AJA*, vol. 47, 1943, pp. 403–36.

——, 'Hagia Sophia and the first minaret erected after the conquest of Constantinople', *AJA*, vol. 54, 1950, pp. 28–40.

——, 'Hagia Sophia: the collapse of the first dome, *Archaeology*, vol. 4, 1951, pp. 94–103.

——, 'Hagia Sophia: The construction of the second dome and its later repairs', *Archaeology*, vol. 4, 1951, pp. 162–71.

Eyice, S., 'Le baptistère de Sainte Sophie d'Istanbul', *9° Congresso di Archeologia Cristiana*, 1975, vol. 2, pp. 257–73.

Fossati, G., *Aya Sofia, Constantinople, as recently restored by order of H.M. the Sultan Abdul Mediid*, London, 1852. (Chiefly a pictorial record with disappointingly little detail of the restoration works, for which see Mango, *Materials*.)

Grelot, G. J., *Relation nouvelle d'un voyage de Constantinople*, Paris, 1860.

Janin, R., 'Le palais patriarcal de Constantinople byzantine', *REB*, vol. 20, 1962, pp. 131–55.

——, *Le géographie ecclésiastique de l'empire byzantine: Constantinople, les églises et les monastères*, Paris, 2nd edn, 1969, pp. 455–70.

Kahler, H. (trans. E. Childs), *Hagia Sophia*, London, 1967. (Valuable chiefly for its wide-angle photographs of the interior and the chapter on the mosaics referred to below.)

Kleiss, W., 'Beobachtungen in der Hagia Sophia in Istanbul', *IM*, vol. 15, 1965, pp. 168–85. (A different hypothesis about the development of the design.)

Lethaby, W. R. and H. Swainson, *The church of Sancta Sophia, Constantinople*, London, 1894. (Superseded in many respects, but an unusually perceptive account with excellent descriptions of architectural details.)

Mainstone, R. J., 'The structure of the church of St Sophia, Istanbul', *Transactions of the Newcomen Society*, vol. 38, 1965–66, pp. 23–49.

——, 'Justinian's church of St Sophia, Istanbul: Recent studies of its construction and first partial reconstruction', *AH*, vol. 12, 1969, pp. 39–49.

——, 'The reconstruction of the tympana of St Sophia at Istanbul', *DOP*, vol. 23/24, 1969–70, pp. 355–68.

Majeska, G. P., 'St Sophia in the fourteenth and fifteenth centuries: the Russian travelers on the relics', *DOP*, vol. 27, 1973, pp. 71–87.

——, 'Notes on the archeology of St Sophia at Constantinople: the green marble bands on the floor', *DOP*, vol. 32, 1978, pp. 299–308.

Mamboury, E., 'Topographie de Sainte-Sophie, le sanctuaire et la soléa, le mitatorion etc.', *Atti del V Congreso di studi byzantini*, Rome 1940, vol. 2, pp. 197–209.

Mango, C., *Materials for the study of the mosaics of St Sophia at Istanbul*, Washington, DC, 1962, Dumbarton Oaks Studies 8. (Also contains considerable material on the structural history of the church.)

Mango, C. and J. Parker, 'A twelfth-century description of St Sophia', *DOP*, vol. 14, 1960, pp. 233–45.

Mathews, T. F., *The early churches of Constantinople: architecture and liturgy*, University Park, 1971, pp. 88–99.

——, *The Byzantine churches of Istanbul, a photographic survey*, University Park, 1976, 262–312.

Millet, G., 'La coupole primitive de Sainte-Sophie', *Revue Belge de Philologie et d'Histoire*, vol. 2, 1923, pp. 599–617. (Like the work by Millet cited previously, valuable chiefly for its collation of the relevant documents.)

Prost, H., 'Sainte-Sophie', *Monuments antiques relevés et restaurés: Supplément*, Paris, 1923. (Reconstruction drawings based on a measured survey.)

Salzenberg, W., *Altchristliche Baudenkmale von Constantinopel vom V bis XII Jahrhundert*, Berlin, 1854.

Sanpaolesi, P., *Santa Sofia a Constantinopoli*, series *Forma e colore*, Florence, 1965. (Album of large colour plates)

Schneider, A. M., 'Die Grabung im Westhof der Sophienkirche zu Istanbul', *IF*, vol. 12, Berlin, 1941.

——, *Die Hagia Sophia zu Konstantinopel*, Berlin, 1939. (Good early photographs)

Strube, C., *Die westliche Eingangsseite der Kirchen von Konstantinopel in justinianscher Zeit*, Wiesbaden, 1973, pp. 13–105.

Swift, E. H., *Hagia Sophia*, New York, 1940.

Thode, D., *Untersuchungen zur Lastabtragung in spätantiken Kuppelbauten*, dissertation, Darmstadt, 1975, pp. 14–125. (Included as the most recently published structural analysis of the church, though it is open to many criticisms chiefly on the grounds that it pays insufficient attention to the considerable changes in behaviour that have taken place and attempts calculations of a type for which there are inadequate data about the properties of the materials and the internal cracking.)

Underwood, P. A., 'Notes on the work of the Byzantine Institute in Istanbul: 1957–1959', *DOP*, vol. 14, 1960, pp. 205–15. (Discusses the *opus sectile* panel above the Imperial door.)

Van Nice, R. L., *St Sophia in Istanbul; an architectural survey*, Washington, 1st instalment 1965, 2nd instalment due 1986. (The fundamental record of the present state of the structure.)

——, 'The structure of St Sophia', *AF*, vol. 118, 1963, pp. 131–9. (Partly retracted in idem, 'St Sophia's structure: a new assessment of the half domes', *AF*, vol. 121, 1964, pp. 45–9.)

Xydis, S. G., 'The chancel barrier, solea and ambo of Hagia Sophia', *AB*, vol. 29, 1947, pp. 1–24.

Zaloziecky, W. R., *Die Sophienkirche in Konstantinopel*, Rome, 1936.

Mosaics

Brekenridge, J. D., 'Christ on the lyre-backed throne', *DOP*, vol. 34/35, 1980–81, pp. 247–60.

Cormack, R., 'Interpreting the mosaics of S Sophia at Istanbul', *Art History*, vol. 4, 1981, pp. 131–49.

——, *Reading Byzantine Art: the Deisis mosaic of St Sophia*, Cambridge, due 1988.

Cormack, R. and E. J. W. Hawkins, 'The mosaics of St Sophia at Istanbul: the rooms above the southwest vestibule and ramp', *DOP*, vol. 31, 1977, pp. 175–251.

Mango, C., *Materials for the study of the mosaics of St Sophia at Istanbul*, Washington, DC, 1962, Dumbarton Oaks Studies 8.

——, 'The mosaics of Hagia Sophia' in Kahler, H., *Hagia Sophia*, London, 1967, pp. 47–60.

Mango, C. and E. J. W. Hawkins, 'The apse mosaic of St Sophia at Istanbul', *DOP*, vol. 19, 1965, pp. 113–51.

——, 'The mosaics of St Sophia at Istanbul. The church fathers in the north tympanum', *DOP*, vol. 26, 1972, pp. 1–41.

Oikonomides, N., 'Leo VI and the narthex mosaic of Saint Sophia', *DOP*, vol. 30, 1976, pp. 151–72.

——, 'The mosaic panel of Constantine IX and Zoe in Saint Sophia', *REB*, vol. 36, 1978, pp. 219–32.

Underwood, P. A. and E. J. W. Hawkins, 'The mosaics of Hagia Sophia at Istanbul 1959–60. The portrait of the Emperor Alexander', *DOP*, vol. 15, 1961, pp. 187–217.

Whittemore, T., *The mosaics of St Sophia at Istanbul 1931–2. The mosaics of the narthex*, Oxford, 1933.

——, *The mosaics of St Sophia at Istanbul 1933–4. The mosaics of the southern vestibule*, Oxford, 1936.

——, *The mosaics of St Sophia at Istanbul 1935–8. The imperial portraits of the south gallery*, Oxford, 1942.

——, *The mosaics of St Sophia at Istanbul 1934–8. The Deisis panel of the south gallery*, Oxford, 1952.

Historical background

Barnes, T. D., *The new empire of Diocletian and Constantine*, Cambridge, Mass., 1982.

Baynes, N. H., *Constantine the Great and the Christian Church*, 2nd edn, London, 1972.

Browning, R., *Justinian and Theodora*, London, 1971.

——, *The Byzantine Empire*, London, 1980.

Bury, J. B., *A history of the later Roman Empire from the death of Theodosius I to the death of Justinian*, 2 vols, London, 1923.

Dagron, G., *Naissance d'une capitale. Constantinople et ses institutions de 330 à 451*, Paris, 1974.

Downey, G., 'Byzantine architects, their training and methods', *Byz*, vol. 18, 1946–8, pp. 99–118.

——, 'Pappus of Alexandria on architectural studies', *Isis*, vol. 38, 1948, pp. 197–200.

——, 'Justinian as builder', *AB*, vol. 32, 1950, pp. 262–6.

——, 'Notes on Procopius, *De aedificiis*', *Studies presented to D. M. Robinson on his seventieth birthday*, St Louis, 1953, vol. 2, pp. 719–25.

——, 'Earthquakes at Constantinople and vicinity AD 342–1454', *Speculum*, vol. 30, 1955, pp. 596–600.

——, *Constantinople in the age of Justinian*, Norman, Oklahoma, 1960.

Heath, T., *A history of Greek mathematics*, 2 vols, Oxford, 1921.

Janin, R., *Le géographie ecclésiastique de l'empire byzantine: Constantinople, les églises et les monastères*, Paris, 2nd edn, 1969.

Jones, A. H. M., *The later Roman Empire 284–602*, 3 vols, Oxford, 1964.

Mainstone, R. J., 'The springs of structural invention', *JRIBA*, vol. 70, 1963, pp. 57–71. (Revised version 'Intuition and the springs of structural invention', *VIA*, vol. 2, 1973, pp. 42–63.)

——, 'Structural theory and design before 1742', *AR*, vol. 143, 1968, pp. 303–10.

Mango, C., *The Brazen House*, Copenhagen, 1959.

——, *Byzantium: the empire of New Rome*, London, 1980.

——, *Le développement urbain de Constantinople (IVe–VIIe siècles)*, Paris, 1985.

Meyendorf, J., 'Justinian, the empire and the church', *DOP*, vol. 22, 1968, pp. 45–60.

Ostrogorsky, G., *History of the Byzantine state*, Oxford, 2nd edn, 1968.

Stein, E., *Histoire du Bas-Empire*, Paris, Brussels, Amsterdam, 2 vols, 1949–59.

Ure, P. N., *Justinian and his age*, Harmondsworth, 1951.

Architectural and structural antecedents

Blake, M. E., *Ancient Roman construction in Italy from the prehistoric period to Augustus*, Washington, DC, 1947.

——, *Roman construction in Italy from Tiberius through the Flavians*, Washington, DC, 1959.

Blake, M. E., and D. T. Bishop, *Roman construction in Italy from Nerva through the Antonines*, Philadelphia, 1973

Butler, H. C., *Early churches in Syria*, Princeton, 1929.

Calderini, A., G. Chierici and C. Cecchelli, *La basilica di S. Lorenzo Maggiore in Milano*, Milan, 1951.

Choisy, A., *L'art de bâtir chez les Romains*, Paris, 1872.

——, *L'art de bâtir chez les Byzantines*, Paris 1883.

Corbo, V. C., *Il Santo Sepulcro di Gerusaleme*, Jersualem, 1981.

Crowfoot, J. W., *Early churches in Palestine*, London, 1941.

Grabar, A., *Martyrium: recherches sur le culte des reliques et l'art chrétien antique*, 2 vols text plus 1 vol. plates, Paris, 1943–6.

Harrison, R. M., *Excavations at Sarachane in Istanbul*, vol. 1, Princeton and Washington, due 1986.

Hoddinot. R. F., *Early Byzantine churhes in Macedonia and southern Serbia*, London, 1963.

Kleinbauer, W. E., 'The origin and functions of the aisled tetraconch churches in Syria and northern Mesopotamia', *DOP*, vol. 27, 1973, pp. 91–114.

Krautheimer, R., 'The Constantinian basilica', *DOP*, vol. 21, 1967, pp. 117–40.

——, 'Constantine's church foundations', *Akten des VII International Kongresses für Christliche Archäologie Trier 1965*, 1969, pp. 237–55.

——, *Early Christian and Byzantine architecture*, Harmondsworth, 3rd edn, 1979.

——, 'Success and failure in Late Antique church planning', *The age of spirituality*, ed. K. Weitzmann, New York, 1980, pp. 121–39.

Krautheimer, R., S. Corbett and A. K. Frazer, *Corpus Basilicarum Christianarum Romae*, vol. 5, Vatican City, 1977.

Lavin, I., 'The house of the Lord: aspects of the role of palace triclinia in the architecture of Late Antiquity and the Early Middle Ages', *AB*, vol. 44, 1962, pp. 1–27.

Lehmann, K., 'The dome of heaven', *AB*, vol. 27, 1945, pp. 1–27.

Licht, K. de F., *The Rotunda in Rome*, Copenhagen, 1968, Jutland Archaeological Society Publications VIII.

Lugli, G., *La tecnica edilizia romana con particolare riguardo a Roma e Lazio*, 2 vols. Rome, 1957 (reprinted 1968).

MacDonald, W., 'Some implications of later Roman construction', *JSAH*, vol. 17, 1958, pp. 2–8.

——, *The architecture of the Roman Empire: an introductory study*, New Haven and London, 1965, Yale Publications in the History of Art 17.

Mainstone, R. J., *Development in structural form*, London and Cambridge, Mass., 1975 (reprinted 1983).

Mango, C., *Byzantine architecture*, New York, 1976.

Nash, E., *Pictorial dictionary of Ancient Rome*, 2 vols, London, 2nd edn, 1968.

Smith, E. B., *The dome: a study in the history of ideas*, Princeton, 1950.

Swift, E. H., *Roman sources of Christian art*, New York, 1951.

Ward-Perkins, J. B., 'The Italian element in Late Roman and Early Medieval architecture', *PBA*, vol. 33, 1947, pp. 163–94.

——, 'Constantine and the origins of the Christian basilica', *PBSR*, vol. 22, 1954, pp. 69–90.

——, 'Notes on the structure and building methods of early Byzantine architecture' in *The Great Palace of the Byzantine emperors*, edited D. Talbot Rice, Edinburgh, 1958, pp. 52–104.

——, 'Imperial mausolea and their possible influence on early Christian central-plan buildings', *JSAH*, vol. 25, 1966, pp. 297–9.

——, 'Memoria, martyr's tomb and martyr's church', *Akten des VII International Kongresses für Christliche Archäologie Trier 1965*, 1969, pp. 3–27.

——, *Roman imperial architecture*, Harmondsworth, 2nd end, 1981.

Liturgy

Dix, G., *The shape of the liturgy*, London, 2nd edn, 1945.

Mateos, J., *Célébration de la parole dans la liturgie byzantine*, Rome, 1971, Orientalia Christiana Analecta 191.

Mathews, T. F., *The early churches of Constantinople: architecture and liturgy*, University Park, 1971, 105–180.

Shepherd, M. H., 'Liturgical expressions of the Constantine triumph', *DOP*, vol. 21, 1967, pp. 59–78.

Taft, R., *The Great Entrance*, Rome, 1975, Orientalia Christiania Analecta 200.

——, 'How liturgies grow: the evolution of the Byzantine Divine Liturgy', *OCP*, vol. 43, 1977, pp. 355–78.

——, 'The liturgy of the Great Church: an initial synthesis of structure and interpretation on the eve of iconoclasm', *DOP*, vol. 34/35, 1980–1, pp. 45–75.

Sequels

Charles, M. A., 'Hagia Sophia and the great imperial mosques', *AB*, vol. 12, 1930, pp. 321–45.

Demus, O., *Byzantine mosaic decoration*, London, 1947.

Goodwin, G., *A history of Ottoman architecture*, London, 1971.

Krautheimer, R., *Early Christian and Byzantine architecture*, Harmondsworth, 3rd edn, 1979.

Mango, C., *Byzantine architecture*, New York, 1976.

Vogt-Goknil, U., *Les mosques turques*, Zurich, 1953.

Index